A CALDECOTT ACTIVITY BOOK FOR

WOLF IN THE SNOW

CLAUDIA KRAUSE

ARCHWAY PUBLISHING

Archway Publishing books may be ordered through booksellers or by contacting:

Archway Publishing
1663 Liberty Drive
Bloomington, IN 47403
www.archwaypublishing.com
844-669-3957

ISBN: 978-1-6657-5220-6 (sc)
ISBN: 978-1-6657-5221-3 (e)

Print information available on the last page.

Archway Publishing rev. date: 12/18/2023

A special thank you to Matthew Cordell, the author of *Wolf in the Snow*, and to Feiwel & Friends, an imprint of Macmillan Publishing Company, for publishing this delightful story.

For facts on the author, visit claudiakrausebooks.com.

To the many students who've inspired me throughout my teaching career. Their thought-provoking questions and responses never ceased to amaze me. I know they're doing wonderful things to improve our world.

INTRODUCTION

Welcome to a story adventure. This Caldecott Activity book was developed to enhance and reinforce skills that develop children's academic skills while reading a delightful story. The enclosed questions and activities for this delightful book can be used by parents, grandparents, guardians, and teachers. The book can be read at any time of the year, allowing the reader to make different choices from the activity book with each reading. The questions section isn't numbered, which allows the reader to pick and choose the questions they'd like to develop, thus giving the reader ownership of the questions and the timeline. The activities are numbered, aligning with the questions.

The questions are designed to develop critical thinking, vocabulary, math skills, and science knowledge, all while deepening the children's understanding of this wonderful story. The activities foster creativity and individual expression, offering various art, writing, and research opportunities. The activities foster creativity and individual expression, offering various art, writing, and research opportunities. The activities can be done at home with parents, grandparents, or guardians, or they can be used by teachers in the classroom. Teachers can use the questions and activities as class assignments, homework assignments, or learning center activities. The activities follow a designated presentation format that states the title of the activity, the objective, and the materials needed. It further relays the things that need to be done prior to the activity, an introductory statement, as well as a review of the children's prior responses. The format introduces the activity and offers extension activities. I suggest creating a reading center in the classroom or at home and providing baskets of books about wolves, survival skills, dogs, snow, trees, and weather. You could also provide pillows, carpet squares, or animal beds, where the children can sit comfortably.

I encourage parents, grandparents, or guardians to take their children to the local library, where they can explore age-appropriate materials related to the activities. Research suggestions are offered throughout the activity book, and most libraries have computers available for children to use. Ask the librarian to suggest additional age-appropriate websites. In addition, I suggest visiting various community locations. The local television station might be willing to let children visit the station, watching the meteorologist describe and predict the weather. Sportswear clothing outlets display a variety of protective clothing, while the local animal shelter has a variety of dogs. It only takes a phone call to inquire about available enrichment opportunities. Many businesses are willing to allow children to visit their facilities, offering guided tours, as well as information. Call these businesses to find out what opportunities might be available. Additionally, contacts with professional organizations may be fruitful. I suggest that teachers contact their local school district to obtain a list of organizations that are willing to enrich the educational experiences of children. Some of these organizations are happy to contribute to special projects and field trips, thus furthering the children's academic knowledge.

I'd love to see how you've developed the enclosed questions and activities. Please feel free to send me pictures, projects, ideas, samples, suggestions, and your responses to the material. I will try to disseminate your ideas to others. I hope you have a wonderful experience reading this book and doing the activity package. Happy learning!

Wolf in the Snow illustration: Front Cover

Direct the children's attention to the front cover. Encourage them to answer the following questions in complete sentences.

QUESTIONS

The brackets around the text indicate questions/instructions an adult should read to the children. Examples of how the children may answer the questions are included in parentheses.

- **[What do you see on the front cover?]** Write the children's responses on a piece of paper and save this for later. (Well, the child and the wolf seem to be approaching each other. The child is holding out her hands to the wolf.) See Art #1 and Writing #1.

- **[How would you describe the child?]** Write the children's responses on a piece of paper and save this for later. (Well, the young child is reaching out to the young wolf, so she must feel comfortable. The young child looks cold.) See Art #2 and Writing #2.

- **[How would you describe the wolf?]** Write the children's responses on a piece of paper and save this for later. (Well, the young wolf looks scared. I think the young wolf is carefully approaching the young child.) See Art #3 and Writing #3.

- **[Do you think there's anything unusual about this scene?]** Write the children's responses on a piece of paper and save this for later. (Well, I think it's unusual that an animal would approach a human. I think the young wolf is lonely.) See Writing #4.

- **[What do you know about wolves?]** Write the children's responses on a piece of paper and save this for later. (Well, I know that wolves live in the wild. I know that wolves have sharp teeth. I know that wolves travel in groups.) See Science #1.

1

- **[Do you think all wolves are gray or black?]** Write the children's responses on a piece of paper and save this for later. (Most wolves are gray. I've seen pictures of wolves that are black.) See Science #2.

- **[How old is the wolf on the cover?]** (Well, the wolf is small, so he or she must be a young wolf.) Allow the children to verbalize their answers.

- **[Do you think his or her mother is nearby? Why or why not?]** (The mother wolf is probably walking ahead of the young wolf. I think the young wolf couldn't keep up with the pack.) Allow the children to verbalize their answers.

- **[Would you say the wolf is trusting? Why or why not?]** (I think the young wolf is very trusting. He or she is coming very close to the young girl.) Allow the children to verbalize their answers.

- **[Would you say the child is brave? Why or why not?]** (I think the young child is also brave. She is willing to have a young wolf come close to her.) Allow the children to verbalize their answers.

- **[How would you describe the weather?]** (Well, it's snowing outside, so it must be cold. The young child is wearing mittens, boots, and a face covering.) Allow the children to verbalize their answers. See Science #3.

- **[What do you think the temperature is outside?]** (Well, if it's snowing, it must be cold outside. I remember seeing the temperature on the thermometer read 30° Fahrenheit last winter.) Allow the children to verbalize their answers. See Science #3. See resource section for weather calendar.

- **[What protective clothing is the child wearing?]** Write the children's responses on a piece of paper and save this for later. (The child is wearing a heavy coat, hat, socks, mittens, a face covering, and boots.) See Science #4.

- **[Do you think the child and the wolf will become friends? Why or why not?]** (Well, it would be unusual for a wild animal to become friends with the child. I don't think they'll become friends. I think they could become friends.) Allow the children to verbalize their answers.

ACTIVITIES

Art

#1. Illustrate the front cover of the book.

- **Objective.** Presenting, Anchor Standard #4. Select, analyze, and interpret artistic work for presentation. Select. Categorize images based on expressive properties.
- **Level of difficulty.** Moderate. (This task may take several days to complete.)
- **Materials needed.** Pencils, paints, brushes, construction paper, and the front cover projected onto a white surface. You may want to have the children do this activity individually, in small groups, or as a whole-class project.
- **Before the activity.** Prepare the materials.
- **Begin the activity by saying,** "Earlier, we described what we saw on the front cover."
- **Review the children's responses.** (The young child is holding out her hands to the young wolf. The young wolf looks scared.)
- **Introduce the activity.** "Today, we're going to draw or paint the front cover." Have the children pencil in their drawing and then have them draw or paint the cover. Attach the children's adjectives from the writing lesson to their picture. (See Writing #1.)

#2. Draw or paint the young child.

- **Objective.** Responding, Anchor Standard #7. Perceive and analyze artistic work. Perceive. Categorize images based on expressive properties.
- **Level of difficulty.** Moderate. (This task may take several days to complete.)
- **Materials needed.** Pencils, paints, brushes, construction paper, and the front cover projected onto a white surface. You may want to have the children do this activity individually, in small groups, or as a whole-class project.
- **Before the activity.** Prepare the materials.
- **Begin the activity by saying,** "Earlier, we described the young child."
- **Review the children's responses.** (The young child looks cold in this picture. The young child is brave to hold out her hands to the young wolf.)
- **Introduce the activity.** "Today, we're going to draw or paint the young child." Have the children pencil in their drawing and then have them draw or paint the young child. Attach the children's descriptions of the young child from the writing lesson to their picture. (See Writing #2.)

#3. Draw or paint the young wolf.

- **Objective.** Responding, Anchor Standard #7. Perceive and analyze artistic work. Perceive. Categorize images based on expressive properties.
- **Level of difficulty.** Moderate. (This task may take several days to complete.)
- **Materials needed.** Pencils, paints, brushes, construction paper, and the front cover projected onto a white surface. You may want

4

to have the children do this activity individually, in small groups, or as a whole-class project.

- **Before the activity.** Prepare the materials.
- **Begin the activity by saying,** "Earlier, we described the young wolf."
- **Review the children's responses.** (The young wolf looks scared. The young wolf looks like he or she is slowly approaching the young child. The young wolf has his or her head lowered.)
- **Introduce the activity.** "Today, we're going to draw or paint the young wolf." Have the children pencil in their drawing and then have them draw or paint the young wolf. Attach the children's descriptions of the young wolf from the writing lesson to their picture. (See Writing #3.)

Writing

#1. Introduce adjectives by describing the scene on the cover.

- **Objective.** Conventions of Standard English. (Demonstrate command of the conventions of standard English grammar and usage when writing or speaking. Use frequently occurring adjectives.)
- **Level of difficulty.** Moderate (This task may take several days to complete.)
- **Materials needed.** Lined paper and pencils for the children.
- **Before the activity.** Place a large piece of white paper on the board. Have a black marker available for writing the children's responses.
- **Begin the activity by saying,** "Earlier, we described the young wolf."
- **Review the children's responses.** (The young child is holding out her hands to the young wolf. The young wolf looks scared.)
- **Introduce the activity.** "Today, we're going to learn about adjectives. When we describe things, we're using adjectives. Adjectives tell us

valuable details about an object. For example, we can say that the child is wearing a red coat. The word red describes the color of the coat. We can say the wolf is small. The word small describes the wolf." Read all the responses of the children and have them copy one sentence on a piece of lined paper. If they'd like to write their own sentence, be available to help them sound out the correct spelling of the words. Attach this sentence to their drawing/painting of the front cover. (See Art #1.)

#2. Practice adjectives by describing the young child.

- **Objective.** Conventions of Standard English (Demonstrate command of the conventions of standard English grammar and usage when writing or speaking. Use frequently occurring adjectives.)
- **Level of difficulty.** Moderate. (This task may take several days to complete.)
- **Materials needed.** Lined paper and pencils for the children.
- **Before the activity.** Place a large piece of white paper on the board. Have a black marker available for writing the children's responses.
- **Begin the activity by saying,** "Earlier, we described the young child."
- **Review the children's responses.** (The young child looks cold in this picture. The young child is brave to hold out her hands to the young wolf.)
- **Introduce the activity.** "Today, we're going to learn about adjectives. When we describe things, we're using adjectives. Adjectives tell us key details about an object. For example, we can say that the child is wearing a red coat. The word *red* describes the color of the coat." Read all the responses of the children and have them copy one sentence on a piece of lined paper. If they'd like to write their own sentence, be available to help them sound out the correct spelling

6

of the words. Attach this sentence to their drawing/painting of the front cover. (See Art #2.)

#3. Practice adjectives by describing the young wolf.

- **Objective.** Conventions of Standard English. Demonstrate command of the conventions of standard English grammar and usage when writing or speaking. Use frequently occurring adjectives.
- **Level of Difficulty.** Moderate. (This task may take several days to complete.)
- **Materials needed.** Lined paper and writing materials for the children.
- **Before the activity.** Place a large piece of white paper on the board. Have a black marker available for writing the children's responses.
- **Begin the activity by saying,** "Earlier, we described the young wolf."
- **Review the children's responses.** (The young wolf looks scared. The young wolf looks like he/she's slowly approaching the young child. The young wolf has his/her head lowered.).
- **Introduce the activity.** "Today, we going to learn about adjectives. When we describe things, we're using adjectives. Adjectives tell us important details about an object. For example, we can say that the small wolf is approaching the child. The word *small* describes the size of the wolf." Read all the responses of the children and have them copy one sentence on a piece of lined paper. If they'd like to write their own sentence, be available to help them sound out the correct spelling of the words. Attach this sentence to their drawing/painting of the front cover. (See Art #3.)

#4. Practice writing skills.

- **Objective.** Production and Distribution of Writing. (With guidance and support from adults, focus on a topic, respond to questions

7

and suggestions from peers, and add details to strengthen writing as needed.)

- **Level of difficulty.** Moderate. (This task may take several days to complete.)
- **Materials needed.** Lined paper and pencils for the children.
- **Before the activity.** Place a large piece of white paper on the board. Have a black marker available for writing the children's responses.
- **Begin the activity by saying,** "Earlier, we said that we thought it was unusual for the wolf to approach the young child."
- **Review the children's responses.** (Wolves are wild animals who avoid humans. The young wolf is looking for food. The young wolf is lonely.)
- **Introduce the activity.** "Today, we're going to practice our writing skills." When we start writing a sentence, we begin the sentence with a capital letter. We end the sentence with a period, a question mark, or an exclamation mark." Read all the responses of the children and point out the capital letters and ending punctuation marks in each of their responses. Have them copy their favorite sentence on a piece of lined paper. If they'd like to write their own sentence, be available to help them sound out the correct spelling of the words. Attach this sentence to their drawing/painting of the front cover. (See Art #1.)

Science

#1. Learn about a KWL *chart*. Create a chart that includes things I *know* about wolves, things I *want* to learn about wolves, and things I *learned* about wolves.

- **Objective.** Life Science. Structure, Functions, and Information Processing. Read texts and use media to determine patterns in behavior of parents and offspring that help offspring survive.

8

- **Level of difficulty.** Moderate. (This task may take several days to complete.)

- **Materials needed.** Place a large piece of white paper on the board. Have a black marker available for writing the children's responses.

- **Before the activity.** Divide a large piece of white paper into three sections. Write the following three designations in the three sections—things I *know* about wolves, things I *want* to know about wolves, and things I *learned* about wolves.

- **Begin the activity by saying,** "Today, we're going to create a KWL chart. First, let's list the things we know about wolves." Have the children relay the things they know about wolves. Write these comments in the designated area.

- **Review the children's responses** (Well, I know that wolves live in the wild. I know that wolves have sharp teeth. I know that wolves travel in groups.)

- **Introduce the activity.** "Now, we're going add information to our KWL chart. To review, this KWL chart contains three lists—(1) things I *know* about wolves, (2) things I *want* to learn about wolves, and (3) things I *learned* about wolves." Review the children's previous responses about what they *know* about wolves once more. Go to the internet and type, "Tell me about wolves." Choose an age-appropriate website for the children that relays important information about wolves. Read and discuss the additional information with the children. Write the information in the two remaining sections of the chart (the things they want to learn about wolves and the things they learned about wolves.) Leave this chart up and continue adding information as it's obtained.

#2. Learn about the color of wolves.

- **Objective.** Life Science. Structure, Function, and Information Processing. Make observations to construct an evidence-based

9

account that young plants and animals are like, but not exactly like, their parents.

- **Level of difficulty.** Moderate. (This task may take several days to complete.)
- **Materials needed.** Paints; pencils; paintbrushes; crayons; glue; and black, gray, and reddish-orange yarn.
- **Before the activity.** Go to the internet and type, "Tell me about the color of wolves." Choose an age-appropriate website that relays valuable information about the color of wolves.
- **Begin the activity by saying,** "Earlier, we discussed the color of wolves. We thought they might be gray or black."
- **Review the children's responses.** (I think most wolves are gray. I've seen pictures of wolves that are black.)
- **Introduce the activity.** "Today, we're going to learn the various colors of wolves." Go to the internet and type, "Tell me about the colors of wolves." Select the age-appropriate website you chose earlier that relays important information about the colors of wolves. Read and discuss this information with the children. Allow the children to draw or paint a wolf, using the various colors described on the internet. Let these pictures dry. You might want to provide some black, gray, and reddish-orange yarn for the children to pull apart and glue onto their finished wolf picture. This will make it appear as fur. (See Art #3.)

#3. Learn about and observe weather.

- **Objective.** Earth and Space Science. Weather and Climate. Use and share observations of local weather conditions to describe patterns over time.
- **Level of difficulty.** Moderate. (This task will take several days to complete.)

- **Materials needed.** Pencils, crayons, stickers, and a weather calendar (see resource section).
- **Before the activity.** Go to the internet and type, "Weather." Choose an age-appropriate website that relays important information about the weather. In addition, there are some videos related to weather the children will enjoy seeing. Preview these before showing them to the children.
- **Begin the activity by saying,** "Earlier, we discussed the weather."
- **Review the children's responses.** (The weather can be sunny, windy, rainy, cloudy, or snowy.)
- **Introduce the activity.** "Today, we're going to make a weather calendar." Go to the internet and type, "Weather." Select the age-appropriate website you chose earlier that relays important information about the weather. Read and discuss this information with the children. Give each child a blank monthly calendar (see resource section). Have them write in the name of the month and dates for a particular month. Then have them look outside each day to determine the weather and draw the appropriate weather sign on their calendar (e.g., sunny, windy, rainy, cloudy, and snowy). You may be able to order weather stickers on the internet. They would enjoy putting these on their calendar.

#4. Learn about protective clothing.

- **Objective.** Earth and Space Science. Weather and Climate. Ask questions to obtain information about the purpose of weather forecasting to prepare for and respond to severe weather.
- **Level of difficulty.** Easy.
- **Materials needed.** None.
- **Before the activity.** Go to the internet and type, "Tell me about protective clothing." Choose an age-appropriate website that relays important information about protective clothing.

- **Begin the activity by saying,** "Earlier, we discussed the protective clothing the young child was wearing."
- **Review the children's responses.** (The young child is wearing a heavy coat, mittens, boots, a head covering, a face covering, and socks.)
- **Introduce the activity.** "Today, we're going to learn some important information about protective clothing." Go to the internet and type, "Tell me about protective clothing." Select the age-appropriate website you chose earlier that relays important information about protective clothing. Read and discuss this information with the children.

QUESTIONS

The brackets around the text indicate questions/instructions an adult should read to the children. Examples of how the children may answer the questions are included in parentheses.

- **[What do you see on this page?]**
- **[There's a large window in the house. Imagine that you live there. What would you see if you were looking outside or inside the house?]** Place a large piece of paper on the board and list all the things you might see if you were looking outside the house. (There are trees, animals going by the window, and birds flying in the air.) Place another piece of paper on the board and list all the things you might see if you were looking inside the house. (There are chairs, the fireplace, and objects on the mantel.) See Art #1 and Writing #1.
- **[How would you describe this family?]** Write the children's responses on a piece of paper and save this for later. (The family looks happy. The family is warm inside their house. The young child is shaking hands with the dog). See Writing #2.
- **[What animal is included in this family scene?]** (The family has a dog.) Have the children relay the name(s) of their dog(s) to a friend.
- **[How many of you have a dog at home?]** Write on a piece of paper how many children have dogs and save this for later (There

are fifteen children in class who have a dog in their family). See Math #1 and #2.

- **[The people inside the house are drinking some beverage. What do you think the people are drinking?]** Write the children's responses on a piece of paper and save this for later. (Well, it's cold outside, so it might be something hot.)

- **[What beverages do you enjoy drinking?]** (Coca-Cola, milk, water, apple juice, hot chocolate, hot apple cider, and hot cranberry juice). List the beverages they personally enjoy. Write the children's responses on a piece of paper and save this for later. See Math #5.

- **[How does the family keep warm in the winter?]** (Well, there's a fireplace in the background, so they probably use this to keep warm.) Allow the children to verbalize their answers.

- **[Do you think some people still use a fireplace to heat their home? Why or why not?]** (I have a fireplace in my house, but we also have a heating system. We have a fireplace in our house, but we only use it on special occasions. Yes, we use our fireplace as the main source of heat. We live in a remote area that doesn't connect to the electrical grid. We don't have a fireplace in our house.) Allow the children to verbalize their answers.

- **[Do you know what a mantel is?]** Have the children raise their hand if they know what a mantel is. (A mantel can be a board or a large piece of stone above the fireplace, where people place special things, such as trophies, books, and statues.). Allow the children to verbalize their answers.

- **[Does your family have a mantel above the fireplace?]** (My family does have a mantel above the fireplace. We don't have a fireplace in our house.) If the children don't have a mantel, have them relay some special things they'd like to place on a mantel. These special things might be in their room, in a picture frame on the wall, or hanging on the refrigerator. Allow the children to verbalize their answers.

- **[What special things does this family place on their mantel?]**
  Write the children' responses on a piece of paper and save this for later. (This family has books, a boat, and a wolf standing on a rock.) See Writing / Oral Language #3.

- **[Do you think this family's house is cozy and comfortable?]**
  (Well, they have a warm fireplace inside the house. The young girl is playing with the dog on a rug. The parents are drinking something from their mugs.) Allow the children to verbalize their answers.

Recreate this scene in one corner of the room by placing rugs, pillows, blankets, and baskets of books about winter and snow. If you create this interior scene during the winter, see if someone has a *safe* electric heater that could be placed in the area. Allow the children to sit and read in this area, with the "fireplace," or electric heater, blazing. You might also introduce hand warmers to the children who've never seen or used them.

ACTIVITIES

Art

#1. Draw two windows showing an inside and outside view.

- **Objective.** Creating. Anchor Standard #1. Generate and conceptualize artistic ideas and work. Investigate, Plan, Make. Elaborate on an imaginative idea.

- **Level of difficulty.** Moderate. (This task may take several days to complete.)

- **Materials needed.** Pencils, paint, paintbrushes, and the window page (see resource section).

- **Before the activity.** Prepare the materials.
- **Begin the activity by saying,** "Earlier, we discussed what we might see when looking outside and inside the window."
- **Review the children's responses.** (If I was looking outside, I'd see trees, animals going by the window, and birds flying in the air). We also discussed what we'd see inside the house. (If I was looking inside the house, I'd see chairs, the fireplace, and objects on the mantel.) (See Art #1 and Writing #1.)
- **Introduce the activity.** "Today, you'll create two separate windows. One window will show things we might see outside, while the other window will show things we might see inside the house. On one window, you'll draw things that might appear outside the window, such as animals, tracks, birds flying in the air, and so on. On the other window, you'll draw things that are inside the house, such as a rug, chairs, the fireplace, and other household items." Tell the children their drawing must fit inside the picture frame area.
- **Extension of the activity.** As an alternative to using the picture drawn on the page, have the children draw a picture of their family inside and outside their house. You could use various materials to frame/highlight the windows, such as felt, popsicle sticks, or cardboard. Let the children's creations dry. When they are finished, allow the children to explain to a friend what is inside and outside their house.

 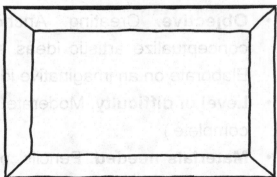

16

#2. Design a mug.

- **Objective.** Creating, Anchor Standard #1. Generate and conceptualize artistic ideas and work. Investigate, Plan, Make. Elaborate on an imaginative idea.
- **Level of difficulty.** Moderate. (This task may take several days to complete.)
- **Materials needed.** Pencils, paint, paintbrushes, construction paper, and mug page (see resource section).
- **Before the activity.** Prepare the materials.
- **Begin the activity by saying,** "Earlier, we observed that the mother and father were drinking something from mugs."
- **Review the children's responses.** (Well, it's cold outside, so it might be something hot. Hot chocolate, hot cider, or hot cranberry juice are a few possibilities.) (See Math #3 and #4.)
- **Introduce the activity.** "Today, we're going to design our own mugs." (See resource section.) Give each child a blank piece of paper and have them practice drawing assorted designs for their individual mug. When they feel they've created their mug design, give them a copy of the mug drawn on the resource page. Allow them to use colored pencils, paint, and pastels to complete their design.

17

#3. Draw or paint a winter scene.

- **Objective.** Creating, Anchor Standard #1. Generate and conceptualize artistic ideas and work. Investigate, Plan, Make. Make art or design with various materials and tools to explore personal interests, questions, and curiosities.
- **Level of difficulty.** Moderate. (This task may take several days to complete.)
- **Materials needed.** Pencils, paint, paintbrushes, glue, cotton balls, and construction paper.
- **Before the activity.** Prepare the materials.
- **Begin the activity by saying,** "Earlier, we observed that the family's house looks cozy and comfortable. However, it appears cold outside."
- **Review the children's responses.** (The family has a warm fireplace inside the house. The young girl is playing with the dog on a rug. The parents are drinking something from their mugs.)
- **Introduce the activity.** "Today, we're going to draw or paint a winter scene on a piece of construction paper." You can project a page from the book onto a white surface or have them create their own winter scene. Have the children sketch their picture with a pencil and then paint the winter scene. Make sure the children's names are on the back of their picture. Let the pictures dry. Give each child several cotton balls. Have them pull off small pieces of cotton from the cotton ball and glue this to their winter scene.

Writing / Oral Language

#1. Write about the things we might see looking outside and inside the window.

- **Objective.** Key Ideas and Details. Ask and answer questions about key details in a text.
- **Level of difficulty.** Moderate. (This task may take several days to complete.)
- **Materials needed.** Lined paper and pencils.
- **Before the activity.** Place a large piece of white paper on the board. Have a black marker available for writing the children's responses. Divide the paper into two portions, one side labeled "Outside the House," and one side labeled "Inside the House." Write the things that the children might see in these two locations. (See Art #1.)
- **Begin the activity by saying,** "Earlier, we discussed things we might see when looking outside the house. We also discussed things we might see inside the house."
- **Review the children's responses.** ("I'd see trees outside, with snow covering them. I'd see squirrels scampering up the trees. Inside, I'd see two comfortable chairs that are next to the fireplace.")
- **Introduce the activity.** "Today, we're going to write about our favorite thing(s) that we might see outside and inside the house." (Outside, I'd see trees, squirrels, and animal tracks. Inside, I'd see a rug, chairs, the fireplace, and things on the mantel.) Have the children copy one or more of their favorite sentences from the discussion onto a piece of lined paper. If they'd like to create their own sentence(s), be available to help them sound out the words. Attach their paper to their window drawings. (See Art #1.)

#2. Describe and write about the family.

- **Objective.** Integration of Knowledge and Ideas. Use illustrations and details in a story to describe its characters, setting, or events.
- **Level of difficulty.** Moderate. (This task may take several days to complete.)
- **Materials needed.** Lined paper and pencils.
- **Before the Activity.** Place a large piece of white paper on the board. Have a black marker available for writing the children's responses.
- **Begin the activity by saying,** "Earlier, we described this family."
- **Review the children's responses.** (The family looks happy. The family is warm inside their home. The young child is shaking hands with the dog.)
- **Introduce the activity.** "Today, you're going to copy one or more of your favorite sentences about the family on a piece of lined paper." If they'd like to create their own sentence(s), be available to help them sound out the words.

#3. Engage in an oral expression activity telling why certain items are important to us.

- **Objective.** Presentation of Knowledge and Ideas. Tell a story or recount an experience with appropriate facts and relevant, descriptive details, speaking audibly in coherent sentences.
- **Level of difficulty.** Easy.
- **Materials needed.** None.
- **Before the activity.** Have the children bring in a special item that's important to them. Talk about how families place things on their mantel that they feel are important.
- **Begin the activity by saying,** "Earlier, we noticed that this family placed special items on their mantel. The family has a boat, a

stuffed animal that looks like a cat, and a figurine of a wolf standing on a rock." What things are important to you?

- **Review the children's responses.** ("I got this blue ribbon when I rode my horse in the horse show. I got this certificate of appreciation for volunteering at my local animal shelter. I got this gardening set because I spent several hours helping at the community garden.")

- **Introduce the activity.** "Today, we're going to explain why the item we brought in is important." Give each child an opportunity to come to the front of the class and explain why that item is significant and important. Do not force the children to participate. Sharing an item should be on a voluntary basis. Discuss the fact that everyone doesn't necessarily appreciate the same things. This gives the children an opportunity to speak in front of their peers and verbalize their thoughts.

Science

#1. Introduce a thermometer.

- **Objective.** Earth and Space Science. Weather and Climate. Use and share observations of local weather conditions to describe patterns over time.

- **Level of difficulty.** Moderate. (This task may take several days to complete.)

- **Materials needed.** Copy of the thermometer page (see resource section) and a red crayon.

- **Before the activity.** Run off copies of the thermometer in the resource section for each child. Go to the internet and type, "How cold does it have to be to start snowing?" Choose an age-appropriate website that relays information about how cold the temperature needs to be to start snowing.

- **Begin the activity by saying,** "Earlier, we discussed what time of year we thought it was in the story. We said that it must be winter because it's snowing outside."

- **Review the children's responses.** ("I think it's winter because there's snow falling outside. Snow falls in the winter.")

- **Introduce the activity.** "Today, we going to examine a thermometer and find out how cold it needs to be to start snowing." Ask the children if anyone knows how cold it must be for snow to form. Go to the internet and type, "How cold does it have to be to start snowing?" Select the age-appropriate website you chose earlier that relays this information. Read and discuss the information with the children. Give each child a copy of the thermometer (see resource section). Have the children draw a red line at thirty-two degrees Fahrenheit (32°F).

- **Extension of the activity.** To extend the lesson, allow them to locate various temperatures on their thermometer (e.g., fifty degrees Fahrenheit [50°F], seventy-five degrees Fahrenheit [75°F]).

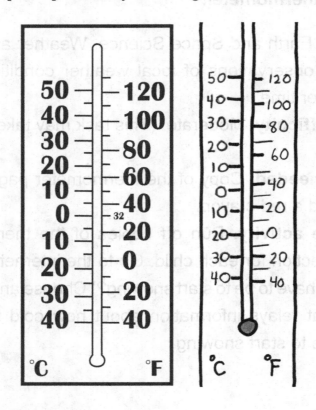

#2. Learn about and make snowflakes.

- **Objective.** Earth and Space Science. Weather, Climate. Obtain and combine information to describe climates in different regions of the world.

- **Level of difficulty.** Moderate. (This task may take several days to complete.)

- **Materials needed.** Place a large piece of white paper on the board. Have a black marker available for writing the information about snowflakes. Have lined paper and pencils available for the children to write the snowflake information. Have scissors and sheets of white paper cut into squares for the children to make snowflakes. In addition, have glue and crayons available.

- **Before the activity.** Go to the internet and type, "Tell me some cool facts about snowflakes." Choose an age-appropriate website that relays this information. There are also videos available. Preview these websites before you show them to the children.

- **Begin the activity by saying,** "Earlier, we learned about how snowflakes are formed and how cold it needs to be for snow to form." (It needs to be thirty-two degrees Fahrenheit (32°F) for snow to form.) "Let's learn a few more cool facts about snowflakes." Read and discuss the information on the website you selected with the children.

- **Review the children's responses.** (We learned that snowflakes are light. Snowflakes are assorted sizes.)

- **Introduce the activity.** "Today, we're going to write our favorite fact(s) about snowflakes on a piece of lined paper. We'll also make snowflakes."

1. Have the children write their favorite fact(s) about snowflakes on the lined paper.

23

2. When they've completed their writing, have them make snowflakes. Give them square pieces of white paper and show them how to fold the paper. (Fold the paper in half, forming a triangle. Fold the paper again and cut along the folded edges.) Have them cut out several snowflakes and save these for later.

3. Give the children a large piece of dark blue construction paper and have them glue their snowflakes to the paper. Have them glue the facts they learned about snowflakes to the back of their picture.

- **Extension of the activity.** They can make small snowflakes and glue these to a piece of construction paper, adding additional details (e.g., trees, animals, and hills). Have them attach the snowflake information from the website to their picture. You could also have them make large snowflakes and hang them from the ceiling.

Math

#1. Write numerals and identify quantity.

- **Objective.** Counting and Cardinality. Know number names and the count sequence. Write numbers from 0 to 20. Represent several objects with a written numeral—0–20 (with 0 representing a count of no objects).
- **Level of difficulty.** Easy.
- **Materials needed.** Markers, whiteboards, crayons, paper.
- **Before the activity.** Ask the children how many of them have a dog. Write this numeral on a piece of paper and save it for later.
- **Begin the activity by saying,** "Earlier, we took a survey to determine how many of you had dogs in your family."
- **Review the children's responses.** (Fifteen children raised their hand when they were asked if they had a dog.)

24

- **Introduce the activity.** "Today, we're going to review how many of you have dogs in your family."
  1. Earlier, I asked you to raise your hand if you had a dog. There were 15 students in class who had a dog. Write this numeral on the board. Point to the numeral on the board. Have the children count aloud to 15.
  2. Have the younger children practice writing the numeral 15 on a whiteboard. Ask the children what 15 means and allow them time to explain. (We can draw 15 things on the board. We can have 15 kids stand up. We can put 15 crayons on the desk.) Have the older children show this number by drawing 15 dog bones on a piece of paper.

#2. Introduce one-to-one correspondence.

- **Objective.** Counting and Cardinality. Count to tell the number of objects. Understand the relationship between numbers and quantities. Connect counting to cardinality.
- **Level of difficulty.** Moderate. (This task may take several days to complete.)
- **Materials needed.** Round peel-off dots, pencils, crayons, and construction paper.
- **Before the activity.** Prepare the materials.
- **Begin the activity by saying,** "Earlier, I asked you to raise your hand if you had a dog."
- **Review the children's responses.** (There were 15 of you who said you had a dog.) Write this numeral on the board.
- **Introduce the activity.** "Today, we're going to match 15 dogs with 15 bowls."
  1. Give each child a piece of construction paper. Distribute one peel-off dot to each child. Have them place the dot on the top, left-hand side of the construction paper. Tell them they'll need

25

to make room for an additional 14 dots/dogs on the construction paper.

2. Have them draw and color a dog next to or below the dot. This dot will represent the dog's bowl. Continue distributing the dots until all 15 dots and dogs are drawn. Make sure the children print their name on the back of the paper. Practice counting the number of "bowls," as well as the dogs near the bowls. Relay the fact that each dog has a bowl. This is called a one-to-one correspondence. There is one bowl for each dog.

#3. Survey what the adults might be drinking.

- **Objective.** Measurement and Data. Represent and interpret data. Draw a picture graph and a bar graph (with single-unit scale) to represent a data set with up to four categories. Solve simple, put-together, take-apart, and compare problems using information presented in a bar graph.
- **Level of difficulty.** Easy.
- **Materials needed.** Sticky notes and pencils.
- **Before the activity.** Place a large piece of white paper on the board and divide it into several sections. These sections will represent the possible beverages the parents are drinking. Ask the children to name some beverages they could be drinking and write them on the board. Tell them that they can only vote one time for a beverage. They will write their choice on a sticky note.
- **Begin the activity by saying,** "Earlier, we observed that the man and woman inside the house were drinking some beverage(s)."
- **Review the children's responses.** (Hot chocolate, hot apple cider, and hot cranberry juice).
- **Introduce the activity.** "Today, we're going to take a survey to determine which of the beverages we think the adults are drinking."

26

1. Give each child a sticky note and have the children print their names on the back of the sticky notes. Have them write the beverage they thought the adults were drinking on the front of the sticky note (e.g., hot chocolate, hot apple cider, hot cranberry juice).

2. Ask the children to come to the front of the class, one at a time, and place their sticky note in the appropriate section. When all the children have placed their sticky notes on the beverage of their choice, have one child come to the front of the room and count the number of sticky notes placed on one of the beverages. Ask a second child to count the same sticky notes to verify the number.

3. Do this same process for the other beverage choices. If both numbers are the same, print that number at the bottom of the paper. Review the results with the children. ("Five of you thought the adults were drinking hot chocolate. Four of you thought they were drinking hot apple cider, and four of you thought they were drinking hot cranberry juice.")

Hot Chocolate	Hot Apple Cider	Hot Cranberry Juice
5 sticky notes	4 sticky notes	4 sticky notes
Total = 5	Total = 4	Total = 4

#4. Make a bar graph of the above hot beverages.

- **Objective.** Measurement and Data. Represent and Interpret data. Draw a picture graph and a bar graph (with single-unit scale) to represent a data set with up to four categories. Solve simple put-together, take-apart, and compare problems using information presented in a bar graph.

- **Level of difficulty.** Moderate. (This task may take several days to complete.)

- **Materials needed.** Examples of bar graphs, survey results from the example above (Math #3), a piece of half-inch graph paper, a piece of one-inch graph paper, pencils, and crayons.
- **Before the Activity.** Distribute the one-inch graph paper, pencils, and crayons.
- **Begin the activity by saying,** "Earlier, we took a survey to determine what we thought the adults were drinking."
- **Review the children's responses.** (Hot chocolate, hot apple cider, and hot cranberry juice).
- **Introduce the activity.** "Today, we're going to create a bar graph of the adult beverages we chose earlier."

1. Show the children various bar graphs so they have an idea of what they look like. Discuss the various features shown on graphs (e.g., the title, the numbers on the left-hand side, the choices at the bottom of the graph).

2. Give them a piece of one-inch graph paper, emphasizing that each one-inch section represents one vote. Explain to them that the bar graph needs to have a title. We could call the graph "Adult Beverage Choices." In addition, it needs to show the total number of votes on the left-hand side of the page. The favorite beverages would appear at the bottom of the graph (e.g., hot chocolate, hot apple cider, hot cranberry juice). The actual votes are listed above the specific beverage. (Five of you thought the adults were drinking hot chocolate. Four of you thought they were drinking hot apple cider. And four of you thought they were drinking hot cranberry juice.)

3. Finally, allow the children to color in the number of votes for each hot beverage.

Adult Beverage Choices

	Hot Chocolate	Hot Apple Cider	Hot Cranberry Juice
5	X		
4	X	X	X
3	X	X	X
2	X	X	X
1	X	X	X

#5. Survey the children's favorite beverages.

- **Objective.** Measurement and Data. Represent and interpret data.
- **Level of difficulty.** Easy.
- **Materials needed.** A large piece of paper placed on the board, sticky notes, and pencils.
- **Before the activity.** Place a large piece of white paper on the board and divide it into several sections. These sections will represent the possible beverages the children enjoy. Have a black marker available. Ask them what beverages they enjoy drinking and write these on the board (e.g., Coca-Cola, milk, water, apple juice, hot chocolate, hot apple cider, and hot cranberry juice). When they've listed all the beverage choices, write these choices in the designated areas on the white paper. Tell them that they can only vote one time for a beverage. They will print their name and choice on a sticky note.
- **Begin the activity by saying,** "Earlier, we discussed what beverages you personally enjoyed drinking."
- **Review the children's responses.** (Coca-Cola, milk, water, apple juice, hot chocolate, hot apple cider, and hot cranberry juice).
- **Introduce the activity.** "Today, we're going to take a survey to determine which of the beverages you enjoy drinking."

1. Give each child a sticky note and have them print their name on the back of the sticky note. Have them write the beverage they enjoy on the front of the sticky note.

2. One at a time, allow them to place their sticky note on the beverage they enjoy drinking. When all the children have placed their sticky notes on the beverage of their choice, have one child come to the front of the room and count the number of sticky notes placed on one of the beverages. Ask a second child to count the same sticky notes to verify the number.

3. Do this same process for the other beverage choices. If both numbers are the same, print that number at the bottom of the paper. Review the results with the children. (Four of you enjoy drinking Coca-Cola, four of you enjoy drinking water, and five of you enjoy drinking milk.)

Note. After the children have completed some of the prior activities, serve some hot chocolate with a candy cane or marshmallows inserted in the cup. This could be a special reward for completing their writing or math activities. (See resource section for permission slips.)

Wolf in the Snow illustration: Young girl walking up a hill

Direct the children's attention to the picture of the young girl walking up the hill, with the dog barking in the background. Encourage them to answer the following questions in complete sentences.

QUESTIONS

The brackets around the text indicate questions/instructions an adult should read to the children. Examples of how the children may answer the questions are included in parentheses.

- **[What do you see on this page?]**
- **[How would you describe the scenery/location of this family's house?]** Write the children's responses on a piece of paper and save this for later. (It has a hill. There are trees near the house. It's snowing. It's located in an isolated area.) See Writing #1.
- **[Why do you think the dog is barking?]** Write the children's responses on a piece of paper and save this for later. (The young child is walking away from the house, so the dog probably wants to come with the young child. The young child and dog live in the same family, so the dog wants to go with the young child.) See Writing #2.
- **[How do you think the dog feels?]** Write the children's responses on a piece of paper and save this for later. (The dog feels lonely. I think the dog wants to go with the young girl. I think the dog is wondering who it will play with during the day.) See Writing #3.
- **[What type of dog do you think the family owns?]** Write the children's responses on a piece of paper and save this for later. (I think it's a hound dog. I think it's a bloodhound.) See Math #3.

31

- **[How would you describe the house?]** Write the children's responses on a piece of paper and save this for later. (It's a square. It's made of wood. It has several windows.) See Math #1.

- **[The house on this page could be described as a square or a rectangle. Are all houses squares or rectangles?]** (No, some houses are round. Some houses have more than four sides.) The house on this page could be described as a square or a rectangle.) See Math #2.

- **[Where is the house located?]** Write the children's responses on a piece of paper and save this for later. (Well, there are trees surrounding the house. I don't see any other houses nearby. I think the house is in a rural area.)

- **[Do you know what kind of trees are around the house?]** Write the children's responses on a piece of paper and save this for later (I think the trees are pine trees. I think the trees are spruce trees.) See Science #1.

- **[Do you think the family has a lot of neighbors? Why or why not?]** (I don't think the family has a lot of neighbors because they're in a forest.)

- **[What time of year do you think it is?]** (Well, the ground isn't completely covered with snow, so it could be early or late fall.)

- **[Do you think it's cold outside?]** (Well, the child is wearing boots, mittens, a coat, and a face covering, so it must be cold.)

- **[The child is walking away from the house. Do you think she'd like the dog to come with her?]** (I think she would like the dog to come with her, but she's probably on her way to school. The dog can't come to school. I think she wants the dog to stay near the house because she's going to school.) See Writing #2.

- **[How would you describe the relationship between the child and the dog?]** (The dog and the young child have a good relationship, because the child is turning back toward the dog to wave goodbye to it. The dog is barking toward the young child, as if to say, "See you later!" The dog seems to be well trained because it's staying near the house. If it hadn't been trained, it would follow the young child.) See Science #2.

- **[What wintry weather clothing is the young child wearing on her hands?]** (The young child is wearing mittens.) See Art #1.

ACTIVITIES

Art

#1. Make a pair of mittens.

- **Objective.** Creating, Anchor Standard #1. Generate and conceptualize artistic ideas and work. Investigate, Plan, Make. Engage in explorative and imaginative play with materials.
- **Level of difficulty.** Moderate. (This task may take several days to complete.)
- **Materials needed.** Mitten pattern (see resource section), poster board, scissors, pencil, glue, colored felt pieces, fabric glue, cotton balls, and yarn.
- **Before the activity.** Prepare the materials.
- **Begin the activity by saying,** "Earlier, we noticed that the young child was wearing mittens."
- **Review the children's responses.** (The young child is wearing mittens.)
- **Introduce the activity.** "Today, we're going to make a pair of mittens."
    1. An older child or parent can help the children with this project. Give each child the mitten pattern from the resource section and have them cut around the mitten.

2. Have them carefully trace two mittens onto a piece of poster board and cut around them. Make sure they print their names on the back of the mittens.

3. Have them glue the mittens onto their favorite color of felt, using fabric glue. Make sure the mittens are placed on the felt so that the thumb sections are facing each other. Make sure their name in facing outward.

4. After the mittens are dry, have the children carefully cut around them. Glue cotton balls to the top edge of the mittens. Let the cotton balls dry. Attach some yarn with glue at the top of each mitten.

- **Extension of the activity.** As an extension of this project, you might want to read the delightful story of *The Mitten* by Jan Brett.

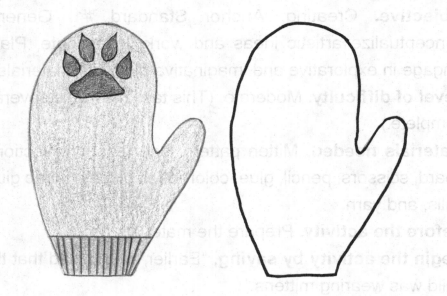

Writing

#1. Write about a place where they'd like to live.

- **Objective.** Knowledge of Language. Use knowledge of language and its conventions when writing, speaking, reading, or listening. Choose words and phrases for effect.

- **Level of difficulty.** Moderate (This task may take several days to complete.)
- **Materials needed.** Paper on bulletin board, marker, pencils, white construction paper, and lined paper.
- **Before the activity.** Place a large piece of paper on the board and have the children describe where they live.
- **Begin the activity by saying,** "Earlier, we described the scenery/location of this family's house."
- **Review the children's responses.** (It has a hill. There are trees near the house. It's snowing. It's located in an isolated area.)
- **Introduce the activity.** "Today, we're going to describe where we live."

1. Place a large piece of paper on the board and have the children describe where they live (I live in an urban area, with lots of people and houses and apartments. People live close together. I live in a rural area, with houses that are far apart. I live in a city area, with apartments that are close together.)
2. Discuss how people live in different areas for a variety of reasons. A job might have brought them to a certain area. They might have lived there all their lives. They might have come to live with a relative in a new area.
3. Have the children write about a place they'd like to live. Maybe they live in a city, but they'd prefer to live in the country. Perhaps they live in the country, and they'd prefer to live in a city.
4. When they've finished writing their story, allow them to draw a house in the location where they'd like to live. Have them attach their story to the house.
5. Have them tell a friend where they'd like to live. (I'd like to live in a cabin in the forest. I'd like to live in an apartment in New York City. I'd like to live in a house by a lake.)

#2. Write why the young girl would like the dog to come to school with her.

- **Objective.** Presentation of Knowledge and Ideas. Describe people, places, things, and events with relevant details, expressing ideas and feelings clearly.
- **Level of difficulty.** Moderate. (This task may take several days to complete.)
- **Materials needed.** Paper on bulletin board, marker, pencils, and lined paper.
- **Before the activity.** Place a large piece of paper on the board.
- **Begin the activity by saying,** "Earlier, we noticed that the young child was walking away from the house, and we wondered if she'd like the dog to come with her." Have the children describe why they think the young child would like to have the dog come with her.
- **Review the children's responses.** (I think she would like the dog to come with her, but she's probably on her way to school. The dog can't come to school. I think she wants the dog to stay near the house because she's going to school.).
- **Introduce the activity.** "Today, we're going to give some reasons why we think the young girl would like the dog to come with her." Review the children's responses. Have the children write their favorite reason why the young child would like to have the dog come with her onto a piece of lined paper. If they'd like to write their own sentence(s), be available to help them sound out the words. Have the children draw a picture of this page and attach it to their writing.

#3. Create conversation bubbles about how the dog might feel being left alone at home.

- **Objective.** Demonstrate command of the conventions of standard English grammar and usage when writing or speaking.

- **Level of difficulty.** Moderate. (This task may take several days to complete.)
- **Materials needed.** Paper on bulletin board, marker, pencils, and conversation bubbles (see resource section).
- **Before the activity.** Place a large piece of paper on the board and have the children describe what the dog might be feeling, saying, or thinking.
- **Begin the activity by saying,** "Earlier we discussed how we thought the dog felt."
- **Review the children's responses.** ("I sure wish I could go with her." "It's lonely staying here alone." "Who will I play with all day?" "I guess I'll have to run after the squirrels.")
- **Introduce the activity.** Today, we're going to create conversation bubbles to express what the dog might be feeling, saying, or thinking. Have the children write what they think the dog is feeling, saying, or thinking on a piece of paper. Help them make any corrections needed. Give each child a conversation bubble for each comment.

#4. Have the children think of reasons it would be a good idea for the dog to go to school with the child.

- **Objective.** Presentation of Knowledge and Ideas. (Produce complete sentences when appropriate to task and situation to provide requested detail or clarification.)
- **Level of difficulty.** Easy.

- **Materials needed.** Paper on bulletin board, marker, pencils, and lined paper.
- **Before the activity.** Place a piece of paper on the board and list a few reasons why it would be beneficial for the dog to come with the child. (The dog could protect the young child in a forest area. The dog has a good sense of smell and knows where to go. The dog also has a good sense of hearing and could hear things that the young child couldn't.)
- **Begin the activity by saying,** "Earlier we wondered if the young child wanted the dog to come with her."
- **Review the children's responses.** (If my dog comes with me, I'll be protected. My dog has a good sense of smell and could smell things I couldn't. The dog might see things that I don't see.)
- **Introduce the activity.** "Today, we're going to think of additional reasons it would be a good idea to have the dog come with the young child." Write the children's responses on a piece of paper. Have the children copy their favorite reason on a piece of lined paper.
- **Extension of the activity.** Do the same above process. However, have the children think of reasons it wouldn't be a good idea to have the dog come with the young child. (If the young child was in school, what would the dog do during the day? Where would the dog stay? The dog might need water and food during the day. What about the barking of the dog? How would the dog have a good relationship with any other dogs?)

Science

#1. Learn about the pinyon pine tree and taste pine nuts.

- **Objective.** Life Science. Interdependent Relationships in Ecosystems. Make observations of plants and animals to compare the diversity of life in different habitats.

- **Level of difficulty.** Easy.
- **Materials needed.** Paper on bulletin board, marker, permission form to taste pine nuts (see resource section), small paper cups, small tray/plate, and pine nuts.
- **Before the activity.** Place a piece of paper on the board and list the types of trees they think are surrounding the house. Go to the internet and type, "Tell me about pinyon pine trees." Choose an age-appropriate website.
- **Begin the activity by saying,** "Earlier, we discussed what type of trees surrounded the house."
- **Review the children's responses.** (The trees are pine trees. I think the trees are spruce trees.)
- **Introduce the activity.** "Today, we're going to learn about one type of tree. It's the pinyon pine tree."
  1. Go to the website that relays information about the pinyon pine tree. Read and discuss this information with the children. There are some interesting videos on the internet that the children might enjoy seeing. Tell them that a special nut comes from this tree.
  2. Ask the children to raise their hand if they've ever eaten a pine nut. Have a few pine nuts on a small tray and show the children what they look like. Make sure that no child has a nut allergy before you show them the nuts.
  3. Place a few pine nuts in a small paper cup and let the children taste them. Make sure you get parental permission before the children taste the pine nuts. (See resource section for permission form.) Ask them what they thought about the taste. Have them relay their opinion to a friend.

#2.Discuss the relationship between the child and the dog to learn about dog training.

- **Objective.** Engineering Design. Structures and Properties of Matter. Use a model to describe that animals receive different types of information through their senses, process the information in their brain, and respond to the information in different ways.

- **Level of difficulty.** Easy.

- **Materials needed.** Place a large piece of white paper on the board. Have a black marker available for writing the children's responses.

- **Before the activity.** Go to the internet and type, "Dog training." Choose an age-appropriate website.

- **Begin the activity by saying,** "Earlier we discussed the relationship between the child and the dog."

- **Review the children's responses.** (The dog and the young child have a good relationship, because the child is turning back toward the dog to wave goodbye to it. The dog is barking toward the young child, as if to say, "See you later!" The dog is well trained because it's staying near the house. If it hadn't been trained, it would follow the young child.)

- **Introduce the activity.** "Today, we going to discuss the relationship between the child and the dog."

  1. "What do you think about their relationship?" Review the children's responses. "You thought the child and the dog had a good relationship. You thought the dog was well trained."

  2. "Do you think all dogs are well trained?" "Today, we're going to learn about dog training."

  3. Go to the internet and type, "Dog training." Select the age-appropriate website you chose earlier. Read and discuss the information with the children. Ask the children if their dog obeys simple commands.

- **Extension of the activity.** Invite a dog trainer to class to discuss and demonstrate some simple commands, such as come, sit, heel, and stay.

Math

#1. Design the inside structure of a house.

- **Objective.** Measurement and Data. Geometric measurement. Understand concepts of area and relate area to multiplication and to addition. A square with side length one unit, called "a unit square," is said to have "one square unit" of area and can be used to measure area.
- **Level of difficulty.** Moderate for the younger children. Challenging for the older children.
- **Materials needed.** White construction paper, pencils, magazines, scissors, and glue.
- **Before the activity.** Go to the internet and type, "Images of simple house designs." Choose an age-appropriate website.
- **Begin the activity by saying,** "Earlier, we described the house."
- **Review the children's responses.** (It has a square shape. It's made of wood. It has several windows.)
- **Introduce the activity.** "Today, we're going to design the inside structure of the house."
  1. Go to the internet website and look at simple house designs. Show the children some of these simple design plans and discuss the various spaces and measurements. Explain to them that they'll create the inside structure of a house, determining where the various rooms will be located (e.g., living room, kitchen, bedrooms, and bathroom).
  2. Use graph paper for this process. For the younger children, give them a piece of construction paper and let them decide where

each room will be located. Have them cut out pictures from a magazine and glue them onto the paper (e.g., a picture of a living room, kitchen, bathroom, and bedrooms).

- **Extension activity for older students.**
  1. For the older children, tell them the total living space for the house should equal 1,400 square feet. Give each child a practice piece of paper and have them sketch out where they think each room should be located. They should indicate the measurements of each room. (The bedroom is 6 feet by 6 feet.) They can sketch out several options. The total measurement of the house should equal 1,400 square feet.
  2. When they're ready to do their final sketch, give them a piece of heavy paper. Have them carefully draw their design on this paper. Have them explain to the class why they chose the various locations for each room. (I put the kitchen away from the living room because the fireplace would make it too warm. I put the living room near the fireplace to keep the area warm.)
  3. As an extension of this lesson, you might want to invite an architect to class to discuss architectural design and drawing.

#2. Learn about various shapes.

- **Objective.** Geometry. Identify and describe shapes (squares, circles, triangles, rectangles, hexagons, cubes, cones, cylinders, and spheres). Correctly name shapes regardless of their orientations or overall size.
- **Level of difficulty.** Moderate. (This task may take several days to complete.)
- **Materials needed.** Shapes page (see resource section), pencils, white construction paper, and glue.
- **Before the activity.** Go to the internet and type, "Tell me about shapes." Choose an age-appropriate website.

- **Begin the activity by saying,** "Earlier, we discussed the shape of houses."
- **Review the children's responses.** (Some houses are round. Some houses have more than four sides.)
- **Introduce the activity.** "Today, we're going to discuss various shapes." Show the children the resource page that shows the various shapes (e.g., circle, square, rectangle, triangle, pentagon [five sides], hexagon [six sides], and octagon [eight sides]. Go to the website you selected. Read and discuss the information with the children. Allow them to cut out and trace around the outside of each shape and count the number of sides. There are several videos on the internet that the children might enjoy seeing about shapes. Choose age-appropriate videos to share.

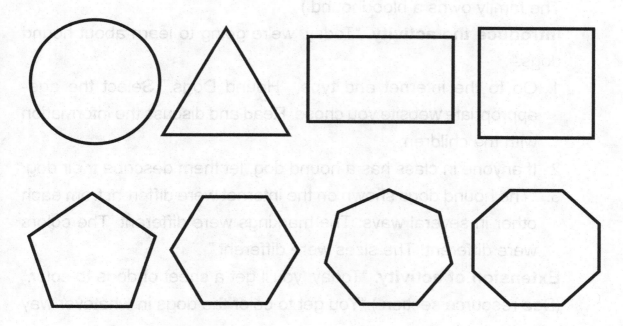

#3. Learn about hound dogs.

- **Objective.** Measurement and Data. Classify objects and count the number of objects in each category. Classify objects into given categories, count the numbers of objects in each category, and sort the categories by count.

- **Level of difficulty.** Moderate. (This task may take several days.)
- **Materials needed.** Place a large piece of white paper on the board. Have tape available so the dogs can be grouped in various ways. Have glue, scissors, construction paper, and crayons available. Have paper bags or small boxes to hold the colored dogs. (See resource section.)
- **Before the activity.** Go to the internet and type, "Hound Dogs." Choose an age-appropriate website.
- **Begin the activity by saying,** "Earlier, we discussed what type of dog the family owns."
- **Review the children's responses.** (The family owns a hound dog. The family owns a bloodhound.)
- **Introduce the activity.** "Today, we're going to learn about hound dogs."
  1. Go to the internet and type, "Hound Dogs." Select the age-appropriate website you chose. Read and discuss the information with the children.
  2. If anyone in class has a hound dog, let them describe their dog.
  3. "The hound dogs shown on the internet were different from each other in several ways. The markings were different. The colors were different. The sizes were different."
- **Extension of activity.** "Today, you'll get a sheet of dogs to color." (See resource section.) "You get to color the dogs in whatever way you choose."

Later, we'll group the dogs in certain ways.

1. Give the children time to color the dogs in different ways. When the children have finished coloring their dogs, ask them to print their name on the back of each dog. Put all the dogs into a box.

2. Put a piece of paper on the board and pick several dogs from the box that have the same attribute (e.g., dogs with brown markings). Tape these dogs onto the paper. Ask the children how the dogs are the same. Allow the children time to think of ways the dogs are the same. (These dogs all have brown markings.)

3. Repeat this process for another attribute. (These dogs all have facial markings.) Repeat this process for another attribute. (These dogs all have black markings.)

4. Allow the children to sort the dogs in the box. Then have two children sit at a table or on the floor with a piece of paper in front of them. Allow the children to sort the dogs in whatever way they choose. The only requirement for this task is that they must tell their partner how the dogs are the same. (The dogs have long fur, facial markings, brown coloring, or black markings.)

5. When all the children have had an opportunity to sort the dogs in the box, you can return their individual dogs. Allow them to sort and glue their dogs into various groups on a piece of construction paper.

Wolf in the Snow illustration: Child walking in the field/forest

Direct the children's attention to the round picture where the child is walking in the field/forest. Encourage them to answer the following questions in complete sentences.

QUESTIONS

The brackets around the text indicate questions/instructions that an adult should read to the children. Examples of how the children may answer the questions are included in parentheses.

- **[What do you see on this page?]**
- **[Where do you think the child is going?]** (The child is going to school. I think the child is going to visit a friend. I think the child is going to the forest to play.)
- **[There's a path where she's walking. Do you think she's going to school or a friend's house?]** (I think she's going to school. She's probably used this path/trail before.)
- **[Do you use the same path to school?]** See Math #1.
- **[Could you tell someone how to go to school?]** See Writing / Oral Language #1.
- **[What do you think the child could do in the forest?]** Make a list of things she could do (e.g., build a snowman, watch birds, collect interesting rocks, or find pine cones). See Art #2 and Writing / Oral Language #2.
- **[Evergreen trees have pine cones attached. How many of you have ever seen a pine cone?]** Record the number on the board. (Nine children have seen a pine cone.) See Science #1.

- **[How could we describe pine cones?]** Write the children's responses on a piece of paper and save this for later. (The pinecones are round. They have round things in the middle.) If the children live in an area where pine cones are available, ask the children to bring in pine cones that have dropped to the ground. See Writing / Oral Language #4 and Science #1.

- **[Do you think pine trees are important to our environment?]** Write the children's responses on a piece of paper and save this for later. (Pine trees are important for our environment/world because they give us food. Trees also produce oxygen for our environment.) See Writing / Oral Language #5.

- **[The child in the story is wearing a red coat. Raise your hand if you have a red coat.]** Write the children's responses on a piece of paper and save this for later. (Thirteen children in class have red coats.) See Art #1 and Math #2.

- **[The child in the story is wearing boots. Raise your hand if you have a pair of boots.]** Write the children's responses on a piece of paper and save this for later. (Thirteen children in class have boots.) See Writing / Oral Language #3 and Math #3.

- **[Why would wearing boots at this time of year and in this location be beneficial?]** Write the children's responses on a piece of paper and save this for later. (Boots would protect her feet in the snow. Boots would keep her feet warm.) See Writing #3.

ACTIVITIES

Art

#1. Design a new red coat for the young child.

- **Objective.** Responding. Anchor Standard #7. Perceive and analyze artistic work. Investigate, Plan, Make. Engage in explorative and imaginative play with materials.
- **Level of difficulty.** Moderate. (This task may take several days to complete.)
- **Materials needed.** Construction paper, poster board, coat page (see resource section), red felt, crayons, chalk, colored pencils, scissors, glue, and paint.
- **Before the activity.** Prepare all the materials.
- **Begin the activity by saying,** "Earlier, we talked about the child wearing a red coat."
- **Introduce the activity.** "Today, we're going to design a red coat for the child." Give the children a piece of paper and let them create different designs. When they think they're ready to draw their design, give them the coat page (see resource section). They can create a heavy paper coat using poster board. Have them use crayons, chalk, colored pencils, or paint to make their design. They can also use red felt to create the new coat, adding designs with a marker. They can draw the young child's face on a separate piece of paper, cut it out, and then glue the face onto the new coat if they'd like. When they're finished, place their coats on the bulletin board.

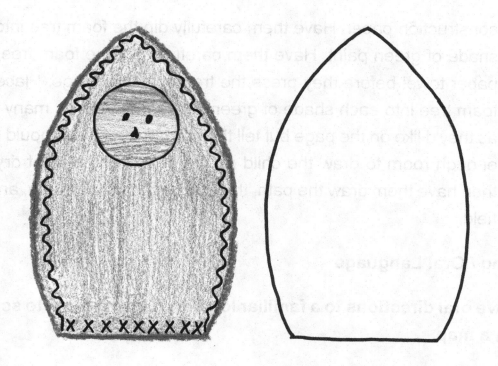

#2. Have the children create a forest scene using sponges and paint.

- **Objective.** Creating. Anchor Standards #2. Organize and develop artistic ideas and work. Investigate. Explore uses of materials and tools to create works of art or design.
- **Level of difficulty.** Moderate. (This task may take several days to complete.)
- **Materials needed.** Foam tree stamps, white construction paper, different shades of green paint, small pie tins to hold the paint, and paper towels.
- **Before the activity.** Prepare all the materials. Cut out the tree shapes from the foam squares.
- **Begin the activity by saying,** "Earlier, we talked about what the young girl could do in the forest."
- **Review the children's responses.** (Build a snowman, watch birds, collect interesting rocks, or find pinecones).
- **Introduce the activity.** "Today, we're going to create our own forest using foam stamps." Give the children a large piece of white

construction paper. Have them carefully dip the foam tree into one shade of green paint. Have them carefully blot the foam tree on a paper towel before they press the tree onto their page. Place one foam tree into each shade of green. Have them put as many trees as they'd like on the page but tell the children that they should leave enough room to draw the child on the path. Let the paint dry and then have them draw the path, the child, birds, a snowman, and the field.

Writing / Oral Language

#1. Give oral directions to a familiar location. Draw a route to school, using a map.

- **Objective.** Presentation of Knowledge and Ideas. Describe familiar people, places, things, and events and, with prompting and support, provide additional detail.
- **Level of difficulty.** Moderate. (This task may take several days to complete.)
- **Materials needed.** Local street map, projector, construction paper, and pencils.
- **Before the activity.** Project the local street map onto a board. Prepare all materials.
- **Begin the activity by saying,** "Earlier, I asked if you could tell someone how you go to school."
- **Review the children's responses.** (I go out my front door, turn left onto 6th Street, turn right onto Maple Avenue, and walk directly to school.)
- **Introduce the activity.** "Today, we're going to look at our local street map, draw a picture, and explain to a friend how we get to school." (See Math #1.) Demonstrate this process with the children on the map. Give the children a piece of paper so they can draw

and name the streets that would get them to school. Have them tell a friend exactly the route they'd take to get to school, using the picture they've drawn. (I leave my house and walk east on Maple Street. Then I turn north on Spruce Street. I walk two blocks on Spruce Street until I arrive at school.)

#2. Have the children write about an activity that could be done in a forest area. Draw a picture of this activity.

- **Objective.** Presentation of Knowledge and Ideas. Speak audibly and express thoughts, feelings, and ideas clearly.

- **Level of difficulty.** Moderate. (This task may take several days to complete.)

- **Materials needed.** Large piece of white paper on the board, black marker, pencils, crayons, and lined paper.

- **Before the activity.** Place a large piece of white paper on the board. Have a black marker available for writing the children's responses.

- **Begin the activity by saying,** "Earlier, we wondered what the child could do in the forest."

- **Review the children's responses.** (She could build a snowman, watch birds, or collect interesting rocks or pine cones.)

- **Introduce the activity.** "Today, we're going to draw and write about our favorite activity in the forest." Have the children tell why they'd do the activity they chose. (I think I'd go bird watching in the forest so I could try to identify the various kinds of birds that live there.) When the children have completed their sentence/paragraph, have them draw a picture of the forest activity. Allow the children to explain their choice to a friend.

#3. Discuss why wearing boots would be a good idea in the snow. Draft a story about where a pair of boots might travel.

- **Objective.** Research to Build and Present Knowledge. With guidance and support from adults, recall information from experiences or gather information from provided sources to answer a question.
- **Level of difficulty.** Moderate (This task may take several days to complete.)
- **Materials needed.** Large piece of white paper on the board, black marker, pencils, crayons, lined paper, boot page (see resource section), cotton balls, string/yarn, and glue.
- **Before the activity.** Place a large piece of white paper on the board. Have a black marker available for writing the children's responses.
- **Begin the activity by saying,** "Earlier, we discussed why we thought wearing boots was a good idea."
- **Review the children's responses.** (Boots would protect her feet in the snow. Boots would keep her feet warm. Boots would prevent injuring the bottom of her feet.).
- **Introduce the activity.** "Today, you're going to write a story about where a pair of boots might go. It doesn't necessarily have to be in the snow, just some location of your choice." (My boots took me on a trail through Yellowstone National Park. I walked along a boardwalk next to a geyser. The geyser was called Old Faithful. It shot hot water into the sky. My boots enjoyed that experience!) Allow the children to make a pair of boots and attach some string to create laces. You could also glue cotton or felt to the top of the boots. Allow them to choose any color construction paper for their boots. Attach their story to the boots. (See resource section.)

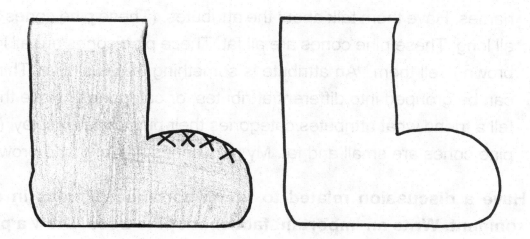

#4. Have the children examine various pine cones and place their pine cones into various groups.

- **Objective.** Presentation of Knowledge and Ideas. Report on a topic or text, tell a story, or recount an experience in an organized manner, using appropriate facts and relevant, descriptive details to support main ideas or themes. Speak clearly at an understandable pace.
- **Level of difficulty.** Easy.
- **Materials needed.** A variety of pine cones to examine (e.g., long, fat, short, light brown, and dark brown).
- **Before the activity.** Ask the children to bring in a variety of pine cones.
- **Begin the activity by saying,** "Earlier, I asked you to describe a pine cone."
- **Review the children's responses.** (The pine cone is round. It has round things in the middle.)
- **Introduce the activity.** "Today, we're going to examine the pine cones that you collected. We're going to put them into groups." Give each child a variety of pine cones (e.g., small, big, long, fat, light brown, and dark brown pine cones). Have them place their pine cones into various groups. Allow them to determine the groups'

names. Have them talk about the attributes. (These pine cones are all long. These pine cones are all fat. These pine cones are all light brown.) Tell them, "An attribute is something that is similar. Things can be grouped into different attributes, or categories." Have them tell a friend what attributes/categories their pine cones display. (My pine cones are small and fat. My pine cones are long and brown.)

#5. Have a discussion related to the importance of trees in our environment. Write an important fact about pine trees. Draw a pine tree.

- **Objective.** Comprehension and Collaboration. Engage effectively in a range of collaborative discussions (one-on-one, in groups, and teacher-led) with diverse partners on topics and texts, building on others' ideas and expressing their own clearly.)
- **Level of difficulty.** Easy.
- **Materials needed.** White construction paper, paints, paintbrushes, crayons, pencils, and lined paper.
- **Before the activity.** Go to the internet and type, "Why are pine trees important to the environment?" Choose a website that's age appropriate.
- **Begin the activity by saying,** "Earlier, we wondered if pine trees were important for our environment."
- **Review the children's responses.** (I think pine trees are important for our environment/world because they give us food. Pine trees also produce oxygen for our environment.)
- **Introduce the activity.** "Today, we're going to learn about pine trees and learn why they're important to our environment." Go to the internet and type, "Why are pine trees important to the environment?" Select the website you chose to use. Read and discuss this information with the children. (Pine trees are important because they keep us cool. They also give us food.) Have the

children draw/paint one type of pine tree and write one important environmental fact about that tree.

Science

#1. Examine a pine cone and learn additional facts about it.

- **Objective.** Life Science. Interdependent Relationships in Ecosystems. Make observations of plants and animals to compare the diversity of life in different habitats.
- **Level of difficulty.** Easy.
- **Materials needed.** Pine cones and pine nuts.
- **Before the activity.** Place a large piece of white paper on the board. Have a black marker available for writing the children's responses.
- **Begin the activity by saying,** "Earlier, we discovered that nine children in class had seen a pine cone.
- **Review the children's responses.** (I've seen a pine cone. It was shaped like an egg. It had little things that look like petals on the outside. It was brown. Some pine cones are egg-shaped and fat, while others are long and thin.)
- **Introduce the activity.** "Today, we're going to learn about and examine various pine cones."
  1. Raise your hand if you've ever seen a pine cone. Record the number on the board. Go to the internet and type, "Show me pine cones with seeds." Choose an age-appropriate website for the children. Read and discuss the information with them. There are also videos that the children will enjoy seeing and hearing. Preview these videos before you show them to the children.
  2. Bring in various pine cones for the children to examine. Have the children verbally describe the pine cone. (e.g., The pine cone is brown. The pine cone has pointy things on the outside. The pine cone has different shapes.). Explain to the children that the

pine cones hold the seeds, which have a soft, meaty substance inside.

3. Heat some of the pine cones in an oven (at approximately 170°) until you can remove some of the seeds. Have the children examine the seeds.

4. Bring in some pine nuts for the children to examine. Make sure no child in class has a nut allergy. Allow them to carefully examine the seeds. Have them taste a few pine nuts. (See resource section for the permission form.)

Extension of the activity. If possible, plant a few pine seeds. The children will enjoy watching them grow.

Math

#1. Determine an alternate route to school on a city street map.

- **Objective.** Geometry. Reason with shapes and their attributes. Partition shapes into parts with equal areas. Express the area of each part as a unit fraction of the whole. For example, partition a shape into four parts with equal area and describe the area of each part as one quarter of the area of the shape.

- **Level of difficulty.** Moderate. (This task may take several days to complete.)

- **Materials needed.** Local city map, white construction paper, pencils, and crayons.

- **Before the activity.** Display a large city map on the board showing the streets near the school.

- **Begin the activity by saying,** "Earlier, we noticed that the young child was walking on a path. She might be on her way to school, to play in the forest, or to visit a friend. When we go to a certain location, we usually have different ways we can get there."

- **Review the children's responses.** (If I live on 9th Street and I want to get to school, I could walk west on 9th Street, turn north on Maple Street, and then walk directly to the school. I could also walk east on 9th Street and then turn north on Spruce Street and walk directly to the school.)

- **Introduce the activity.** "Today, we're going to find a different way to get to school. You usually go in the same direction. Today, we're going to look at a map to see if you could get to school using a different route. Display a large city map on the board showing the streets near the school. Show them how they could take different routes to reach the same destination. (If I live on 9th Street and I want to get to school, I could walk west on 9th Street, turn north on Maple Street, and then walk directly to the school. I could also walk east on 9th Street and then turn north on Spruce Street and walk directly to the school.) "Today, we're going to determine the easiest and safest way to get to school." Give each child a piece of white construction paper. Have each child come up to the map and determine the safest and easiest way to get to school. Then have them draw this route to school on the construction paper. They can add additional streets to their map if they'd like to. Have them explain to a friend the route they'd take to school. If the city map has a scale designation, have the children determine the distance from their house to the school.

#2. Practice writing the numeral determined by the survey question, "Who owns a red coat?" Practice writing number sentences that would equal that number.

- **Objective.** Counting and Cardinality. Know number names and the count sequence. Write numbers from 0 to 20. Represent a number of objects with a written numeral from 0 to 20 (with 0 representing a count of no objects). Operations and Algebraic Thinking. Understand

and apply properties of operations and the relationship between addition and subtraction.

- **Level of difficulty.** Easy.
- **Materials needed.** Markers, whiteboard, pencils, and paper.
- **Before the activity.** Display the paper showing the survey results to the question, "Who owns a red coat?"
- **Review the children's responses.** (Thirteen children owned a red coat.)
- **Introduce the activity.** "Today, we're going to practice writing the numeral 13 on a whiteboard." Have the children practice writing that number on a whiteboard. For the younger children, have them practice counting from 0 to 13.
- **Extension of the activity.** For the older students, have them write number sentences that would equal thirteen (0 + 13 = 13, 1 + 12 = 13, 2 + 11 = 13, 3 + 10 = 13, 4 + 9 = 13, 5 + 8 = 13, 6 + 7 = 13, 7 + 6 = 13, 8 + 5 + 13, 9 + 4 = 13, 10 + 3 = 13, 11 + 2 = 13, 12 + 1 = 13, 13 + 0 = 13).

#3. Practice writing the numeral determined by the survey question, "Who owns a pair of boots?" Practice writing number sentences that would equal that number.

- **Objective.** Counting and Cardinality. Know number names and the count sequence. Write numbers from 0 to 20. Represent several objects with a written numeral from 0 to 20 (with 0 representing a count of no objects). Operations and Algebraic Thinking. Understand and apply properties of operations and the relationship between addition and subtraction.
- **Level of difficulty.** Easy.
- **Materials needed.** Markers, whiteboard, pencils, and paper.
- **Before the activity.** Display the paper showing the survey results to the question, "Who owns a pair of boots?"

- **Begin the activity by saying,** "Earlier, we took a survey to determine who owned a pair of boots."
- **Review the children's responses.** (Thirteen children owned a pair of boots.)
- **Introduce the activity.** "Today, we're going to practice writing the numeral 13 on a whiteboard. Have the children practice writing that number on a whiteboard. For the younger children, have them practice counting from zero to thirteen.
- **Extension of the activity.** For the older students, have them write number sentences that would equal thirteen (0 + 13 = 13, 1 + 12 = 13, 2 + 11 = 13. See the number sentence combinations in Math #2).

QUESTIONS

The brackets around the text indicate questions/instructions an adult should read to the children. Examples of how the children may answer the questions are included in parentheses.

- **[What do you see on this page?]**
- **[How many wolves are on this page?]** Write the children's response on a piece of paper and save this for later. (There are five wolves on this page.) See Math #1.
- **[Do you think the wolves on this page are all the same age? Why or why not?]** Write the children's comments on a piece of paper and save this for later. (Well, the wolf in the middle looks smaller. He or she must be the youngest. I don't think the wolves are all the same age.) See Science #1.
- **[Why do you think the smallest wolf is in the center?]** Write the children's comments on a piece of paper and save this for later (I think the older wolves may be protecting the younger wolf. The older wolves may be letting the younger wolf rest.) See Science #2.
- **[How many wolves are howling?]** (It looks like one wolf in the background is howling.)
- **[Why do wolves howl?]** Write the children's comments on a piece of paper and save this for later. (I think wolves howl because they're trying to find members of their pack. I think wolves howl because

they're warning other wolves to stay out of their territory.). See Science #3.

- **[Do you think these wolves belong to the same wolf pack? Why or why not?]** Write the children's comments on a piece of paper and save this for later. (These wolves belong to the same wolf pack because wolves usually travel together. I don't think the wolves would allow wolves outside their pack to travel with them.) See Science #4.

- **[What do we call a gathering of wolves?]** (We call them a pack, a family, or a rout.)

- Point out that there are five wolves on this page. **[Can you think of a number sentence that would equal five (5)?]** Write the children's comments on a piece of paper and save this for later. ($0 + 5 = 5$, $1 + 4 = 5$, $2 + 3 = 5$, $3 + 2 = 5$, $4 + 1 = 5$, $5 + 0 = 5$.) See Math #2. Have the younger children hold up five fingers. See Math #3.

- Note that the wolves on this page are all facing the same direction. **[How can we determine which way the wolves are headed?]** Hold up a picture of the compass rose (see resource section). Draw a large compass rose on the board so the children can easily see it. A compass rose shows us direction. **[In which direction are the wolves headed?]** Note that they should assume the top of the page is north. (Well, they're headed west.) See Art #1.

- **[The young child on the left-hand side of the page is headed in which direction?]** (She's headed east.) Repeat the prior process. See Art #1.

- **[Do you think the wolves are able to travel a long distance?]** Write the children's responses on a piece of paper and save this for later. (I think wolves can travel a long distance. I think they can travel ten miles a day. I think wolves can travel fifteen miles per day.) See Math #4.

- **[Do you think wolves can run fast?]** Write the children's responses on a piece of paper and save this for later. (I think wolves can run fast. I think wolves can run five miles per hour. I think wolves can run ten miles per hour.). See Math #5.

- **[Do you think the wolves and the young child will run into each other?]** Write the children's responses on a piece of paper and save this for later. (I think the young child will stay on the path and won't run into the wolves. I think the wolves would avoid the young child if they heard or smelled her. I think the wolves might come close to the young child, but I think they'd move away from her.) See Writing #1.

- **[Do you think wolves can communicate with each other?]** Write the children's responses on a piece of paper and save this for later. (I think wolves do communicate with each other. I think it would be important for wolves to be able to communicate with each other.) See Science #6.

ACTIVITIES

Art

#1. Learn about and decorate a compass rose.

- **Objective.** Responding. Anchor Standard #8. Interpret intent and meaning in artistic work. Analyze. Interpret art by identifying subject matter and describing relevant details.

- **Level of difficulty.** Moderate. (This task may take several days to complete.)

- **Materials needed.** Compass rose sheets (see resource section), crayons, markers, large map of the United States, scissors, and construction paper.

- **Before the activity.** Put the map of the United States on a bulletin board. Assemble the materials to color the compass rose.

- **Begin the activity by saying,** "Earlier, we noticed that all the wolves were facing the same direction. We wondered about the direction the wolves were headed."

- **Introduce the activity.** "Today, we're going to learn about and decorate a compass rose." Hold up the picture of the compass rose (see resource section.) "A compass rose tells us which direction we're headed. The top of the compass rose is facing north. The bottom of the compass rose is facing south. The right-hand point is facing east, and the left-hand point is facing west." Give the children the compass rose sheet and allow them to color it. Give them colored pencils, pastels, or crayons to use. Have them cut out the compass rose and glue it onto a piece of construction paper. For the extension activity below, have a large map of the United States available for each child.

- **Extension of the activity.** "If I wanted to go to Nebraska, and I lived in Texas, which direction would I go?" Point to Texas and Nebraska on the map and have the children place their compass rose on Texas. Allow them to verbalize their responses. (Well, Nebraska is above Texas, so I'd head north.) "If I lived in California, and I wanted to go to Virginia, which direction would I go?" Allow the children to answer. (I would head east.) Continue this same process until you've demonstrated north, south, east, and west. As the children get more proficient with locating various directions, you can introduce northeast (NE), northwest (NW), southeast (SE), and southwest (SW). Have the children explain to a friend how the compass rose directs us in a certain direction.

Writing

#1. Write a prediction about whether the young child and the wolves will run into each other.

- **Objective.** Text Types and Purposes. Write opinion pieces on topics or texts, supporting a point of view with reasons. Provide reasons that support the opinion.
- **Level of difficulty.** Moderate. (This task may take several days to complete.)
- **Materials needed.** Pencils, lined paper, crayons, and white construction paper.
- **Before the activity.** Prepare the materials.
- **Begin the activity by saying,** "Earlier, I asked you if you thought the child and the wolves would run into each other."
- **Review the children's responses.** (I think the young child will stay on the path and won't run into the wolves. I think the wolves would avoid the young child if they heard or smelled her. I think the wolves might come close to the young child, but I think they'd move away from her.)
- **Introduce the activity.** "Today, you're going to write about what you think will happen in this situation." Review the children's responses. "You can write one of the prior responses on a piece of lined paper or you can write your own sentence." Be available to help them sound out the words. Allow the children to draw a picture of their response.

Science

#1. Determine whether wolves of different ages travel together.

- **Objective.** Engineering Design. Life Science. Interdependent Relationships in Ecosystems. Construct an argument that some animals form groups that help members survive.
- **Level of difficulty.** Easy.
- **Materials needed.** None.
- **Before the activity.** Go to the internet and type, "Do wolves of different ages travel together in a pack?" Choose an age-appropriate website.
- **Begin the activity by saying,** "Earlier, I asked you if you thought the wolves on the page were all the same age."
- **Review the children's responses.** (Well, the wolf in the middle looks smaller. It's probably the youngest. I don't think the wolves are all the same age.)
- **Introduce the activity.** "Today, we're going to learn if wolves of different ages travel together." Go to the internet and type, "Do wolves of different ages travel together in a pack?" Select the age-appropriate website you chose that relays information about wolves traveling together. Read and discuss the information with the children. "Wolves in the pack can be different ages."

#2. Determine if older wolves protect younger wolves.

- **Objective.** Engineering Design. Life Science. Interdependent Relationships in Ecosystems. Construct an argument that some animals form groups that help members survive.
- **Level of difficulty.** Easy.
- **Materials Needed.** None.

- **Before the activity.** Go to the internet and type, "Do older wolves protect younger wolves?" Choose an age-appropriate website.
- **Begin the activity by saying,** "Earlier, we wondered why the smallest wolf was in the center of the pack."
- **Review the children's responses.** (I think the older wolves may be protecting the younger wolf. The older wolves may be letting the younger wolf rest.)
- **Introduce the activity.** "Today, we're going to discover if the older wolves protect the younger wolves." Go to the internet and type, "Do older wolves protect younger wolves?" Select the age-appropriate website you chose for the children. Read and discuss this information with the children. The International Wolf Center has lots of information the children will enjoy hearing and reading. They even have a live "wolf cam" they'll enjoy watching. Have the children relay their favorite fact to one of their friends.

#3. Determine why wolves howl.

- **Objective.** Engineering Design. Life Science. Interdependent Relationships in Ecosystems. Construct an argument that some animals form groups that help members survive.
- **Level of difficulty.** Moderate. (This task may take several days to complete.)
- **Materials needed.** White construction paper, paints, paintbrushes, crayons, pencils, and the book turned to the right-hand side of the page showing the darker wolf howling.
- **Before the activity.** Go to the internet and type, "Why do wolves howl?" Choose an age-appropriate website.
- **Begin the activity by saying,** "Earlier, we wondered why wolves howl."

66

- **Review the children's responses.** (I think wolves howl because they're trying to find members of their pack. I think wolves howl because they're warning other wolves to stay out of their territory.)
- **Introduce the activity.** "Today, we're going to find out why wolves howl." Go to the internet and type, "Why do wolves howl?" Select the age-appropriate website you chose. Read and discuss the information with the children. "They howl for a variety of reasons. They howl to gather the pack together. They howl to find a mate. They howl as a warning to other wolves, and they howl to indicate their location, as well as for other reasons." Have the children recreate the picture on the right-hand side of the page, with the darker wolf howling. Have the children relay their favorite fact to a friend.

#4. Determine if wolves travel in the same wolf pack.

- **Objective.** Engineering Design. Life Science. Interdependent Relationships in Ecosystems. Construct an argument that some animals form groups that help members survive.
- **Level of difficulty.** Easy.
- **Materials needed.** None.
- **Before the activity.** Go to the internet and type, "Do wolves travel in the same wolf pack?" Choose an age-appropriate website.
- **Begin the activity by saying,** "Earlier, we wondered if the wolves belonged to the same wolf pack."
- **Review the children's responses.** (These wolves belong to the same wolf pack because wolves usually travel together. I don't think the wolves would allow wolves outside their pack to travel with them.)
- **Introduce the activity.** "Today, we're going to find out if wolves travel in the same wolf pack." Go to the internet and type, "Do wolves travel in the same wolf pack? Select the age-appropriate

website you chose. Read and discuss the information with the children. Have the children relay their favorite fact to a friend.

#5. Determine how fast a wolf can run.

- **Objective.** Life Science. Interdependent Relationships in Ecosystems, Animals, Plants, and their Environment. Use materials to design a solution to a human problem by mimicking how plants and/or animals use their external parts to help them survive, grow, and meet their needs.
- **Level of difficulty.** Easy.
- **Materials needed.** None.
- **Before the activity.** Go to the internet and type, "How fast can a wolf run?" Choose an age-appropriate website.
- **Begin the activity by saying,** "Earlier, we wondered whether wolves could run fast."
- **Review the children's responses.** (I think wolves can run fast. I think wolves can run five miles per hour. I think wolves can run ten miles per hour.)
- **Introduce the activity.** "Today, we're going to find out if wolves can run fast." Go to the internet and type, "How fast can a wolf run?" Select the age-appropriate website you chose. Read and discuss the information with the children. Have the children relay this information to a friend.

#6. Determine whether wolves communicate with each other.

- **Objective.** Life Science. Interdependent Relationships in Ecosystems, Animals, Plants, and their Environment. Use materials to design a solution to a human problem by mimicking how plants and/or animals use their external parts to help them survive, grow, and meet their needs.

- **Level of difficulty.** Moderate. (This task may take several days to complete.)
- **Materials needed.** White construction paper, crayons, paints, paintbrushes, and the website showing the wolf postures for communication projected onto a piece of white paper.
- **Before the activity.** Go to the internet and type, "Do wolves communicate?" Choose an age-appropriate website.
- **Begin the activity by saying,** "Earlier, we wondered if wolves communicate with each other."
- **Review the children's responses.** (I think wolves do communicate with each other. I think it would be important for wolves to be able to communicate with each other.)
- **Introduce the activity.** "Today, we're going to learn if wolves communicate with each other." Go to the internet and type, do wolves communicate? Select the age-appropriate website you chose. Read and discuss this information with the children. The International Wolf Center has lots of information that the children will enjoy hearing and reading. There are also videos that the children will enjoy seeing. Have the children draw one wolf posture that communicates to the other wolves (e.g., tail between its legs, ears turned down).

Math

#1. Practice writing the numerals 0 to 5. Practice writing number sentences that would equal 5.

- **Objective.** Counting and Cardinality. Know number names and the count sequence. Write numbers from 0 to 20. Represent several objects with a written numeral from 0 to 20 (with 0 representing a count of no objects). Operations and Algebraic Thinking. Understand

69

and apply properties of operations and the relationship between addition and subtraction.

- **Level of difficulty.** Moderate. (This task may take several days to complete.)
- **Materials needed.** Whiteboards, markers, pencils, and paper.
- **Before the activity.** Prepare the materials.
- **Begin the activity by saying,** "Earlier, we counted 5 wolves on the right-hand side of the page."
- **Introduce the activity.** "Today, we're going to practice writing the numerals 0 to 5." For the younger children, give them whiteboards and markers and have them practice writing these numerals. For the older children, have them write number sentences on a piece of paper that would equal 5. (0 + 5 = 5, 1 + 4 = 5, 2 + 3 = 5, 3 + 2 = 5, 4 + 1 = 5, 5 + 0 = 5)

#2. Learn about number sentences. Write number sentences that would equal 5.

- **Objective.** Operations and Algebraic Thinking. Understand and apply properties of operations and the relationship between addition and subtraction.
- **Level of difficulty.** Moderate. (This task may take several days to complete.)
- **Materials needed.** Paper, pencils, and wolf stickers if available.
- **Before the activity.** Go to the internet and type, "Show me a video that explains number sentences." Choose an age-appropriate website.
- **Begin the activity by saying,** "Earlier, we talked about number sentences that would equal 5." (0 + 5 = 5, 1 + 4 = 5, 2 + 3 = 5 3 + 2 = 5, 4 + 1 = 5, 5 + 0 = 5.)
- **Review the children's responses.** (I know that 2 + 3 = 5 and 4 + 1 = 5.)

- **Introduce the activity.** "Today, we're going to watch a video that explains number sentences." Go to the internet and type, "Show me a video that explains number sentences." Select the age-appropriate website. We observed that there were 5 wolves on the page. Can you think of a way to write a number sentence that equals 5? Give the children an opportunity to think of different ways. (0 + 5 = 5, 1 + 4 = 5, 2 + 3 = 5, 3 + 2 = 5, 4 + 1 = 5, 5 + 0 = 5). Write their responses on a piece of paper. Give them a piece of paper. Have them write different number sentences that would equal 5. (1 + 4 = 5, 2 + 3 = 5). Have the children write number sentences with wolf stickers (if available) or wolves drawn below the spelled out numbers (one wolf + two wolves = three wolves).

#3. Demonstrate how a number sentence can be represented by two numbers, using your hands.

- **Objective.** Operations and Algebraic Thinking. Represent and solve problems involving addition and subtraction. Use addition and subtraction within twenty to solve word problems involving situations of adding to, taking from, putting together, taking apart, and comparing, with unknowns in all positions (by using objects, drawings, and equations with a symbol for the unknown number to represent the problem).
- **Level of difficulty.** Easy.
- **Materials needed.** None.
- **Begin the activity by saying,** "Earlier, we decided there were 5 wolves on this page. Can you hold up 5 fingers?"
- **Review the children's responses.** The children will hold up their hands to show the number 5.
- **Introduce the activity.** "Today, you're going to use both of your hands to show me how you can make the number 5." The teacher should hold up both of his or her hands so the children understand

that they're to use both hands to show you how 5 can be created. Ask them to show you 5 using two hands (e.g., 2 fingers on one hand and 3 fingers on the other hand). Let them practice using various combinations of numbers on both hands. Have them explain to a friend their number sentence. (I have 2 fingers up on one hand and 3 fingers up on my other hand. That equals 5 fingers.)

#4. Determine how far wolves can travel in a day.

- **Objective.** Number and Operations in Base Ten. Extend the counting sequence. Count to 120, starting at any number less than 120. In this range, read and write numerals and represent several objects with a written numeral.
- **Level of difficulty.** Moderate to challenging. (This task may take several days to complete.)
- **Materials needed.** Local map, paper, and pencils.
- **Before the activity.** Go to the internet and type, "How far can wolves travel in a day?" Choose an age-appropriate website.
- **Begin the activity by saying,** "Earlier, we discussed whether wolves could travel a long distance."
- **Review the children's responses.** (I think wolves can travel a long distance. I think they can travel ten miles a day. I think wolves can travel fifteen miles per day.)
- **Introduce the activity.** "Today, we're going to find out how far wolves can travel in a day." Go to the internet and type, "How far can wolves travel in a day?" Choose an age-appropriate website. Read and discuss this information with the children. Wolves can travel up to 50 miles per day in search of food. For the younger children, give them specific locations that would explain 50 miles. (It's 50 miles from our school to the city of Mayfield or from our school to the city of Emery.) Have them ask their parents to drive them from their house to a location 50 miles away. Or they could

find out how far it is from their house to a familiar location (e.g., to the theater). Then they could find out how many trips to this location they could take (e.g., Fifty miles would be four, twelve-mile trips to the theater, with two miles remaining. That would be one-way trips. If you use the return mileage, it would be two round trips, with two miles remaining.) This will give them an idea of how far 50 miles is.

- **Extension of the activity.** Ask the children if they know how far a mile is. (A mile is 5,280 feet.) For the older children, convert 50 miles to feet (50 x 5,280 feet = 264,00 feet).

#5. Determine how fast a wolf can run.

- **Objective.** Counting and Cardinality. Know number names and the count sequence. Write numbers from 0 to 20. Represent several objects with a written numeral from 0 to 20 (with 0 representing a count of no objects).
- **Level of difficulty.** Easy.
- **Materials needed.** Local map, paper, and pencils.
- **Before the activity.** Go to the internet and type, "How fast can a wolf run?" Choose an age-appropriate website.
- **Begin the activity by saying,** "Earlier, we wondered if wolves could run fast."
- **Review the children's responses.** (I think wolves can run fast. I think wolves can run 5 miles per hour. I think wolves can run 10 miles per hour.)
- **Introduce the activity.** "Today, we're going to find out how fast a wolf can run." Go to the internet and type, "How fast can a wolf run?" Select the age-appropriate website you chose. Read and discuss this information with the children. "Wolves can run approximately 20 miles per hour to catch their prey." For the younger children, have them write this numeral on a whiteboard and then give them specific locations that would explain 20 miles. (It's 20 miles from our school

to Hillside Park. It's 20 miles from our school to the museum.) Have them ask their parents to drive them from their house to a location 20 miles away or determine how many trips to a familiar location (e.g., to the market) they could take. (The market is five miles away, so we could take four one-way trips or two round trips). This will give them an idea of how far 20 miles is.

- **Extension of the activity.** Ask the children if they know how far a mile is. (A mile is 5,280 feet.) Have them convert 20 miles to feet (20 x 5,280 feet = 105,600 feet).

QUESTIONS

The brackets around the text indicate questions/instructions an adult
should read to the children. Examples of how the children may answer
the questions are included in parentheses.

- **[What do you see on this page?]**

- **[How many children do you think attend this school?]** (Well, it
  looks like there are nine children close to the school and the young
  child walking away from the school. That would be ten children.
  There might be more children inside the school.) See Math #1.

- **[Do you think it's morning or afternoon?]** (Well, the child is
  waving at the other children, so perhaps it's afternoon, and she's
  going home. However, the other children seem to be staying near
  the school.)

- **[When do you get out of school?]** Write the time the children get
  out of school on the board (e.g., 2:15 p.m.). See Math #2.

- Note that the child is walking home alone. **[Why doesn't she
  walk with a friend?]** Write the children's responses on a piece of
  paper. Save this paper for later. (The child lives away from the other
  children. I think the child left school early. I think the child wants to
  be alone today.) See Writing #1.

- **[How would you describe the look on the child's face?]** Write
  the children's responses on a piece of paper and save this for later.

(The child looks unhappy. I think the child looks tired. I think the child looks cold.). See Writing #2.

- Point out that the child has a frown on her face. **[Why do you think she's frowning?]** Write the children's responses on a piece of paper and save this for later. (I think the child is frowning because it's so cold outside. I think the child is frowning because she is walking home alone. I think the child is frowning because she didn't understand something the teacher talked about in school.) See Writing #3.

- Have the children look carefully at the young child walking up the hill. Note that she has very pink cheeks. **[Why are her cheeks so pink?]** Write the children's responses on a piece of paper and save for later. (Well, when you go out in the cold, your cheeks turn pink.) See Science #1.

- Point out that the young child in the picture has a very bright red coat. Ask the children to stand up if they have a red coat or jacket. Have them look carefully at the children near the school. **[Do any other children near the school have a red coat?]** (Well, it looks like one other child has a red coat.)

- **[What other coat colors are the children wearing?]** (Pink, green, aqua, yellow, avocado, gold, purple, blue, and red.) See Art #4.

- **[How do you know that this building is the school?]** (Well, there is a sign above the door that reads, "School.")

- **[What flag do you think is flying at the top of their school flagpole?]** Write the children's responses on a piece of paper and save this for later. (Their state flag is flying at the top of the flagpole.

- **[Do we have a flag(s) flying at our school?]** (Yes, we have a state and US flag flying at the top of our flagpole.) Have the children draw or paint the US flag. See Art #2 and #3.

76

- **Why does each state and country have its own flag?]** (It's a symbol that represents the state or country.) Create a display of flags on a bulletin board. (See Art #1.)
- **[How is our school the same and different from the school in the picture?]** Write the children's responses on a piece of paper.

How is our school the same?

Our school has windows.

Our school has trees nearby.

How is our school different?

Our school doesn't have stairs.

Our school doesn't have a fence around it.

- Point out that it appears that the child is walking home alone in the snow. **[What do you think about this?]**
- **[Why doesn't this school have a bus to take the children home?]** (Well, maybe there's only one school in the area, and the school district can't afford to buy a bus.)

ACTIVITIES

Art

#1. Learn about a state's flag. Paint/draw their state flag.

- **Objective.** Responding. Anchor Standard #7. Perceive and analyze artistic work. Perceive. Determine messages communicated by an image.
- **Level of difficulty.** Moderate. (This task may take several days to complete.)
- **Materials needed.** White construction paper, paints, paintbrushes, and pencils.

- **Before the activity.** Go to the internet and type, "Tell me about the Colorado state flag." Choose an age-appropriate website.
- **Begin the activity by saying,** "Earlier, we talked about why each country or state has its own flag."
- **Review the children's responses.** (The flag is a symbol that represents a state or country.)
- **Introduce the activity.** "Today, we're going to learn about the state flag of Colorado." Go to the internet and type, "Tell me about the Colorado state flag." Select the age-appropriate website you chose. Read and discuss this information with the children. "Colorado's flag has two blue stripes, which represent the sky, and one white stripe, which represents the snow on the mountains. The red C on the flag represents the 'ruddy' earth. It also has three other meanings (Colorado, columbine, and centennial). The yellow inside the letter C represents the sunshine." Talk about the importance of each state or country having its own flag. "People can recognize the flag of their state or country. Each state or country's flag is different from other flags." Go to the internet and type in the children's home state (e.g., California, Oregon, Maine, or New Jersey). Read and discuss this information with the children. Have the children draw or paint their state flag.
- **Extension of the activity.** Have the older children research what the colors and symbols of their state flag represent and share with the class what they learned. Create a display of the children's flags on a bulletin board.

#2. Learn about our country's flag. Make the American flag.

- **Objective.** Responding. Anchor Standard #7. Perceive and analyze artistic work. Perceive. Determine messages communicated by an image.
- **Level of difficulty.** Easy.

- **Materials needed.** White construction paper, rulers, pencils, crayons, colored pencils, paintbrushes, and paints.
- **Before the activity.** Go to the internet and type, "Are public schools required to fly the American flag?" Choose an age-appropriate website. In addition, go to the internet and type, "Who designed the American flag?" Choose an age-appropriate website. Place a large piece of white paper on the board. Have a black marker available for writing the children's responses.
- **Begin the activity by saying,** "Earlier, we observed that there was a flag flying from the top of the school."
- **Review the children's responses.** (Yes, there is a flag flying from the school, but I don't know which flag. It looks like the flag is white. I see a flag flying from the top of the school, but it doesn't have any markings on it.)
- **Introduce the activity.** "Today, we're going to learn about flying our country's flag."
  1. Ask the children if their state is required to fly the American flag. Write their responses on a piece of paper. Go to the internet and type, "Are public schools required to fly the American flag?" Select the age-appropriate website you chose. Read and discuss this information with the children.
  2. "Who designed the American flag?" Write the children's responses on a piece of paper. Go to the internet and type, "Who designed the American flag?" Select the age-appropriate website you chose. Read and discuss this information with the children. There is some controversy as to who designed the flag.
  3. "What do the stars and stripes represent? What do the colors of the flag represent?" Write the children's responses on a piece of paper. Go to the internet and type, "What do the stars and stripes on the American flag represent?" Select the age-appropriate website you chose. Read and discuss this information with the

children. "Now that we know some important information about the American flag, we're going to draw/paint our country's flag."

- **Extension of the activity.** The older children could do this same process for countries outside the United States. Display these flags throughout the room.

#3. Learn if our state flag is the same as the US flag.

- **Objective.** Responding. Anchor Standard #7. Perceive and analyze artistic work. Perceive. Determine messages communicated by an image.
- **Level of difficulty.** Easy.
- **Materials needed.** White construction paper, pencils, paints, paintbrushes, colored pencils, and crayons.
- **Before the activity.** Go to the internet and search for your state's flag. Choose an age-appropriate website.
- **Begin the activity by saying,** "Earlier, I asked whether our state's flag was the same as the US Flag."
- **Review the children's responses.** (No, the state flag is different from the US flag. Our state's flag doesn't look like the American flag. The American flag has stripes, but our state flag has other things on it.)
- **Introduce the activity.** "Today, we're going to determine if our state flag is the same as the American flag." Go to the internet and search for your state's flag. Select the age-appropriate website you chose. Read and discuss this information with the children and then have them draw/paint their state flag.
- **Extension of the activity.** For the older children, have them do a comparison-and-contrast task related to their state's flag compared to the American flag. "Is our state flag the same as the US flag?" (Our state flag doesn't have stripes. Our state flag doesn't have stars. Both flags have blue in them. Both flags have red in them.)

80

Go to the internet and look up the information about your state flag. Read and discuss this information with the children and then have them draw/paint their state flag.

#4. Recreate a picture from the book. Learn about mixing colors.

- **Objective.** Connecting. Anchor Standard #10. Synthesize and relate knowledge and personal experiences to art. Synthesize. Create works of art about events in home, school, or community life.
- **Level of difficulty.** Moderate. (This task may take several days to complete.)
- **Materials needed.** White construction paper, paints, paintbrushes, crayons, colored pencils, scissors, and glue.
- **Before the activity.** Prepare all the materials.
- **Begin the activity by saying,** "Earlier, we noticed that the children near the school were wearing different colored coats."
- **Review the children's responses.** (One child is wearing a pink coat. One child is wearing a green coat.)
- **Introduce the activity.** "Today, we're going to color the various colors of the children's coats and place them near the school." Give the children a piece of white construction paper. Have them draw the school in pencil. You could create a template of the school and have the children trace around the template. When they're satisfied with their school drawing, have them use colored pencils to shade in the details. Give them another piece of white construction paper to draw/paint the children with the different colored coats (e.g., pink, green, aqua, yellow, avocado, gold, purple, blue, and red). Let these dry. Have the children cut out the children wearing the different colored coats and glue them near the school.
- **Extension of the activity.** This would be a good opportunity to show the children how colors can be mixed to create new colors. For example, white paint mixed with a dab of red creates pink. Blue

and red mixed together will create purple. Green and blue mixed together will create aqua. Allow them an opportunity to mix a few colors together. You can place cotton swabs in small containers so the children can experiment with various color combinations.

Writing

#1. Write why you think the young child left school early.

- **Objective.** Text Types and Purposes. Write opinion pieces on topics or texts, supporting a point of view with reasons. Provide reasons that support the opinion.
- **Level of difficulty.** Moderate. (This task may take several days to complete.)
- **Materials needed.** A piece of paper on the bulletin board, a black marker, pencils, and lined paper.
- **Before the activity.** Place a large piece of white paper on the board. Have a black marker available for writing the children's responses.
- **Begin the activity by saying,** "Earlier, we talked about why we thought the young child was walking home alone."
- **Review the children's responses.** (The young child lives away from the other children. I think the young child left school early because she wasn't feeling well. I think the child wants to be alone today.).
- **Introduce the activity.** "Today, we're going to write one reason why we think the young child left school early. You can copy one of the sentences from the paper we discussed earlier or write your own sentence(s)." Be available to help them sound out the spellings for each word.

#2. Describe the look on the child's face. Understand that adjectives give us important information about a picture/object.

- **Objective.** Key Ideas and Details. Describe characters in a story (e.g., their traits, motivations, or feelings) and explain how their actions contribute to the sequence of events.
- **Level of difficulty.** Moderate. (This task may take several days to complete.)
- **Materials needed.** A large piece of paper on the board, markers, pencils, and lined paper.
- **Before the activity.** Place a large piece of white paper on the board. Have a black marker available for writing the children's responses.
- **Begin the activity by saying,** "Earlier, we described the look on the child's face."
- **Review the children's responses.** (The child looks cold. The child looks tired. I think the child looks unhappy.).
- **Introduce the activity.** "Today, we're going to describe the look on the child's face." When we describe things, we're using adjectives. Adjectives give us valuable information about a picture. You said the child looks cold, tired, and unhappy. Have the children copy one of the sentences from the paper. If they'd like to write their own sentence(s), be available to help them sound out the letters for each word.

#3. Make a prediction as to why the child might be frowning.

- **Objective.** Key Ideas and Details. Describe characters in a story (e.g., their traits, motivations, or feelings) and explain how their actions contribute to the sequence of events.
- **Level of difficulty.** (This task may take several days to complete.)
- **Materials needed.** A large piece of paper on the board, markers, pencils, and lined paper.

- **Before the activity.** Place a large piece of white paper on the board. Have a black marker available for writing the children's responses.
- **Begin the activity by saying,** "Earlier, we noticed that the child had a frown on her face."
- **Review the children's responses.** (The child is frowning because it's so cold outside. I think the child is frowning because she's walking home alone. I think the child is frowning because she doesn't feel well.).
- **Introduce the activity.** "Today, we're going to write some sentences as to why the child might be frowning." Write their responses on a piece of paper. Have the children copy one of the sentences from the paper. If they'd like to write their own sentence(s), you should be available to help them sound out the letters for each word.

Science

#1. Find out why our cheeks turn pink/red when we go out in cold weather.

- **Objective.** Earth and Space Science. Weather and Climate. Use and share observations of local weather conditions to describe patterns over time.
- **Level of difficulty.** Moderate. (This task may take several days to complete.)
- **Materials needed.** A large piece of paper on the board, markers, pencils, and lined paper.
- **Before the activity.** Go to the internet and type, "What causes our cheeks to get pink/red in cold weather?" Choose an age-appropriate website. Place a large piece of white paper on the board. Have a black marker available for writing down the facts from the website, as well as the children's responses.

- **Begin the activity by saying,** "Earlier, we observed that the young child had very pink cheeks. What causes our cheeks to turn pink?"
- **Review the children's responses.** (The wintry weather makes our cheeks turn pink. Well, when we go out in the cold, our cheeks turn pink.)
- **Introduce the activity.** "Today, we're going to find out why our cheeks turn pink/red in cold weather." Go to the internet and type, "What causes our cheeks to get pink/red in cold weather?" Select the age-appropriate website you chose. Read and discuss this information with the children. Have the children write their favorite fact on a piece of lined paper and then tell a friend that fact.

Math

#1. Count the number of children they see near the school. Write the numerals 0 to 9.

- **Objective.** Counting and Cardinality. Know number names and the count sequence. Write numbers from 0 to 20. Represent several objects with a written numeral from 0 to 20 (with 0 representing a count of no objects).
- **Level of difficulty.** Easy.
- **Materials needed.** A piece of paper on the board, black markers, and whiteboards.
- **Before the activity.** Place a large piece of white paper on the board. Have a black marker available for writing the numerals on the board.
- **Begin the activity by saying,** "Earlier, we wondered how many children went to this school."
- **Review the children's responses.** (Well, it looks like there are nine (9) children close to the school and the young child walking away from the school. That would be ten (10) children. There might

be more children inside the school. However, we'll only count the number of children we see outside the school.)

- **Introduce the activity.** "Today, we're going to count the number of children we see near the school. We'll also practice writing the numerals 0 to 9." Have one child come up to the book and count the number of children they see on the page. You might project this page onto a piece of white paper so the children can see the image. Have a second child verify the number. (There are nine (9) children near the school.) Give each child a whiteboard and have them practice writing the numeral 9 on the whiteboard. Have them practice writing other numerals (e.g., 0 to 8), one numeral at a time, making sure each numeral is written correctly. The children can sit together and ask each other to write a specific numeral. (Write the numeral 3. Write the numeral 5.) Have them take turns asking the other children to write the numerals.

- **Extension of the activity.** For the older children, have them write various number sentences that would equal nine (9). ($0 + 9 = 9$, $1 + 8 = 9$, $2 + 7 = 9$, $3 + 6 = 9$, $4 + 5 = 9$, $5 + 4 = 9$, $6 + 3 = 9$, $7 + 2 = 9$, $8 + 1 = 9$, and $9 + 0 = 9$). If you wanted to include the young child who's walking away from school, that would equal ten (10). You could write various number sentences that would equal ten (10). ($0 + 10 = 10$, $1 + 9 = 10$, $2 + 8 = 10$, $3 + 7 = 10$, $4 + 6 = 10$, $5 + 5 = 10$, $6 + 4 = 10$, $7 + 3 = 10$, $8 + 2 = 10$, $9 + 1 = 10$, and $10 + 0 = 10$.)

#2. Learn to tell time. Make a clock.

- **Objective.** Measurement and Data. Work with time and money. Tell and write time from analog and digital clocks to the nearest five minutes, using a.m. and p.m.

- **Level of difficulty.** Moderate. (This task may take several days to complete.)

- **Materials needed.** A large clock that the children can see, individual clocks (see resource section), half-inch brads, and scissors.

- **Before the activity.** Run off copies of the clock in the resource section for each child. Place a large piece of white paper on the board. Have a black marker available for writing the children's responses.

- **Begin the activity by saying,** "Earlier, we wondered when the children got out of school."

- **Review the children's responses.** (I think they get out of school at about the same time as we get out of school. We get out of school at 2:15 p.m. We get out of school at 3:00 p.m.)

- **Introduce the activity.** "Today, we're going to discuss possible times when the children could get out of school. When do we get out of school?" Write the children's responses on a piece of paper. (We get out of school at 2:15 p.m. We get out of school at 3:00 p.m.) "Does everyone get out of school at the same time?" Allow the children time to respond. Demonstrate on a large clock the time the children get out of school. Talk about the hour and minute hands on a clock. The small hand on a clock shows us the hour, while the large hand shows us the minutes on a clock. Give each child a copy of the clock with the hour and minute hands. (See resource section.) Have the children carefully cut out all three portions of the clock. An older student or adult could help with this process. Have them put the minute and hour hands on the clock, using a half-inch brad to attach the minute and hour hands to the larger clock. Have them fold back the brad on the backside of the clock. Have the children practice showing various times when they think the children could get out of school (e.g., 2:15 p.m., 2:30 p.m., or 2:45 p.m.).

QUESTIONS

The brackets around the text indicate questions/instructions an adult
should read to the children. Examples of how the children may answer
the questions are included in parentheses.

- **[What do you see on this page?]** See Art #1.

- **[In which direction are the wolves headed?]** (If the top of the
  page is north, then the wolves must be heading west.) The children
  learned earlier that the compass rose indicated that the wolves were
  heading west.

- **[Do you think a wolf can run fast?]** Write the children's responses
  on a piece of paper and save this for later. (I think a wolf can run
  ten miles per hour. I think a wolf can run fifteen miles per hour.) See
  Math #1.

- **[We can see from the illustration that it's snowing. What's
  another way we can determine that it's cold outside?]** (Well,
  three wolves are breathing out and creating condensation/steam.)
  See Science #1.

- **[How would you describe the wolves?]** Write the children's
  responses on a piece of paper and save this for later. (The wolves
  look tired, determined, and strong.) See Writing #1.

- **[Where is the youngest wolf?]** (The smallest wolf, who is the
  youngest, is walking behind the older wolves.) See Writing #2.

- Have the children look carefully at the illustration. Direct them to notice that one wolf is looking at the biggest wolf. **[Do you think there's a reason why he or she is looking at the biggest wolf?]** (The biggest wolf is the leader of the wolf pack.) See Science #2.

- **[How is the youngest wolf different from the other wolves?]** (Well, he or she is smaller and darker. He or she doesn't seem to be able to keep up with the older wolves. The young wolf has dark fur all over his or her body.) See Art #2.

- **[How would you describe the teeth of the wolf in the foreground?]** (The teeth look long. The teeth look sharp. It looks like the wolf has a lot of teeth.) See Science #3.

- **[How many teeth does a wolf have?]** Write the children's responses on a piece of paper and save this for later. (A wolf has twenty teeth. A wolf has thirty teeth.). See Science #4.

- **[How many teeth do you have?]** Write the children's responses on a piece of paper and save this for later. (I think I have twenty teeth. I think I have thirty teeth.) See Science #5.

- **[Why are some of the wolf's teeth larger than the others?]** Write the children's responses on a piece of paper and save this for later. (I think some of the wolf's teeth are larger because they hold onto its prey. I think some of the wolf's teeth are larger because they tear the meat off the animal.) See Science #6.

- **[Do you think wolves have good hearing?]** Write the children's responses on a piece of paper and save this for later. (I think wolves have good hearing. I think wolves can hear a long way away.) See Art #3.

89

ACTIVITIES

Art

#1. Paint/draw the wolves.

- **Objective.** Responding. Anchor Standard #8. Interpret intent and meaning in artistic work. Analyze. Interpret art by identifying subject matter and describing relevant work.
- **Level of difficulty.** Moderate. (This task may take several days to complete.)
- **Materials needed.** White construction paper, paints, paintbrushes, and crayons.
- **Before the activity.** Have books available that show various wolves.
- **Begin the activity by saying,** "This page shows the wolves heading west. It's snowing and cold."
- **Introduce the activity.** "Today, we're going to paint/draw the wolves. We've learned a lot of information about wolves, and we've discovered that they're amazing animals. We'll keep these pictures for our next writing assignment that describes these wolves." (The wolves look fierce. They look tired. They look determined.)

#2. Make a "wolf mobile."

- **Objective.** Presentation. Anchor Standard #4. Select, analyze, and interpret artistic work for presentation. Select. Select art objects for personal portfolio and display, explaining why they were chosen.
- **Level of difficulty.** Moderate. (This task may take several days to complete.)
- **Materials needed.** White poster board, paints, paintbrushes, crayons, string, scissors, glue, hole punch, and paper clips.
- **Before the activity.** Prepare the materials.

- **Begin the activity by saying,** "Earlier, we noticed that the young wolf was different from the other wolves."
- **Review the children's responses.** (He or she was smaller. He or she didn't seem able to keep up with the older wolves. The young wolf has dark fur all over his or her body.)
- **Introduce the activity.** "Today, we're going to make a mobile of the wolf pack, starting with the biggest wolf." Have the children draw each of the wolves on poster board and punch holes at the top and bottom portion of each wolf. Starting with the biggest wolf, attach string to the top and bottom. Attach the second wolf to the first wolf and continue with each wolf. The young wolf should be attached last. Hang the wolf mobiles throughout the room. The children may want to color/paint both sides, as they will be turning at various times when there's a wind source, so both sides will be seen. Place a paper clip through the string at the top of the mobile and hang it from the ceiling.

#3. Learn about a wolf's sense of hearing. Make wolf ears.

- **Objective.** Connecting. Anchor Standard #11. Artistic ideas and works with societal, cultural, and historical context to deepen understanding. Relate. Identify a purpose of an artwork.
- **Level of difficulty.** Moderate. (This task may take several days to complete.)
- **Materials needed.** Wolf ears (see resource section), two bamboo sticks, scissors, brown/gray/black felt (optional), crayons, and glue.
- **Before the activity.** Go to the internet and type, "Do wolves have good hearing?" Choose an age-appropriate website. Place a large piece of white paper on the board. Have a black marker available for writing the children's responses.
- **Begin the activity by saying,** "Earlier, we wondered if wolves had good hearing."

- **Review the children's responses.** (Wolves have good hearing. I think wolves can hear a long way away.)
- **Introduce the activity.** "Today, we're going to find out if wolves have good hearing." Go to the internet and type, "Do wolves have good hearing?" Select the age-appropriate website you chose. Read and discuss the information with the children. "We discovered that wolves have amazing hearing. They also have amazing ears. They can move their ears in many directions." Have the children make some felt or paper ears on two bamboo sticks (see resource section.) The children can turn the bamboo sticks to bend the ears downward and backward. They can turn the bamboo sticks sideways and tilt the ears forward. Allow them to verbalize what the wolf might be hearing.

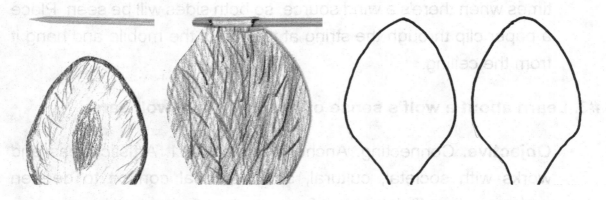

Writing

#1. Learn about adjectives. Use adjectives to describe the wolves.

- **Objective.** Conventions of Standard English. Use frequently occurring adjectives.
- **Level of difficulty.** Easy.
- **Materials needed.** Strips of paper to write their adjectives/sentences, markers, pencils, and a stapler.
- **Before the activity.** Place a large piece of white paper on the board. Have a black marker available for writing the children's responses.

- **Begin the activity by saying,** "Earlier, we described how we thought the wolves looked."
- **Review the children's responses.** (The wolves look tired. The wolves look determined. The wolves look strong.)
- **Introduce the activity.** "Today, we're going to learn about adjectives and describe how the wolves look on this page." When we describe something, we're using adjectives. Adjectives give us valuable information about an object. Have the children write the words/ sentences they used earlier to describe the wolves. (The wolves look fierce. The wolves look determined. The wolves look hungry. The wolves look tired.). Attach these words/sentences to the painting they did earlier of their wolf/wolves. (See Art #1.)

#2. Write conversation bubbles of what the young wolf might be thinking.

- **Objective.** Demonstrate command of the conventions of standard English grammar and usage when writing or speaking.
- **Level of difficulty.** Moderate. (This task may take several days to complete.)
- **Materials needed.** Conversation bubbles (see resource section) and pencils.
- **Before the activity.** Place a large piece of white paper on the board. Have a black marker available for writing the children's responses.
- **Begin the activity by saying,** "Earlier, we observed that the youngest wolf was behind the three older wolves. We wondered what the young wolf might be saying/thinking."
- **Review the children's responses.** ("Man, oh man, I'm tired!" "My older brothers and sisters can move faster than I can." "I wish I could stop and take a short rest." "I'm hungry!")
- **Introduce the activity.** "Today, we're going to write conversation bubbles to imagine what the young wolf might be saying/thinking."

(See resource section.) ("Man, oh man, I'm tired!" "My older brother and sisters can move faster than I can." "I wish I could stop and take a short rest." "I'm hungry!") Have the children write what they think the young wolf might be saying or thinking on the conversation bubble. Place the children's conversation bubbles on the bulletin board for them to read.

Science

#1. Learn why "fog" forms when it's cold outside.

- **Objective.** Earth and Space Science. Weather and Climate. Use and share observations of local weather conditions to describe patterns over time.
- **Level of difficulty.** Easy.
- **Materials needed.** None.
- **Before the activity.** Go to the internet and type, "Tell me about condensation." Choose an age-appropriate website for the children.
- **Begin the activity by saying,** "Earlier, we talked about how we knew it was cold outside. For humans, our cheeks turn pink, and we wear heavy clothing when it's windy or snowing outside. How do we know that it's cold outside for the wolves in this picture?"
- **Review the children's responses.** (The wolves are breathing and forming "fog" near their mouth.) Explain that the fog is called condensation or steam.
- **Introduce the activity.** "Today, we're going to learn why 'fog' (called condensation or steam) forms near our mouth when we're out in the cold weather." Go to the internet and type, "Tell me about condensation." Choose an age-appropriate website for the children. Read and discuss this information with them. There is a National Geographic website that has information the children will enjoy hearing. There are several videos available if you type,

94

"Condensation for kids." Preview the videos before you show them to the children. Have them relay their favorite fact to a friend.

#2. Learn about the power structure of a wolf pack.

- **Objective.** Engineering Design. Life Science. Interdependent Relationships in Ecosystems. Construct an argument that some animals form groups that help members survive.
- **Level of difficulty.** Easy.
- **Materials needed.** None.
- **Before the activity.** Go to the internet and type, "Tell me about an alpha wolf." Choose an age-appropriate website for the children.
- **Begin the activity by saying,** "Earlier, we discussed why we thought one of the wolves in the pack was looking at the biggest wolf."
- **Review the children's responses.** (The smaller wolf is getting information and direction from the bigger wolf. The smaller wolf wants to know what to do. The smaller wolf is learning from the bigger wolf.)
- **Introduce the activity.** "Today, we're going to learn if one wolf is more powerful than another wolf." Go to the internet and type, "Tell me about an alpha wolf." Select the age-appropriate website you chose. Read and discuss this information with the children. Have the children relay their favorite fact to a friend. There are also some videos the children will enjoy seeing and hearing. Preview these before you show them to the children.

#3. Learn about a wolf's teeth.

- **Objective.** Life Science. Interdependent Relationships in Ecosystems, Animals, Plants, and their Environment. Use observations to describe patterns of what plants, animals (including humans) need to survive.

- **Level of difficulty.** Easy to moderate. (If the children draw the teeth, it will be more challenging.)
- **Materials needed.** White construction paper and pencils.
- **Before the activity.** Go to the internet and type, "Tell me about wolves' teeth." Choose an age-appropriate website for the children.
- **Begin the activity by saying,** "Earlier, we observed that some of the teeth on the wolves were larger."
- **Review the children's responses.** (The teeth look long. The teeth look sharp. It looks like the wolf has a lot of teeth.)
- **Introduce the activity.** "Today, we're going to learn about wolves' teeth." Go to the internet and type, "Tell me about wolves' teeth." Select the age-appropriate website you chose. Read and discuss this information with the children. There are some videos the children might enjoy seeing and hearing. Preview these videos before you show them to the children. Perhaps the children could draw the upper or lower portion of the wolves jaw/teeth. Have the children tell a friend the names of two teeth (e.g., incisors or canines).

#4. Learn how many teeth a wolf has. Learn the names of some of the teeth.

- **Objective.** Life Science. Interdependent Relationships in Ecosystems, Animals, Plants, and their Environment. Use observations to describe patterns of what plants, animals (including humans) need to survive.
- **Level of difficulty.** Easy.
- **Materials needed.** None.
- **Before the activity.** Go to the internet and type, "How many teeth does a wolf have?" Choose an age-appropriate website for the children.
- **Begin the activity by saying,** "Earlier we discussed how many teeth a wolf has."

- **Review the children's responses.** (A wolf has twenty teeth. A wolf has thirty teeth.)
- **Introduce the activity.** "Today, we're going to learn how many teeth a wolf has." Go to the internet and type, "How many teeth does a wolf have?" Select the age-appropriate website you chose. Read and discuss this information with the children. "A wolf has forty-two teeth." Challenge them to learn the names of some of the teeth (e.g., incisors, canines, premolars, and molars).

#5. Learn how many teeth an adult has.

- **Objective.** Life Science. Interdependent Relationships in Ecosystems, Animals, Plants, and their Environment. Use observations to describe patterns of what plants, animals (including humans) need to survive.
- **Level of difficulty.** Easy.
- **Materials needed.** White construction paper and pencils.
- **Before the activity.** Go to the internet and type, "How many teeth does a human have?" Choose an age-appropriate website for the children.
- **Begin the activity by saying,** "Earlier, we discussed how many teeth a human has."
- **Review the children's responses.** (A human has twenty teeth. A human has thirty teeth.)
- **Introduce the activity.** "Today, we're going to learn how many teeth a human has." Go to the internet and type, "How many teeth does a human have?" Select the age-appropriate website you chose. Read and discuss the information with the children. Challenge them to learn the names of some of their teeth (e.g., incisors, canines, premolars, and molars). Have the children draw some of these teeth.

#6. Learn why some of the wolves' teeth are larger than others.

- **Objective.** Life Science. Structure, Function, and Information Processing. Make observations of plants and animals to compare the diversity of life in different habitats.
- **Level of difficulty.** Moderate. (This task may take several days to complete.)
- **Materials needed.** White construction paper and pencils.
- **Before the activity.** Go to the internet and type, "Why are some of the wolves' teeth larger?" Choose an age-appropriate website for the children.
- **Begin the activity by saying,** "Earlier, we discussed why some of the wolves' teeth are larger."
- **Review the children's responses.** (I think some of the wolf's teeth are larger because they hold onto its prey. I think some of the wolf's teeth are larger because they tear the meat off the animal.)
- **Introduce the activity.** "Today, we're going to learn why some of the wolves' teeth are larger." Go to the internet and type, "Why are some of the wolf's teeth larger?" Read and discuss the information with the children. "Wolves' teeth are used for attacking their prey and getting to the nutritious parts of their meal, which is in the bones. They need strong, sharp teeth to crush these bones." Have the children draw some of the wolves' teeth.

Math

#1. Learn how fast a wolf can run. Learn how to use a scale marking on a map.

- **Objective.** To learn how to use a map scale.
- **Level of difficulty.** Easy.

- **Materials needed.** A local map and a scale designation for each child.
- **Before the activity.** Go to the internet and type, "How fast can a wolf run?" Choose an age-appropriate website. Have a local map of the city on the bulletin board. Copy the scale marking on the map and make copies of this for each child.
- **Begin the activity by saying,** "Earlier, we discussed whether a wolf could run fast."
- **Review the children's responses.** (I think a wolf can run ten miles per hour. I think a wolf can run fifteen miles per hour.)
- **Introduce the activity.** "Today, we're going to learn how fast a wolf can run."
  1. Go to the internet and type, "How fast can a wolf run?" Choose an age-appropriate website. Read and discuss this information with the children. They can run approximately 24 to 40 miles per hour. This means that a wolf can run 24 miles in one hour. "For example, it's 24 miles from our school to Emery Elementary School. It's 24 miles from our school to East Willow Street."
  2. Get maps of your local area and show them the scale marking on the map. "This scale marking allows people to measure the distance from one location to another." Copy this scale marking and give a copy to each child. Let them practice using this measurement tool to determine various locations on the map. They should try to locate places that are 24 miles away from school. The scale designation may show various distances, so help the children find the general scale location for 24 miles "Some scales show 0 to a 100 miles, while others show smaller distances."
  3. Demonstrate this process by taping a local map to the bulletin board. Find the location of the school and place the scale on the map, starting with the 0 designation directly at the school.

Locate a place that is 24 miles away. Mark this location. Allow the children to relay various locations that are 24 miles from the school. You can do this same exercise using various distances (e.g., 30, 35, and 40 miles).

Direct the children's attention to the page where the child is walking in a field with the snow falling. Encourage them to answer the following questions in complete sentences.

QUESTIONS

The brackets around the text indicate questions/instructions that an adult should read to the children. Examples of how the children may answer the questions are included in parentheses.

- **[What do you see on this page?]**

- **[How would you describe this page?]** (It looks like it's snowing heavily. The child looks cold and tired. I bet the child is tired from walking in the snow.) See Art #1 and Writing #1.

- **[What do you think is unusual about where she's walking?]** Write down the children's responses on a piece of paper and save this for later. (She's not walking on a path. The dried grasses and the snow are blowing toward the child. The young child must be walking into the storm. She looks very cold and tired. She might not be able to see in the snow.) See Science #1.

- **[Could the fact that she isn't on a path pose a problem?]** (Well, the snow probably covered any path, so she wouldn't know where it was. Perhaps she wandered off the path and she's lost.)

- **[What would you do in this situation?]** Ask the children to make a list of five to ten possible solutions in this situation. (There are trees nearby, so I'd head toward the trees for protection. I would pull off the branches of the tree to create a shelter. I'd use the tree branches to cover the snow, so I'd have a dry place to sit.)

- **[Have you ever been really tired, cold, or lost?]** Write the children's responses on a piece of paper and save this for later. (I was very tired when we took a hike in Oregon. My family walked for miles. I thought we'd never stop! I was wearing a thin jacket and I was very cold. I got lost one time when I was walking to my friend's house. I didn't know what to do.) See Writing #1.

- **[What survival techniques would you use if you were lost in the forest?]** Write the children's responses on a piece of paper and save this for later. (I would try to find shelter. I would walk to the trees and use the tree branches for protection. I would sit in some dense branches to protect me from the snow. I would eat the snow to replenish the water lost from walking so long. I would curl up in a ball to save my body heat and protect my body from the wind.) See Science #1.

- **[If the child is lost, what could she do to alert others where she's located?]** Write the children's responses on the board. (Find some tree branches and create a large X in an open area. The large X would be visible from the air.)

- Bring in survival books for the children to examine and read. **[What items would be important to have in a survival kit?]** Make a list of the children's responses and save them for later. (Bottled water, a whistle, a first aid kit, a flashlight, and snacks.) See Art #2 and Science #1.

- Invite an outdoor survival expert to class to discuss survival techniques. You might contact a large sporting goods store to ask if someone would come to class to discuss various survival techniques. See Writing #2.

ACTIVITIES

Art

#1. Experiment with an art technique (i.e., splatter painting).

- **Objective.** Creating. Anchor Standard #2. Organize and develop artistic ideas and work. Investigate. Create personally satisfying artwork using a variety of artistic processes and materials.
- **Level of difficulty.** Moderate. (This task may take several days to complete.)
- **Materials needed.** Dry grass or brush material; crayons; white, watery paint; paintbrushes; glue; and construction paper.
- **Before the activity.** Have the children collect some dry grass or brush material for this project.
- **Begin the activity by saying,** "Earlier, we described this page."
- **Review the children's responses.** (It looks like it's snowing heavily. The child looks cold and tired. I bet the child is tired of walking in the field.)
- **Introduce the activity.** "Today, we're going to recreate this page. It appears that it's a field, with some trees." Have the children collect some dry grass or brush material for this project. First, we're going to glue some dry grass or brush material onto the paper and let this dry. Then, we'll dip a paintbrush into some watery, white paint and splatter the picture with the white paint." Demonstrate how to gently splatter the paint onto a paper towel. You may want to have an older child or adult help with this process. Let the paint dry. On a separate piece of paper, have the children draw and cut out the young child and some trees. Glue these onto the field of grass so it's slightly lifted off the picture. You could use small pieces of sponge to have it lifted further off the page. Gently splatter the young child and the

trees with the watery white paint and allow the picture to dry. Save this picture for later.

#2. Create a survival collage.

- **Objective.** Creating. Anchor Standard #2. Organize and develop artistic ideas and work. Investigate. Create personally satisfying artwork using a variety of artistic processes and materials.
- **Level of difficulty.** Moderate. (This task may take several days to complete.)
- **Materials needed.** Magazines, construction paper, scissors, glue, and paintbrushes.
- **Before the activity.** Prepare the materials.
- **Begin the activity by saying,** "Earlier, we talked about what items we thought would be important to have in a survival kit."
- **Review the children's responses.** (Bottled water, a whistle, a first aid kit, a flashlight, and snacks.)
- **Introduce the activity.** "Today, we're going to cut out items from magazines that you think could be included in a survival kit. We're going to make a survival collage." Have the children look in different magazines for items they think would be good in a survival kit (e.g., bottled water, a whistle, a first-aid kit, a flashlight, and snacks); cut the items out; and glue them onto a piece of construction paper. Cover the entire picture with these items and then cover the entire picture with a watery mixture of glue and water. This mixture will seal the edges. Let the pictures dry and place them in an area with other survival materials, such as books, equipment, and specific survival items.

Writing

#1. Write about a personal experience.

- **Objective.** Comprehension and Collaboration. Recount or describe key ideas or details from a text read aloud or information presented orally or through other media.
- **Level of difficulty.** Moderate. (This task may take several days to complete.)
- **Materials needed.** Lined paper and pencils.
- **Before the activity.** Place a large piece of white paper on the board. Have a black marker available for writing the children's responses.
- **Begin the activity by saying,** "Earlier, we talked about the child being very tired from walking in the snow."
- **Review the children's responses.** (She must be very cold. She's walked for a long time. She's probably tired because she's walked a long distance in the snow. I think she's lost because she's been walking a very long time.)
- **Introduce the activity.** "Today, we're going to talk about a time when you were cold, tired, or perhaps lost. Has there ever been a time when you were cold, tired, or lost?" Allow the children to explain these situations. Write a few of the children's responses on the paper. (I was very tired when we took a hike in Oregon. My family walked for miles. I thought we'd never stop! I was wearing a thin jacket and I was very cold. I got lost one time when I was walking to my friend's house. I didn't know what to do.) Give them a piece of lined paper and have them copy one of the sentences. If they'd like to write their own sentence(s) be available to help them sound out the words. Have them attach their writing to Art #1.

#2. Learn how to write a thank you note. Learn how to address an envelope.

- **Objective.** Produce clear and coherent writing in which the development, organization, and style are appropriate to task, purpose, and audience.
- **Level of difficulty.** Moderate. (This task may take several days to complete.)
- **Materials needed.** Thank you notes, pens, pencils, and stamps.
- **Before the activity.** Place a large piece of white paper on the board. Have a black marker available for writing the children's responses. Go to the internet and type, "How to write a thank you note." Choose an age-appropriate website.
- **Begin the activity by saying,** "Earlier, we had Mr./Mrs. _____ come to our class to discuss survival techniques."
- **Review the children's responses.** (I learned that it's important to find shelter in the cold. I learned that keeping my body warm is important. I learned that using the materials around me to keep me comfortable is important.)
- **Introduce the activity.** "Today, we're going to write thank you notes to him/her, thanking him/her for coming to our class and telling us about how we could survive in a cold environment." (I learned that it's important to find shelter in the cold. I learned that keeping my body warm is important. I learned that using the materials around me to keep me comfortable is important.) Go to the internet and type, "How to write a thank you note." Select the age-appropriate website you chose. Read and discuss this information with the children and demonstrate how to write a thank you note. Have the children practice writing their note, and when they think they're ready to write their final copy, give them a nice thank you note/card to write their message. Have the children carefully write the address

on the front of the envelope, along with the school's return address. Give each child a stamp to put on the envelope and mail them.

Science

#1. Discuss survival techniques in a cold-weather area.

- **Objective.** Engineering Design. Weather and Climate. Obtain and combine information to describe climates in different regions of the world.
- **Level of difficulty.** Easy.
- **Materials needed.** None.
- **Before the activity.** Place a large piece of white paper on the board. Have a black marker available for writing the children's responses. Go to the internet and type, "How to survive in the cold." Choose an age-appropriate website for the children.
- **Begin the activity by saying,** "Earlier, we talked about where the child was walking and possible survival techniques."
- **Review the children's responses.** (She isn't walking on a path. The field material and the snow are blowing toward the child. The young child must be walking into the storm. She looks very cold and tired. She might not be able to see in the snow.)
- **Introduce the activity.** "Today, we're going to discuss some things the young child could do to protect herself in the storm/cold. Do you think the young child is lost? What things could she do to protect herself from the cold?" Write down the children's comments. (I could try to find shelter. I could walk to the trees and use the tree branches to protect me. I could eat the buried layers of the snow to replenish some of the water lost from walking so long. I could curl up in a ball to save my body heat and protect my body from the wind.). Go to the internet and type, "How to survive in the cold." Select the age-appropriate website you chose. Read and discuss this information

with the children and discuss any additional things or items they think would be helpful if they were lost in the cold. There are several videos about cold-weather survival the children will enjoy seeing. Choose an age-appropriate website. Preview the videos before you show them to the children. Have the children relay to a friend what they'd do in this situation.

> ## *Wolf in the Snow* illustration: Wolves walking west, with one small wolf following them
>
> Direct the children's attention to the page where four wolves are walking west, while one small wolf is following behind them. Encourage them to answer the following questions in complete sentences.

QUESTIONS

The brackets around the text indicate questions/instructions an adult should read to the children. Examples of how the children may answer the questions are included in parentheses.

- **[What do you see on this page?]**
- **[How would you describe this page?]**
- **[Do you think the four wolves in the front of the pack know the smallest wolf is falling behind?]** Write the children's responses on a piece of paper and save this for later. (I think they're so busy looking for food they don't realize the young wolf is falling behind! I think the wolves are so used to traveling fast they don't realize the young wolf is falling behind. I think the older wolves should be more considerate.) See Writing #1.
- **[How could the small wolf let the other wolves know that he or she wasn't keeping up with them?]** Write the children's responses on a piece of paper and save this for later. (The small wolf could howl to the four wolves ahead of him or her. The small wolf could simply sit down and rest, hoping the older wolves would realize he or she was falling behind.) See Writing #2.
- **[How do you know that the wolves have traveled in a certain direction?]** (Well, their footprints are heading in the same direction.) See Science #1.

- Go to the internet and type, "Show me some animal footprints." Examine and discuss these prints. See Science #2.
- **[Do you think it's unusual that the four wolves who are ahead of the smaller wolf would let it fall behind?]** (I think the older wolves should know the young wolf is falling behind. The older wolves know the young wolf is smaller, so they should move a little slower.)
- **[How far do you think wolves can travel in a day?]** Write the children's responses on a piece of paper and save this for later. (I think wolves can travel five miles per day. I think wolves can travel ten miles per day.)
- **[What do you think the small wolf is feeling or thinking?]** Write the children's responses on a piece of paper and save this for later. (My brothers and sisters move too fast. I wonder if they know how hard I'm trying to keep up with them. I am getting so hungry. I hope we'll stop soon.) See Writing #3.
- **[Do you think one of the larger wolves is the mother of the small wolf? Why or why not?]** (Well, if the young wolf is traveling with this group, it makes sense that one of the wolves would be the young wolf's mother.)
- The National Park Service has some wonderful information regarding a variety of issues related to wolves. Go to the internet and type, "National Park Service/wolves." Preview this website before you show it to the children. Read and discuss this information with them.

ACTIVITIES

Writing

#1. Learn about some punctuation marks (a period, a question mark, and an exclamation mark).

- **Objective.** Conventions of Standard English. Demonstrate command of the conventions of standard English capitalization, punctuation, and spelling when writing.) Use end punctuation for sentences.
- **Level of difficulty.** Moderate. (This task may take several days to complete.)
- **Materials needed.** Lined paper and pencils.
- **Before the activity.** Place a large piece of white paper on the board. Have a black marker available for writing the children's responses.
- **Begin the activity by saying,** "Earlier, we wondered if the four wolves in the front of the pack realized they were moving so fast the young wolf was falling behind."
- **Review the children's responses.** (I think they're so busy looking for food they don't realize the young wolf is falling behind! I think the wolves are so used to traveling fast they don't realize they've left the young wolf behind. I think the older wolves should be more considerate.)
- **Introduce the activity.** "Today, we're going to discuss whether the four wolves in the front of the pack realize they're moving so fast the young wolf is falling behind. We'll also discuss what you think they might be thinking."
- 1. "Do you think the four wolves in the front of the pack realize the young wolf is falling behind?" Write the children's comments on a piece of paper and save this for later. (I don't think they realize how fast they're moving. I don't think they're paying attention to the young wolf. I think they're hoping to find something to eat.)

111

2. "What do you think the wolf pack might be thinking?" Write the children's comments on a piece of paper and save this for later. (The baby of the family is slowing us down. I wish he or she were older so he or she could keep up with us. I wonder when we'll have to stop so the baby of the family can rest.)

3. "Today, we're going to write a few of these sentences." Explain to the children that we start a sentence with a capital letter. There must be some type of ending punctuation at the end of the sentence, such as a period, a question mark, or an exclamation mark. Explain to them that a period at the end of a sentence shows us that the sentence is complete. A question mark at the end of a sentence shows us that a question has been asked, and an exclamation mark at the end of a sentence shows us that the sentence has described an exciting event. Have the children write one sentence using each of these forms of punctuation (a period, a question mark, and an exclamation mark).

#2. Create an acrostic or free-verse poem.

- **Objective.** Range of Reading and Level of Text Complexity. By the end of the year, read and comprehend literature, including stories, dramas, and poetry at the high end of the grade text complexity band independently and proficiently.

- **Level of difficulty.** Moderate. (This task may take several days to complete.)

- **Materials needed.** Paper and pencils.

- **Before the activity.** Place a large piece of white paper on the board. Have a black marker available for writing the children's responses.

- **Begin the activity by saying,** "Earlier, we talked about how the young wolf could let the wolf pack know that he or she wasn't keeping up."

112

- **Review the children's responses.** (The small wolf could howl to the four wolves ahead of him or her. The small wolf could simply sit down and rest, hoping the older wolves would realize he or she was falling behind.)
- **Introduce the activity.** "Today, we're going to write a 'HELP' poem to the wolf pack from the young wolf." See the following example.

    H   Help me please! I'm much smaller than you. I'm trying so hard to keep up with you.

    E   Everyone is ahead of me. I can't seem to move as fast as you guys do, so give me a break!

    L   Let's stop for a small rest and take a minute or two to rest our bodies and renew ourselves.

    P   Please remember I'm much smaller than you, but one day, I'll be as strong as you.

#3. Introduce and create a paragraph about the young wolf's feeling and thoughts.

- **Objective.** Text Types and Purposes. Write narratives in which they recount a well-elaborated event or short sequence of events; include details to describe actions, thoughts, and feeling; use temporal words to signal event order; and provide a sense of closure.
- **Level of difficulty.** Moderate. (This task may take several days to complete.)
- **Materials needed.** Paper and pencils.
- **Before the activity.** Place a large piece of white paper on the board. Have a black marker available for writing the children's responses. Go to the internet and type, "What is a paragraph?" Choose an age-appropriate website for the children.

113

- **Begin the activity by saying,** "Earlier, we talked about what the small wolf was feeling or thinking as he or she was trailing behind the older wolves."
- **Review the children's responses.** (I think my brother's and sister's move too fast. I wonder if they know how hard I'm trying to keep up with them. I'm getting so hungry. I hope we'll stop soon.)
- **Introduce the activity.** "Today, we're going to learn about a paragraph. We're also going to write a paragraph about the feelings and thoughts of the young wolf." Go to the internet and type, "What is a paragraph?" Select the age-appropriate website you chose. Read and discuss the information with the children. "A paragraph is a group of sentences that are related, dealing with a single topic. Writing involves putting our thoughts on paper." Tell the children they first decide what they want to say and then organize their ideas. Review the sentences they created earlier and tell them that they're going to put their sentences in some type of order. They're going to create a paragraph about what the small wolf is feeling or thinking. Do the following.
  1. Ask them to think of a good start for their paragraph. (I am Little Wolf, and I am having a difficult journey.) Start telling the reader why little wolf is having such a hard time on this journey. (My brothers and sisters move too fast. I wonder if they know how hard I'm trying to keep up with them.) Start arranging their sentences in a logical order. Complete the paragraph with a good ending statement. (This journey will certainly be a challenge and a learning experience for me.)
  2. Explain to the children that we can combine our thoughts into a whole paragraph. Read the finished paragraph to the children. Have them write their individual paragraph by writing sentences for a specified period. They could write a few sentences each

day until the paragraph is finished. Encourage them to give their paragraph a title, perhaps "Little Wolf's Difficult Journey."

Science

#1. Draw a wolf's footprint.

- **Objective.** Life Science. Interdependent Relationships in Ecosystems, Animals, Plants, and their Environment. Use observations to describe patterns of what plants and animals (including humans) need to survive.
- **Level of difficulty.** Moderate. (This task may take several days to complete.)
- **Materials needed.** White construction paper, pencils, black colored pencils, and black markers.
- **Before the activity.** Place a large piece of white paper on the board. Have a black marker available for writing the children's responses. Go to the internet and type, "Show me a wolf's footprints." Choose an age-appropriate website for the children.
- **Begin the activity by saying,** "Earlier, we discussed how we knew the wolves were moving in a certain direction."
- **Review the children's responses.** (The footprints were all heading in one direction.)
- **Introduce the activity.** "Today, we're going to examine and draw a wolf's footprint." Go to the internet and type, "Show me a wolf's footprints." Select the age-appropriate website you chose. Read and discuss this information with the children. In addition, there are some videos the children would enjoy seeing. Preview these videos before you show them to the children. When you've seen and discussed the videos, give each child a piece of white construction paper. Have the children do a freehand drawing of a wolf footprint with a pencil, so they can erase as needed. When they feel they've

115

created the footprint they want, have them carefully trace around the print with a black colored pencil and color it in with a black marker.

#2. Learn about and create various animal footprints.

- **Objective.** Life Science. Interdependent Relationships in Ecosystems, Animals, Plants, and their Environment. Use observations to describe patterns of what plants and animals (including humans) need to survive.
- **Level of difficulty.** Moderate. (This task may take several days to complete.)
- **Materials needed.** White construction paper, pencils, black colored pencils, and black markers.
- **Before the activity.** Place a large piece of white paper on the board. Have a black marker available for writing the children's responses. Go to the internet and type, "Show me some animal footprints." Choose an age-appropriate website for the children.
- **Begin the activity by saying,** "Earlier, we discussed how we knew that the wolves were moving in a certain direction."
- **Review the children's responses.** (The footprints were all heading in one direction.)
- **Introduce the activity.** "Today, we're going to learn about other animal footprints. We're going to examine and draw a different animal's footprint." Go to the internet and type, "Show me some animal footprints." Select the age-appropriate website you chose. Read and discuss this information with the children. In addition, there are some videos the children would enjoy seeing. Preview these videos before you show them to the children. When you've seen and discussed the videos, give each child a piece of white construction paper. Have the children do a freehand drawing of

116

the animal footprint of their choice with a pencil, so they can erase as needed. When they feel they've created the footprint they want, have them carefully trace around the print with a black colored pencil and color it in with a black marker.

Direct the children's attention to the two circular pages where the young child and young wolf are walking in the snow, heading toward the trees. Encourage them to answer the following questions in complete sentences.

QUESTIONS

The brackets around the text indicate questions/instructions that an adult should read to the children. Examples of how the children may answer the questions are included in parentheses.

- **[What do you see on this page?]**
- Talk about predicting future events. Give examples of situations where the children could make predictions. **[After winning a soccer game, what might the players do?]** (They might come together to have a group cheer. They might verbally congratulate each other. They might pat each other on the back.) Have the children examine the two pages in the book, making some predictions as to what might happen to the young child and the young wolf. Write the children's responses on a piece of paper and save it for later. (If the young child and the young wolf are traveling in the same direction, they might run into each other. The young wolf might smell the young child and try to avoid her. The young child might see the young wolf and try to avoid him or her.) See Art #1 and Writing #1.
- Have the children look carefully at the right-hand side of the page. **[What do you see behind the young wolf?]** (There are tracks.) See Science #1.
- Note that both the young child and the young wolf made tracks in the snow. **[How many steps do you think it would take you to

walk one hundred yards?] Explain that one hundred yards is the length of a football field. (I think it would take two hundred steps to go across the field. I think it would take 225 steps to walk the length of the field. I think it would take 450 steps to walk the length of the field.) Place a piece of paper on the board and list all the children's responses. Save this for later. See Math #1.

- **[Do you think wolves have special qualities that help them survive?]** Write the children's responses on a piece of paper and save this for later. (Wolves have a good sense of smell. Wolves have thick fur. Wolves can travel a long distance.) See Writing #2.

ACTIVITIES

Art

1. Recreate the two pictures on this page.

- **Objective.** Creating. Anchor Standards #1. Generate and conceptualize artistic ideas and work. Investigate, Plan, Make. Make art or design with various materials and tools to explore personal interests, questions, and curiosities.
- **Level of difficulty.** Moderate. (This task may take several days to complete.)
- **Materials needed.** White construction paper circles, colored construction paper, glue, pencils, colored pencils, paints, paintbrushes, and crayons.
- **Before the activity.** Place a large piece of white paper on the board. Have a black marker available for writing the children's responses.
- **Begin the activity by saying,** "Earlier, we talked about making future predictions. We said that after winning a soccer game, the players might come together to have a group cheer. They might

verbally congratulate each other. They might pat each other on the back." The two pictures on these pages show the young child and the young wolf walking toward the trees. What might happen? Write the children's responses on the paper.

- **Review the children's responses.** (Well, if the young child and the young wolf are in the same general area, they could run into each other. I think they might see each other. I think they might get scared. I think they might travel together.)

- **Introduce the activity.** "Today, we're going to talk about making predictions. Then we'll create these two circle pictures."

  1. Making predictions means we're trying to use the pictures in this book, along with our own personal experiences to guess what might happen. We predicted that the young wolf and the young girl might run into each other in the forest.

  2. "Now, we'll draw or paint these pictures. Then in our writing activity (Writing #1), we'll write some predictions. We'll do one circle drawing of the young child and one circle drawing of the young wolf." Give each child two circular pieces of white construction paper. On these pages, have them draw/paint each of the pictures (the young child approaching the trees and the young wolf walking toward the trees). Let the pictures dry.

  3. Have the children glue their pictures to another piece of colored construction paper. Let them choose the paper color. Attach the children's writing (predictions) to their pictures. (See Writing #1.)

#2. Learn about various animal tracks. Create a place mat with animal tracks.

- **Objective.** Creating. Anchor Standards #1. Generate and conceptualize artistic ideas and work. Investigate, Plan, Make. Make art or design with various materials and tools to explore personal interests, questions, and curiosities.

- **Level of difficulty.** Moderate to challenging. (This task may take several days to complete.)
- **Materials needed.** Various colors of construction paper, markers, crayons, pencils, plastic wrap, rulers, laminator or plastic material to cover place mats, clay, small tubs, paper towels, wet sand, and plaster of Paris.
- **Before the activity.** Place a large piece of white paper on the board. Have a black marker available for writing the children's responses. Go to the internet and type, "Animal tracks/kids." Choose an age-appropriate website for the children.
- **Begin the activity by saying,** "Earlier, we noticed there were tracks behind the young wolf. Why do tracks appear in the snow?"
- **Review the children's responses.** (The weight of the animal pushes its body into the snow, creating a track.)
- **Introduce the activity.** "Today, we're going to learn about animal tracks."
1. Go to the internet and type, "Animal tracks." Select the age-appropriate website you chose. Read and discuss the information with the children. Write some facts on a large piece of paper.
2. Go to the internet and type, "Animal Track Detective/Science for Kids/YouTube." This will lead you to a video that discusses various animal tracks. Choose an age-appropriate website for the children.
3. Have the children create place mats with a border of various animal tracks. Give each child a piece of colored construction paper. Have them gently and carefully draw a line with a ruler around the top edge of the construction paper, creating a three-inch border around the construction paper. Have the children draw their favorite tracks around the border with a pencil. Erase any drawn lines that may appear around the border. Have the children use a black crayon or marker to highlight the tracks.

4. If you have access to a laminator, you can laminate the place mat to preserve their drawings. If a laminator isn't available, you can purchase rolls of peel-off plastic material that can be used to preserve their drawings.

5. Have the children tell a friend about the various tracks they drew on their place mat.

- **Extension of the activity.**

1. As an extension of the lesson, give the children a chunk of clay and have them create the animal track(s) of their choice. Give each child a piece of plastic wrap. Have them gently smooth out the plastic wrap onto a table or desk. Give each child a piece of clay and have the children lightly press the clay into the plastic wrap. They should gently smooth the clay with a few drops of water, creating a flat surface. Have the children carefully carve out the track(s) with their pencil.

2. The children might want to investigate additional facts about the animal/animal track they've chosen and present these facts to the class. Have the children write some specific information associated with that track and save this information for the following display.

3. Place the children's dry tracks on pieces of colored construction paper and display each child's track in the science area, along with the information they found.

4. If possible, take the children to a muddy area where animal tracks might appear. Carefully examine the tracks and discuss which animal(s) they think created the track.

5. Plaster of Paris molds can be made of their footprint if no animal tracks are available. Have a tub of wet sand material available where the children can place their foot. They should press their foot into the wet sand material, making a clear footprint. Then

have the children step into a tub of warm water, cleaning their foot with paper towels.

6. Mix the plaster of Paris, using the directions on the box. It will be two parts plaster of Paris to one part water. Mix thoroughly and carefully pour this mixture over the footprint or track.

7. Place a large paper clip in the end of the mold so the children can hang it on their wall when it's dry. Allow the print to dry thoroughly and then carefully remove the mold. Brush off the excess debris. The children might enjoy painting their footprint / animal track.

Writing

#1.Predict what the young child and the young wolf might do in this situation.

- **Objective.** Integration of Knowledge and Ideas. Explain how specific aspects of a text's illustrations contribute to what is conveyed by the words in a story (e.g., create mood or emphasize aspects of a character or setting).
- **Level of difficulty.** Moderate. (This task may take several days to complete.)
- **Materials needed.** Lined paper and pencils.
- **Before the activity.** Place a large piece of white paper on the board. Have a black marker available for writing the children's responses.
- **Begin the activity by saying,** "Earlier, we talked about predicting future events."
- **Review the children's responses.** (If the young child and young wolf are traveling in the same direction, they might run into each other. The young wolf might smell the young child and try to avoid her. The young child might see the young wolf and try to avoid him or her.)

- **Introduce the activity.** "Today, we're going to predict what the young child and the young wolf might do in this situation." Put a large piece of paper on the board and draw a line down the middle. On one side, write "Young Child" and on the other side write "Young Wolf."

1. Ask the children to predict what they think is going to happen. (I think the young child will stop for a short break. I think the young child will try to get some protection from the snowstorm. I think the young wolf will try to catch up with the pack. I think the young wolf may stop for a rest.) Write their comments on the paper. Discuss why they chose their predictions. (I chose my prediction because there's a snowstorm, and it seems likely that the young child would try to find protection. I chose my prediction because the young wolf was starting to fall behind the fast-moving pack.)

2. When you've finished discussing the predictions, have the children write their favorite prediction on a piece of lined paper. If they'd like to write their own prediction(s), be available to help them sound out the words.

3. Attach the children's predictions to their pictures in Art #1.

#2. Create Wolf Survival Cards.

- **Objective.** Life Science. Structure, Function, and Information Processing. Read texts and use media to determine patterns in behavior of parents and offspring that help offspring survive.
- **Level of difficulty.** Moderate to challenging. (This task may take several days to complete.)
- **Materials needed.** Wolf Survival Cards (see resource section), scissors, pencils, crayons, and colored pencils.
- **Before the activity.** Place a large piece of white paper on the board. Have a black marker available for writing the children's responses.

- **Begin the activity by saying,** "Earlier, we discussed whether wolves had special qualities that help them survive."
- **Review the children's responses.** (Wolves have a good sense of smell. Wolves have thick fur. Wolves can travel a long distance.)
- **Introduce the activity.** "Today, we're going to find out if wolves have special qualities that help them survive in the wild."

1. Go to the internet and type, "Do wolves have special survival skills?" Choose an age-appropriate website for the children. Read and discuss this information with the children. Write the information on a large piece of paper. The children will have a better understanding of how and why wolves are able to survive in such cold weather. There are also videos available that the children will enjoy watching. Preview these videos before you show them to the children.

2. Give each child several Wolf Survival Cards (see the resource section). Have the children cut out the cards. Have them draw and write information about a wolf's survival skill(s) on each card. (Wolves can use their powerful jaws to tear meat off their prey. Wolves can travel a long distance. Wolves have an incredible sense of smell.) You may want to glue these cards onto colored pieces of construction paper and then glue them onto pieces of poster board. Make sure they print their name on the back of each card.

3. Allow the children to share their Wolf Survival Cards with their friends. Wolf stickers can be purchased on the internet to stick to the Wolf Survival Cards. This would be a fun way to reward the children for their hard work in this area. The stickers could be used on the front of their cards with the specific survival skill written on the back of the card.

There are seven different kinds of wolves. There's the Gray, Arctic, Eastern, Ethiopian, Indian, Red, and Himalayan Wolf.

When a wolf pup is born, their eyes are blue. They change to yellow when they turn eight months old.

Science

#1. Observe and learn about wolf tracks.

- **Objective.** Life Science. Structure, Function, and Information Processing. Read texts and use media to determine patterns in behavior of parents and offspring that help offspring survive.

- **Level of difficulty.** Moderate. (This task may take several days to complete.)

- **Materials needed.** White construction paper, pencils, and erasers.

- **Before the activity.** Place a large piece of white paper on the board. Have a black marker available for writing the children's responses. Go to the internet and type, "Wolf tracks." Choose an age-appropriate website for the children.

- **Begin the activity by saying,** "Earlier, we observed that the young child and the young wolf made different prints or tracks in the snow."

- **Review the children's responses.** (I've seen my footprints in the mud, and they're wider than the wolf tracks. The young wolf has smaller tracks.)

- **Introduce the activity.** "Today, we're going to observe and learn about wolf tracks." Go to the internet and type, "Wolf tracks." Select the age-appropriate website you chose. Read and discuss the information with them. There are also videos that the children will enjoy watching. Preview the videos before you show them to the children. Hold up the picture of the wolf tracks (see resource

126

section). Have the children draw these tracks on a piece of paper. Have additional books available for them to see various animal tracks. Allow them to draw other animal tracks.

Math

#1. Learn how to record data. Learn about a mode.

- **Objective.** Measurement and Data. Measure and estimate lengths in standard units. Measure the length of an object by selecting and using appropriate tools such as rulers, yardsticks, meter sticks, and measuring tapes.
- **Level of difficulty.** Moderate. (This task may take several days to complete.)
- **Materials needed.** Pedometer, marker, pencils, and three-by-five-inch cards.
- **Before the activity.** Invite an adult or older student to help record the measurements. Measure off one hundred yards on the playground. Clearly mark a "start" position and a "stop" position.
- **Begin the activity by saying,** "Earlier, we noticed that both the young child and the young wolf made tracks in the snow. We predicted how many steps it would take us to walk one hundred yards."
- **Review the children's responses.** (I think it would take 200 steps to walk across the field. I think it would take 225 steps to walk the length of the field. I think it would take 450 steps to walk the length of the field.)
- **Introduce the activity.** "Today, we're going to count the number of steps it takes us to walk one hundred yards." Have the children walk the one hundred yards one student at a time, with an adult or friend to record the number of steps it takes them to reach the end of the field.

1. Give each child a three-by-five-inch card and have them put their names on the back.

2. Have the children line up at the position marked "start." If you have access to a pedometer, attach it to the child whose turn it is to walk. It will be fun to compare the recorded steps on the pedometer with the number of steps the adult or friend recorded.

3. Have the child whose turn it is to walk hand the adult or friend the card with their name on it. Have the children start their walk at the "start" location and continue walking until they cross the "stop" location. Have an adult or friend record the number of steps it took them to walk the one hundred yards on the front of the card.

4. Examine the pedometer and record the number of steps on the back of the card. Have them do this exercise twice to see if their numbers are similar. Have them record both numbers on the card (e.g., first walk and second walk). How do the numbers on the pedometer compare to the recorded numbers?

5. Collect these cards from the children and determine if the numbers seem reasonable. Record the numbers on a piece of paper (e.g., John, 400 steps; Mary, 350 steps; Tim, 375 steps; Sue, 400 steps; Amy, 400 steps). Determine which number had the greatest number of responses and share this with the children. "There were more kids whose card read 400 steps than any other number." Talk about why this number is important "This number is important because it shows us which number appeared the most. Mathematicians call this number the *mode*. It means that 400 steps were the numbers most recorded."

6. Do this same process for the second group of numbers. What was the difference between the first group of numbers and the second group of numbers? Were they similar? Were they dissimilar?

Direct the children's attention to the page where the child is walking in the forest, huffing, with the young wolf approaching her. Encourage them to answer the following questions in complete sentences.

QUESTIONS

The brackets around the text indicate questions/instructions an adult should read to the children. Examples of how the children may answer the questions are included in parentheses.

- **[What do you see on this page?]** Write the children's comments on a piece of paper and save this for later. (It looks like both the young child and the young wolf are very cold and tired. The young girl is huffing, and the young wolf is whining.) See Art #1.

- **[How would you say the child and the wolf are alike?]** Write the children's comments on a piece of paper and save this for later. (They both look cold and tired. They're both making noises. The child is huffing, and the wolf is whining. They both look unhappy because they're lost. They both look scared.) See Writing #1.

- Note that the child is huffing along the trail. **[What advice would you give the child?]** Write the children's comments on a piece of paper and save this for later. (I would tell the young child to take a break. She needs a rest. I would tell the young child to find a place to get warm.). See Writing #2.

- Have the children observe that the wolf is whining along the trail. **[What advice would you give the wolf?]** Write the children's comments on a piece of paper and save this for later. (You need to start howling! If you howl loudly enough, perhaps your family will hear you. I think you need to rest for a while because you've traveled a very long way.) See Writing #3.

- Note that being lost in the forest would be a very scary situation. Talk about some survival techniques that might be used in this situation. Write the children's comments on a piece of paper and save this for later. (You could take shelter near the trees. You could collect broken pine branches and pile them up to create a cave. Putting snow on top of the pine branches would help to insulate the shelter.) See Writing #4 and Science #1.

- **[How do you think people survive being stranded in the snow?]** Write the children's comments on a piece of paper and save it for later. (They stay in their vehicles. They take special gear and supplies with them. They create shelters in the snow.) See Science #1.

- After the children have heard the snow survival information in the science section, create a snow shelter within the classroom. A tent could be a way to trap warm air in the snow, with branches surrounding it. Set up a tent in the classroom and put books related to snow survival, wolves, and cold weather information inside the tent. Allow the children some time to read in the "snow cave."

- Go to the internet and type, "How does a wolf survive in the snow?" Read and review the information with the children. There are also videos for the children to watch. Write the children's comments on a piece of paper and save this for later. See Science #2.

- **[How far can a wolf travel in the snow?]** (I think a wolf can travel three miles. I think a wolf can travel five miles. I think a wolf can travel eight miles.) See Math #1.

- **[Raise your hand if you've ever seen a snow globe?]** (My family has a snow globe that we put up during the holiday. We have a winter snow globe that we put up during the winter.) Have the children create a snow globe (see resource section). See Art #2.

ACTIVITIES

Art

#1. Paint/draw this page.

- **Objective.** Creating. Anchor Standard #1. Generate and conceptualize artistic ideas and work. Investigate, Plan, Make. Make art or design with various materials and tools to explore personal interests, questions, and curiosities.
- **Level of difficulty.** Moderate. (This task may take several days to complete.)
- **Materials needed.** White construction paper, paints, paintbrushes, crayons, pencils, and lined paper.
- **Before the activity.** Prepare the materials.
- **Begin the activity by saying,** "Earlier we described what we saw on this page."
- **Review the children's responses.** (It looked like both the young child and the young wolf were very cold and tired. The young girl is huffing, and the young wolf is whining.)
- **Introduce the activity.** "Today, we're going to recreate this page, with the young child and young wolf huffing and whining in the snow." They can draw or paint the page. Have them write one sentence they've learned from their prior discussions. (It looked like both the young child and the young wolf were very cold and tired. The young girl is huffing, and the young wolf is whining.) Have the children attach their sentence to their drawing/painting. Display their work on the bulletin board.

#2. To create a snow globe.

- **Objective.** Presenting. Anchor Standard #4. Select, analyze, and interpret artistic work for presentation. Select. Select art objects for personal portfolio and display, explaining why they were chosen.
- **Level of difficulty.** Challenging. (This task may need additional adult/older student supervision, and it could take several days to complete.)
- **Materials needed.** Snow globe template (see resource section), white construction paper, crayons, colored pencils, paints, glue, glitter, and scissors.
- **Before the activity.** Place a large piece of white paper on the board. Have a black marker available for writing the children's responses. Go to the internet and type, "How to make a snow globe." Choose an age-appropriate website for the children.
- **Begin the activity by saying,** "Throughout the year, many people display a snow globe in their house." Does your family have a snow globe? Write the children's responses on a piece of paper.
- **Review the children's responses.** (My family has a snow globe. We put it on the table during the winter. It's fun to shake it and see the "snow" falling. I like to watch it.)
- **Introduce the activity.** "Today, we're going to create a snow globe. This story takes place in a location where there's a lot of snow, so it will be fun to make one of these decorative globes."
1. Have the children cut out the snow globe template. (See resource section.) Have them print their name on the back of the snow globe and base. Have them draw or paint the young child and the young wolf in the center of the circular globe. Have them draw/paint some trees and small animals around the young child and the young wolf. If they prefer to draw another scene, allow them to create their own winter scene. Let this dry.

2. Have them spread a thin layer of glue over their picture with a paintbrush and sprinkle with silver glitter. Shake the picture and save the excess glitter. Let the picture dry.

3. Decorate the base or cut out some felt to attach to it. Glue the felt onto the bottom of the base. (See resource section.) Let this dry. You might want to glue the entire snow globe onto a piece of poster board.

4. You could also create a snow globe in a jar. Go to the internet and type, "How to make a snow globe in a jar." Choose an age-appropriate website for the children. They would enjoy creating this snow globe.

Writing

#1. Compare the appearance of the young child and the young wolf. Contrast the appearance of the young child and the young wolf.

- **Objective.** Integration of Knowledge and Ideas (Compare and contrast the adventures and experiences of characters in stories.)
- **Level of difficulty.** Moderate. (This task may take several days to complete.)

- **Materials needed.** Lined paper and pencils.
- **Before the activity.** Place a large piece of white paper on the board. Have a black marker available for writing the children's responses. Draw a line down the center and label one side "How they're alike." On the other side write, "How they're different."
- **Begin the activity by saying,** "Earlier, we discussed how the young child, and the wolf were alike. We also discussed how the young child and the young wolf were different."
- **Review the children's responses.** (They're alike because they both look cold and tired. They're both making noises. The child is huffing, and the wolf is whining. They both look unhappy because they're lost. They both look scared. They're different because the young child is a human. The young child is wearing clothes. The young wolf is an animal. The young wolf isn't wearing clothes.).
- **Introduce the activity.** "Today, we're going to compare and contrast the young child and the young wolf."
  1. "To compare means we find things that make them the same. To contrast means that we find things that are different. We'll start by finding out how they're the same. We call these comparison statements. We said they both look tired. They both made noises." (The child is huffing, and the wolf is whining.) Have the children write a sentence about how they think the young child and the young wolf are similar. If the children want to write their own sentence, be available to help them sound out any words.
  2. "Now, we'll contrast the young child and the young wolf. A contrast statement shows how they're different. For example, the young child is a human. The young child is wearing clothes. The young wolf is an animal. The young wolf isn't wearing clothes. Write a contrast sentence to show how they're different." If the children want to write their own sentence, be available to help them sound out any words.

- **Extension of the activity.** You could create some dialogue statements about how the young child and young wolf feel at this point in their journey. Here are some examples:

Young Child
- I feel miserable.
- I feel like I'll never find my way home.
- I feel exhausted.

Young Wolf
- I feel like I'm all alone.
- I miss my wolf pack family.
- I wonder if I'll ever catch up to the pack.

Have the children write a few dialogue statements on a piece of lined paper.

#2. Write a few sentences of advice to the child.

- **Objective.** Text Types and Purposes. Write opinion pieces on topics or texts, supporting a point of view with reasons. Provide reasons that support the opinion.
- **Level of difficulty.** Moderate. (This task may take several days to complete.)
- **Materials needed.** Lined paper and pencils.
- **Before the activity.** Place a large piece of white paper on the board. Have a black marker available for writing the children's responses.
- **Begin the activity by saying,** "Earlier, we discussed how the child was huffing along the trail. We offered some advice to the young child."
- **Review the children's responses.** (I would tell the young child to take a break. She needs a rest. I would tell the young child to find a place to keep herself warm.)

- **Introduce the activity.** "Today, we're going to write a few sentences of advice to the child." Review the children's comments and add any additional comments on a piece of paper. (I think you need to slow down and observe your environment. I think you need to breathe deeply. I think you need to rest your feet.) Have the children write their favorite piece of advice from the list on a piece of lined paper or allow them to write their own sentence(s). Be available to help them sound out the words.

#3. Write a few sentences of advice to the young wolf.

- **Objective.** Text Types and Purposes. Write opinion pieces on topics or texts, supporting a point of view with reasons. Provide reasons that support the opinion.
- **Level of difficulty.** Moderate. (This task may take several days to complete.)
- **Materials needed.** Lined paper and pencils.
- **Before the activity.** Place a large piece of white paper on the board. Have a black marker available for writing the children's responses.
- **Begin the activity by saying,** "Earlier, we discussed how the young wolf was whining along the trail. We offered some advice to the young wolf."
- **Review the children's responses.** (You need to start howling! If you howl loudly enough, your family will hear you. I think you need to rest for a while because you've traveled a very long way.)
- **Introduce the activity.** "Today, we're going to write a few sentences of advice to the young wolf." Review the children's comments and add any additional comments on a piece of paper (I think you need to shake off the snow that's on your back. I think you need to smell the area to see if you can locate the wolf pack. I think you need to stop and listen for the wolf pack.). Have the children write their

favorite piece of advice from the list on a piece of lined paper or allow them to write their own sentence(s). Be available to help them sound out the words.

#4. Engage in a discussion of how it would feel if we were lost in the forest.

- **Objective.** Craft and Structure. Identify words and phrases in stories or poems that suggest feelings or appeal to the senses.
- **Level of difficulty.** Moderate. (This task may take several days to complete.)
- **Materials needed.** Lined paper and pencils.
- **Before the activity.** Place a large piece of white paper on the board. Have a black marker available for writing the children's responses.
- **Begin the activity by saying,** "Earlier, we discussed that it would feel scary if we were lost in the forest. We talked about some survival techniques that could be used in this situation."
- **Review the children's responses.** (You could take shelter near the trees. You could collect broken pine branches and pile them up to create a cave. Putting snow on top of the pine branches would help to insulate the shelter.)
- **Introduce the activity.** "Today, we're going to write a few sentences about what we'd do in this situation." Help the children come up with some examples. (First, I'd find or create a shelter. I'd sit and think about what I should do. I'd find a water source.). Have the children write their favorite survival technique from the list on a piece of lined paper or allow them to write their own sentence(s). Be available to help them sound out the words.

Science

#1. To learn about a lean-to as a survival shelter in the cold weather.

- **Objective.** Engineering Design. Earth and Space Science. Weather and Climate. Obtain and combine information to describe climates in different regions of the world.

- **Level of difficulty.** Moderate. (This task may take several days to complete.)

- **Materials needed.** Three-inch strips of construction paper, pencils, crayons, and colored pencils.

- **Before the activity.** Go to the internet and type, "How to build a lean-to shelter." Choose an age-appropriate website for the children.

- **Begin the activity by saying,** "Earlier, we discussed how being lost in the forest could be very scary. We thought of things we could do to survive in the snow."

- **Review the children's responses.** (We could stay near a protected area. We could take special gear and supplies with us. We could create shelters in the snow.)

- **Introduce the activity.** "Today, we're going to see and read some information about building a lean-to."

1. Go to the internet and type, "How to build a lean-to shelter." Choose an age-appropriate website for the children. Read and review the information.

2. Have the children create panel pictures showing the steps involved in the creation of the lean-to. There may be several ways to create this shelter, so the picture panels would be different. For example, the first panel might show the collection of small tree branches to create a lean-to. The second panel might show tree branches propped up against the lean-to to insulate it. The third panel might show tree branches covering it, with snow over the

tree branches. The fourth panel might show a snow protection shield built of larger branches around the shelter on the snow.

- **Extension of the activity.** A snow cave might be another way to survive in the snow. Go to the internet and type, "Creating a snow shelter." Choose an age-appropriate website for the children. Preview this website before showing it to the children. Read and discuss the information. You could create another set of panel pictures showing how to create a snow shelter.

#2. Learn how wolves survive in very cold weather.

- **Objective.** Engineering Science. Earth and Space Science. Weather and Climate. Obtain and combine information to describe climates in different regions of the world.
- **Level of difficulty.** Moderate. (This task may take several days to complete.)
- **Materials needed.** Lined paper, pencils, crayons, and colored pencils.
- **Before the activity.** Go to the internet and type, "How does a wolf survive in the snow?" Choose an age-appropriate website for the children. Place a large piece of white paper on the board. Have a black marker available for writing the children's responses.
- **Begin the activity by saying,** "How do you think a wolf survives in the snow?" Write down the children's responses on a piece of paper.
- **Review the children's responses.** (The wolves huddle close together to keep warm. I think they try to find a sheltered area to keep warm. I think they find an opening in the rocks.)
- **Introduce the activity.** "Today, we're going to find out how a wolf survives in the snow."
  1. Go to the internet and type, "How does a wolf survive in the snow?" Select the age-appropriate website you chose. Read and discuss the information with the children. There are some videos

139

the children might enjoy watching for additional information. Preview these videos before you show them to the children.

2. "What are some of the things you remember from the website and video?" Write what the children remember from the website and video on a piece of paper. Have them choose the fact they think was the most important and write down that fact. Then have them draw a picture to represent the fact. (Wolves have very thick fur. It keeps them warm in wintry conditions. Their long tails cover their noses/faces at night to keep them warm.)

Math

#1. Estimate how far a wolf can travel.

- **Objective.** Number and Operations in Base Ten. Extend the counting sequence. Count to 120, starting at any number less than 120. In this range, read and write numerals and represent several objects with a written numeral. Measurement and Data. Represent and interpret data. Organize, represent, and interpret data with up to three categories. Ask and answer questions about the total number of data points, how many in each category, and how many more or less are in one category than in another.

- **Level of difficulty.** Moderate. (This task may take several days to complete.)

- **Materials needed.** Lined paper, sticky notes, graph paper, pencils, colored pencils, and crayons.

- **Before the activity.** Place a large piece of white paper on the board. Have a black marker available for writing the children's responses. Divide the paper into sections to represent the number of miles they think a wolf can travel (e.g., 2 miles, 3 miles, 4 miles.)

- **Begin the activity by saying,** "Earlier, we discussed how far we think a wolf can travel in the snow."

- **Review the children's responses.** (I think a wolf can travel 3 miles in the snow. I think a wolf can travel 5 miles in the snow.)
- **Introduce the activity.** "Today, we're going to estimate how far we think a wolf can travel in the snow."

1. Have the children write their name on the back of a sticky note, with their estimate written on the front. Have them come to the board one at a time and place their sticky note on the estimated distance.

   How Far Can a Wolf Travel?

2 miles = Susan, Mary	2 miles = two children
3 miles = Tim, John	3 miles =two children
4 miles = Sean	4 miles = one child
5 miles = Miley, George, Stephen	5 miles = three children
6 miles = Linda, Joe, Amy, James	6 miles = four children

2. A wolf can travel approximately 30 miles in a day. Review the children's comments. Create a chart or bar graph indicating the distances they thought a wolf could travel. (See the prior example.)

Direct the children's attention to the pages where the young child is kneeling on the snow with her arms outstretched. The young wolf is crouched on the ground, whining. Encourage them to answer the following questions in complete sentences.

QUESTIONS

The brackets around the text indicate questions/instructions an adult should read to the children. Examples of how the children may answer the questions are included in parentheses.

- **[What do you see on this page?]**
- **[How would you describe the child?]** Write the children's comments on a piece of paper and save this for later. (The young child looks concerned. The young child looks like she wants to help the young wolf. The young child has her hands outstretched to encourage the young wolf to come closer.) See Writing #1.
- **[How would you describe the young wolf?]** Write the children's comments on a piece of paper and save this for later. (The young wolf looks scared. The young wolf looks like he or she is afraid to come near the young child. The young wolf is making loud whining sounds.) See Writing #2.
- Have the children look carefully at the young wolf's ears. **[What do you see?]** (The young wolf's ears are folded flat against the young wolf's head. This means that he or she is frightened. See Science #1.

- **[Have any of your pets folded their ears back against their body?]** Have the children tell a partner about a time when their pet displayed this behavior.

- **[How do you show fear?]** Invite a child to demonstrate how they personally show fear Children might cover their face with their hands. They might close their eyes and hide from the perceived fear. Have them show a friend how they show fear. See Science #2.

- **[What do you think the child is thinking?]** Write the children's comments on a piece of paper and save this for later. See Writing #3.

- **[What do you think the young wolf is thinking?]** Write the children's comments on a piece of paper and save this for later. See Writing #4.

- **[The author shows us that the wolf was whining.]** Discuss and write down some of the reasons why the young wolf would "whine" in this situation. (It's so cold here. I've walked so many miles. My feet hurt! I'm hungry. I miss my family.). Save this paper for later. See Writing #5.

ACTIVITIES

Writing

#1. Review adjectives.

- **Objective.** Conventions of Standard English. Demonstrate command of the conventions of standard English grammar and usage when writing or speaking. Use frequently occurring adjectives.
- **Level of difficulty.** Easy.
- **Materials needed.** Lined paper and pencils.
- **Before the activity.** Place a large piece of white paper on the board. Have a black marker available for writing the children's responses.

- **Begin the activity by saying,** "Earlier, we described the young child."
- **Review the children's responses.** (The young child looks concerned. The young child looks like she wants to help the young wolf. The young child has her hands outstretched to encourage the young wolf to come closer.)
- **Introduce the activity.** "Today, we're going to talk about and review adjectives. Adjectives describe something." Give them an example of adjectives by holding up a pencil. "We could describe this pencil as thin, yellow, and round. Today, we're going to make a list of adjectives we could use to describe the young child's expression." Use the children's comments to write a list of adjectives and have the children choose their favorite three adjectives to write on a piece of paper (e.g., concerned, exhausted, frightened or tired, scared, worried).

#2. Discuss fear.

- **Objective.** Comprehension and Collaboration. Describe people, places, things, and events with relevant details, expressing ideas and feelings clearly.
- **Level of difficulty.** Easy.
- **Materials needed.** White construction paper, pencils, crayons, colored pencils, and small balloons.
- **Before the activity.** Place a large piece of white paper on the board. Have a black marker available for writing the children's responses. Go to the internet and type, "Childhood fears." Choose an age-appropriate website for the children.
- **Begin the activity by saying,** "Earlier, we described the young wolf."

- **Review the children's responses.** (The young wolf looks scared. The young wolf looks like he or she is afraid to come near the young child. The young wolf is making loud whining sounds.)
- **Introduce the activity.** "Today, we're going to talk about fears."
  1. "Have you ever experienced fear?" Have the children relay a time when they experienced fear. (I was fearful when I walked past a big dog. I felt fear when my brother showed me his snake. I felt fear when I saw a big spider.) Go to the internet and type, "Childhood fears." Choose an age-appropriate website for the children. Read and discuss the information with the children.
  2. YouTube also has some videos related to childhood fears. Preview these before you show them to the children.
  3. Have the children draw a picture of a fear they've experienced.
  4. Ask the children if they can think of ways to help overcome the fear. (I'm afraid of the dark, so I have a night-light near my bed at night to make me feel safe. I'm afraid of bugs, so my mom put some bugs in a glass jar, and I watched them. I discovered that it was fun to watch them! I'm afraid of thunder, so I sat inside one night and looked out the window. The lightning made interesting patterns in the sky.)
  5. Have the children find other children in the class who have the same fear as they have. Have them sit together and discuss how they've dealt with the fear. (I'm afraid of loud noises, but I've learned to quickly cover my ears until the loud noise stops. I used to run away, but now I just wait.)
- **Extension of the activity.** Play a fear stomping game. Have the children write their fears on small pieces of paper and place each fear inside a balloon. Slightly blow up the balloon and tie it off. Repeat this process for all their fears. When the children have blown up all their balloons, have them go outside and let them stomp their fears. They get to stomp each balloon until it pops. Explain to them

that the stomping process may not alleviate their fear, but it helps to put the fear in perspective.

#3. Write what the young child might be thinking.

- **Objective.** Presentation of Knowledge and Ideas. Describe familiar people, places, things, and events with relevant details, expressing ideas and feelings clearly.
- **Level of difficulty.** Easy.
- **Materials needed.** Lined paper and pencils.
- **Before the activity.** Place a large piece of white paper on the board. Have a black marker available for writing the children's responses.
- **Begin the activity by saying,** "Earlier, we imagined what the child might be thinking."
- **Review the children's responses.** (I wonder if the young wolf will come to me. I wonder if the young wolf will let me touch him or her. I wonder if the young wolf is as tired as I am.)
- **Introduce the activity.** "Today, we're going to imagine what the young child might be thinking." Add to the children's reviewed comments. Have the children write their favorite comment(s) on a piece of paper.

#4. Write what the young wolf might be thinking.

- **Objective.** Presentation of Knowledge and Ideas. Describe familiar people, places, things, and events with relevant details, expressing ideas and feeling clearly.
- **Level of difficulty.** Easy.
- **Materials needed.** Lined paper and pencils.
- **Before the activity.** Place a large piece of white paper on the board. Have a black marker available for writing the children's responses.

- **Begin the activity by saying,** "Earlier, we imagined what the young wolf might be thinking."
- **Review the children's responses.** (The child wants to be my friend. The young child looks tired. I hope the young child doesn't hurt me. I hope the young child wants to be my friend.)
- **Introduce the activity.** "Today, we're going to imagine what the young wolf might be thinking." Add to the children's reviewed comments. Have the children write their favorite comment(s) on a piece of paper.

#5. Create a class poem reflecting the feelings of the young wolf.

- **Objective.** Craft and Structure. Identify words and phrases in stories or poems that suggest feelings or appeal to the senses.
- **Level of difficulty.** Moderate. (This task may take several days to complete.)
- **Materials needed.** Lined paper and pencils.
- **Before the activity.** Place a large piece of white paper on the board. Have a black marker available for writing the children's responses.
- **Begin the activity by saying,** "Earlier, we noticed that the young wolf was whining and discussed why that might be."
- **Review the children's responses.** (It's so cold here. I've walked so many miles. My feet hurt! I'm hungry. I miss my family.)
- **Introduce the activity.** "Today, we're going to create a class poem reflecting the feelings of the wolf." If the children want to create their own poem, be available to help them sound out the words. Talk about different poetic styles (e.g., haiku, or free verse). Write some ideas on the board. Create a class poem from the wolf's point of view. See the example included here:

Mile after mile,
I've walked by myself.

147

Trying to keep up,

With my fast-moving family.

Cold, hunger, and pain,

Have been my companions.

Have the children carefully write the class poem on a piece of lined paper.

Science

#1. Discover if wolves show fear.

- **Objective.** Life Science. Interdependent Relationships in Ecosystems. Communicate solutions that will reduce the impact of humans on the land, water, air, and/or other living things in the local environment.
- **Level of difficulty.** Easy.
- **Materials needed.** None.
- **Before the activity.** Place a large piece of white paper on the board. Have a black marker available for writing the information about wolves showing fear. Go to the internet and type, "Do wolves show fear?" Choose an age-appropriate website for the children.
- **Begin the activity by saying,** "Earlier, we observed that the young wolf had his or her ears folded flat against his or her head. We thought he or she was showing fear."
- **Review the children's responses.** (The young wolf is lying flat down on the snow. The young wolf has his or her head on the ground. The young wolf has his or her ears folded flat back on his or her head.)
- **Introduce the activity.** "Today, we're going to discover if wolves show fear."
  1. Go to the internet and type, "Do wolves show fear? Select the age-appropriate website you chose. Read and discuss the

148

information with the children. Write down the important facts they learned on the internet website about fear. Understanding that animals experience fear may help the children deal with their own fears.

2. Have the children relay to a friend their favorite fact about wolves showing fear. (A wolf will try to make itself look small. It will flatten its ears against its body. It will arch its back.)

#2. Discuss the ways in which the children show and deal with fear.

- **Objective.** Life Science. Structure, Function, and Information Processing. Read texts and use media to determine patterns in behavior of parents and offspring that help offspring survive.
- **Level of difficulty.** Easy.
- **Materials needed.** White construction paper, pencils, crayons, and colored pencils.
- **Before the activity.** Place a large piece of white paper on the board. Have a black marker available for writing the children's comments.
- **Begin the activity by saying,** "Earlier, we discussed how we show fear."
- **Review the children's responses.** (We yell. We cover our eyes. We try to find something to defend ourselves with. We pull the covers over our head.)
- **Introduce the activity.** "Today, we're going to discuss and draw a picture of how we show fear. How do you show fear?" (I show fear by covering my face with my hands. I show fear by covering my head with the sheet. I show fear by hiding.). Have the children draw a picture of their fear and how they deal with the fear. Allow the children to explain their picture to a friend.

> *Wolf in the Snow* **illustration: Three-panel pictures on the left-hand side of the page and a picture of the young child holding the young wolf with a question mark above her head on the right-hand side of the page**
>
> Direct the children's attention to the pages where the young wolf is walking in the snow, sinks, and the child picks the young wolf up in her arms. Encourage them to answer the following questions in complete sentences.

QUESTIONS

The brackets around the text indicate questions/instructions an adult should read to the children. Examples of how the children may answer the questions are included in parentheses.

- **[What do you see on this page?]**
- Direct the children to look at the first picture on the top left-hand side of the page. **[What do you think is happening?]** Write the children's comments on a piece of paper and save this for later. (I think the young wolf jumped down because it was getting tired of being carried. I think the young child was so tired she dropped the young wolf. The expression on the young child's face looks frightened.) See Writing #1.
- Have the children look at the second picture in the middle of the left-hand side of the page. **[What do you think is happening?]** Write the children's comments on a piece of paper and save this for later. (I think the young child is surprised the young wolf has walked away and started sinking in the snow. I think the young wolf is not happy about sinking in the snow.) See Writing #1.

- Point out that the young wolf in the second picture is sinking into the snow. **[Why did this happen?]** Write the children's comments on a piece of paper and save this for later. (The young wolf is sinking in the snow because of his or her weight. The young wolf is sinking in the snow because there's more snow in this spot.) See Science #1.

- Direct the children's attention to the bottom picture on the left-hand side of the page. **[What do you think is happening?]** Write the children's comments on a piece of paper and save this for later. (The bottom picture shows the young wolf in the child's arms. I wonder if he or she jumped up into the arms of the child or if the child picked him or her up.) See Writing #1.

- Note that there's a special punctuation mark above the child's head on the right-hand side of the page. Have the children raise their hands if they know what punctuation mark is shown. Have one of the children tell what punctuation mark is shown. It's a question mark. A question mark asks a question. For example, I could ask you a question. What is your favorite food? Do you have a pet? Where do you live? How many animals are in your family? Who is your favorite musical artist? Words such as who, what, why, where, when, and how are words that ask questions. Allow the children to ask a friend a few questions. See Writing #2.

- **[How would you describe the young wolf and child on the right-hand side of the page?]** Write the children's comments on a piece of paper and save this for later. (The young wolf looks comfortable. The young wolf doesn't look afraid. The young wolf seems content to be in the child's arms. The child seems comfortable with the young wolf in her arms. The child seems protective.) See Science #4.

- **[What is happening off in the distance?]** Write the children's comments on a piece of paper and save this for later. (The wolves are howling. The sound is traveling through the air.) See Science #2 and Math #1.

- **[Do you think wolves can communicate?]** Write the children's comments on a piece of paper and save this for later. (The wolf pack is trying to communicate with the young wolf. I think they're howling, so the young wolf will know they're trying to find him or her.) See Science #3.

- **[What do you think the young child is thinking?]** Write the children's comments on a piece of paper. (I wonder if it's a good idea to be walking in the direction of howling wolves. I hope the young wolf doesn't jump down and start running toward the wolf pack. I hope the wolf pack knows I'm trying to help the young wolf.)

- **[What do you think the young wolf is thinking?]** Write the children's comments on a piece of paper. (I sure hope that's my wolf pack family howling! I wonder if they know how far this young child has walked to help me.)

- **[What do you think will happen?]** Write the children's comments on a piece of paper (I think the howling in the distance is the young wolf's family. I think they're coming to find him or her.)

ACTIVITIES

Writing

#1. Discuss outcomes of the events in the story.

- **Objective.** Key Ideas and Details. Describe characters in a story (e.g., their traits, motivations, or feelings) and explain how their actions contribute to the sequence of events.

- **Level of difficulty.** Moderate. (This task may take several days to complete.)

- **Materials needed.** Lined paper and pencils.

- **Before the activity.** Place a large piece of white paper on the board. Have a black marker available for writing the children's responses.
- **Begin the activity by saying,** "Earlier, we discussed what we thought was happening on the left-hand side of the page."
  1. "The top picture/panel shows the young wolf walking in the snow. We wondered if the young wolf jumped down on his or her own or if the young child was so tired she dropped the young wolf. The expression on the young child's face looks frightened." Review the children's comments.
  2. "The middle picture/panel shows the young wolf walking away from the young child and the young wolf starts to sink. We wondered if the young wolf was unhappy about his or her decision to walk away from the young child. It looks like he or she is starting to whine." Review the children's comments.
  3. "The bottom picture/panel shows the young wolf in the child's arms. We wondered if the young wolf jumped up into the arms of the child or whether it was picked up by the young child?"
- **Review the children's responses.** (Young Wolf: I decided to jump into the young child's arms because I was beginning to sink into the snow! I couldn't walk another step. The snow was beginning to cover me. Young Child: I'm so glad the young wolf decided to jump back into my arms. I was afraid he/she might run away.)
- **Introduce the activity.** "Today, we're going to write what we think happened in the story."
  1. Have the children write a few sentences from both the child's perspective and the young wolf's perspective.
  2. Let the children choose which picture/panel they'd like to write about. For example, if they choose the bottom picture and to write from the perspective of the young wolf, they might write, Young Wolf: I decided to jump into the young child's arms because I was beginning to sink into the snow! I couldn't walk another step. The

snow was beginning to cover me. If they choose the top picture and to write from the perspective of the young child, they might write, Young Child: I'm so glad the young wolf decided to jump back into my arms. I was afraid he/she might run away. I don't mind carrying the young wolf.

#2. Discuss a punctuation mark, specifically the question mark.

- **Objective.** Conventions of Standard English. Use end punctuation for sentences.
- **Level of difficulty.** Easy.
- **Materials needed.** Lined paper, pencils, colored markers, or pencils.
- **Before the activity.** Place a large piece of white paper on the board. Have a black marker available for writing a few questions on the paper. (What is your favorite food? Do you have any animals at home? What is your favorite sport?)
- **Begin the activity by saying,** "Earlier, we discussed the punctuation mark above the child's head on the right-hand side of the page. We said it was a question mark."
- **Introduce the activity.** "Today, we're going to sit in double circles and ask questions."
  1. You might want to draw two circles on the board to demonstrate the inner/outer circle concept. Have the children form an inner and an outer circle, with the same number of children in both circles. You could count one, two; one, two; and so on. Have all the ones go to the inner circle, while the twos go to the outer circle.
  2. Have the children face each other. The child in the inner circle asks a question, while the child on the outer circle answers the question. When the children have completed the question, a bell is rung. The inner circle moves one spot to their right, facing a new child. The children on the outside of the circle stay in the

same location. You could reverse this process and have the outer circle moving, while the inner circle remains seated. The same could be done for the questions. Continue this process until the children run out of questions.

- **Extension of the activity.** As an additional activity, have the children write two to three questions on a piece of paper. Have them use brightly colored pencils or markers to make the question marks at the end of the question.

Science

#1. Discuss why a heavy object will sink in the snow.

- **Objective.** Earth and Space Science. Weather and Climate. Ask questions to obtain information about the purpose of weather forecasting to prepare for and respond to severe weather.
- **Level of difficulty.** Easy.
- **Materials needed.** A pair of snowshoes if available.
- **Before the activity.** Place a large piece of white paper on the board. Have a black marker available for writing the children's responses. Go to the internet and type, "Why do things sink in the snow?" Choose an age-appropriate website for the children. Invite a local sporting goods store to send a representative to demonstrate how a snowshoe works.
- **Begin the activity by saying,** "Earlier, we talked about why we thought the young wolf sank into the snow."
- **Review the children's responses.** (The young wolf is sinking in the snow because of his or her weight. The young wolf is sinking in the snow because it's deeper in this spot.)
- **Introduce the activity.** "Today, we're going to discuss why we think the young wolf sank into the snow." Go to the internet and type, "Why do things sink in the snow?" Select the age-appropriate website you

chose. Read and discuss this information with the children. Talk about how weight can be distributed over a large area to prevent sinking. Talk about how a pair of snowshoes can accomplish this.

- **Extension of the activity.** If possible, bring in a pair of snowshoes to show the children. Perhaps a local sporting goods store would send a representative to demonstrate a snowshoe and this principle.

#2. Discuss and discover how far a wolf's howl can travel.

- **Objective.** Physical Science. Waves. Light and Sound. Plan and conduct investigations to provide evidence that vibrating materials can make sound and that sound can make materials vibrate.
- **Level of difficulty.** Easy.
- **Materials needed.** Sticky notes and pencils.
- **Before the activity.** Place a large piece of white paper on the board. Have a black marker available for writing the children's responses. Go to the internet and type, "How far can a wolf's howl travel?" Choose an age-appropriate website for the children.
- **Begin the activity by saying,** "Earlier, we noticed that the wolves were howling in the distance. We wondered how far a wolf's howl could travel."
- **Review the children's responses.** (I think a wolf's howl can travel one mile. I think it can travel three miles. I think it can be heard five miles away.)
- **Introduce the activity.** "Today, we're going to find out how far a wolf's howl can travel. We noticed in the picture that a wolf or wolves were howling in the distance."
  1. "How far do you think a wolf's howl can travel?" Give each child a sticky note and have them put their name and distance prediction on it (e.g., one mile, two miles, three miles). Place a piece of paper on the board, dividing it into the various distance sections (e.g., one mile, two miles, three miles).

2. Have the children place their sticky note in the appropriate section. Go to the internet and type, "How far can a wolf's howl travel?" Choose an age-appropriate website for the children. Read and discuss this information with the children. "A wolf's howl can travel several miles. It can travel approximately ten miles."

3. Have the children examine the various distance sections on the paper that was placed on the board earlier to see whose prediction came the closest to the actual distance. Have a group howl for the winner(s). Perhaps a wolf sticker or wolf calendar could be given to the winner(s).

#3. Discuss and learn if wolves can communicate with each other.

- **Objective.** Engineering Design. Life Science. Structure, Function, and Information Processing. Use a model to describe that animals receive different types of information through their senses, process the information in their brain, and respond to the information in different ways.

- **Level of difficulty.** Easy.

- **Materials needed.** None.

- **Before the activity.** Place a large piece of white paper on the board. Have a black marker available for writing the children's responses. Go to the internet and type, "Can wolves communicate with each other?" Choose an age-appropriate website for the children.

- **Begin the activity by saying,** "Earlier, we discussed whether wolves could communicate with each other."

- **Review the children's responses.** (I think wolves can communicate with each other. Wolves have their own way of communicating with other members of the pack. Their movements are telling each other what they're thinking and feeling.)

- **Introduce the activity.** "Today, we're going to find out if wolves communicate with each other."

1. Go to the internet and type, "Can wolves communicate with each other?" Select the age-appropriate website you chose. Read and discuss this information with the children. "We know that wolves can communicate with each other. For example, wolves can whine, whimper, growl, bark, and make yipping sounds."

2. If the wolf pack realized the young wolf was missing, what sounds do you think they'd make? Allow the children to make different sounds to relay to the young wolf that they're on their way to rescue him or her. What do you think these sounds could relay? Write the children's comments on a piece of paper (Don't worry, young wolf; we're coming in your direction. We know you're nearby. We can smell you.)

#4. Discuss what makes us feel safe and comfortable.

- **Objective.** Life Science. Interdependent Relationships in Ecosystems. Use a model to represent the relationship between the needs of different plants and animals (including humans) and the places they live.
- **Level of difficulty.** Easy.
- **Materials needed.** Potatoes.
- **Before the activity.** Place a large piece of white paper on the board. Have a black marker available for writing the children's responses. Go to the internet and type, "Kids feeling safe." Choose an age-appropriate website for the children.
- **Begin the activity by saying,** "Earlier, we observed that the young wolf looked comfortable. He or she didn't look afraid and seemed content to be in the child's arms."
- **Review the children's responses.** (The wolf looks comfortable. The wolf doesn't look afraid. The wolf seems content to be in the

child's arms. The child seems comfortable with the wolf in her arms. The child seems protective.)

- **Introduce the activity.** "Today, we're going to discuss whether we think the young wolf is comfortable in the young girl's arms."

  1. "We'll talked about what makes us feel safe and comfortable. What makes you feel safe and comfortable?" (I feel safe when I'm with my family. I feel safe with my older brother. I feel safe in my room.) "The young wolf doesn't look afraid and seems content to be in the child's arms." Review the children's comments again. (The wolf looks comfortable. The wolf doesn't look afraid. The wolf seems content to be in the child's arms. The child seems comfortable with the wolf in her arms. The child seems protective.).

  2. "Today, we're going to learn what makes us feel safe and comfortable." Go to the internet and type, "Kids feeling safe." Select the age-appropriate website you chose. Read and discuss the information with the children. There are several videos that the children will enjoy seeing and hearing. Preview these videos before you show them to the children.

  3. Discuss what makes the children happy. Ask them, "What makes you happy?" (I feel happy when my friend listens to me. I feel safe when I have people around me who want the best for me. I feel good when I can help a friend learn something that's difficult for them.)

  4. There are several websites that have activities that will address fear, anxiety, and bullying. Again, preview these websites to make sure they're appropriate for the children.

- **Extension of the activity.** "Today, we're going to do an activity that shows how we're all similar, yet different."

  1. Give each child a potato. Let the children name their potato. Ask the children to stand up with their potato. Have the children find

other potatoes that have similar qualities or attributes. First, ask them to describe attributes their potatoes have. (My potato is small. My potato has spots at the top. My potato has rough skin. My potato has smooth skin.) Allow the children to find several friends whose potato is like theirs.

2. Then, have the children find other potatoes that have different attributes. Have them tell each other about these differences. (My potato has spots on the top, while your potato doesn't have spots on the top. My potato has smooth skin, while your potato has rough skin. My potato is small, while your potato is large.)

3. Eventually, have the children place their potatoes in a basket. Have the children tell how their potatoes were the same and different. Discuss how people are similar yet different.

Math

#1. Learn and discuss a wolf's sense of hearing. Convert miles into feet.

- **Objective.** Presentation of Knowledge and Ideas. Speaking and Listening Standards. Tell a story or recount an experience with appropriate facts and relevant, descriptive details, speaking audibly in coherent sentences.

- **Level of difficulty.** Easy for the younger children. Moderate to challenging for the older students. (This task may take several days to complete for the older children.)

- **Materials needed.** Paper and pencils.

- **Before the activity.** Place a large piece of white paper on the board. Have a black marker available for writing the information about a wolf's sense of hearing. Go to the internet and type, "Tell me about a wolf's hearing." Choose an age-appropriate website for the children.

- **Begin the activity by saying,** "Earlier, we noticed that the wolves were howling off in the distance. The young wolf in this picture made a whining and howling sound."
- **Review the children's responses.** (The wolves are trying to communicate with the young wolf. I think they're howling to let the young wolf know they're nearby. I think the young wolf is whining and howling because he or she is frustrated.)
- **Introduce the activity.** "Today, we're going to learn about a wolf's sense of hearing. The young wolf in this picture made a whining/howling sound. Do you think the mother wolf heard the young wolf whining and howling? Wolves have amazing hearing." Go to the internet and type, "Tell me about a wolf's hearing." Select the age-appropriate website you chose. Read and discuss this information with the children. "It appears wolves can hear sounds six to ten miles away. Have the children relay their favorite fact to a friend."
- **Extension of the activity.** For the older children, have them determine the number of feet this would represent. They will need to multiply 5,280 feet by 6, 7, 8, 9, and 10). See the example included here:

5,280 x 6 = 31,680 feet   5,280 x 7 = 36,960 feet   5,280 x 8 = 42,240 feet
5,280 x 9 = 47,520 feet   5,280 x 10 = 52,800 feet

> ## *Wolf in the Snow* illustration: Long trail of footprints
>
> Direct the children's attention to the pages where you see a long trail of footprints. The young child is carrying the young wolf and howling sounds can be heard in the distance. Encourage them to answer the following questions in complete sentences.

QUESTIONS

The brackets around the text indicate questions/instructions an adult should read to the children. Examples of how the children may answer the questions are included in parentheses.

- **[What do you see on this page?]**
- **[How far do you think the young child can walk in the snow?]** Give each child a sticky note and have them put their name and distance prediction on it. Collect these notes for a later activity. See Math #1.
- **[Can our weight be distributed over the surface of the snow, so we don't sink?]** Write the children's comments on a piece of paper and save this for later. (I've seen people use snowshoes to walk in the snow. They don't sink.) See Math #2.
- **[What do you think the young child is thinking at this point?]** Write the children's comments on a piece of paper and save this for later. (I wonder if I should be heading in the direction where the wolves are howling? I wonder if I should let the young wolf go on his or her own way? I'm getting very tired of walking.) See Writing #1.
- **[What do you think the young wolf is thinking at this point?]** Write the children's comments on a piece of paper and save this for later. (This has been an incredible journey. The young child has

walked such a long way. I don't know how far she can continue to walk and carry me.) See Writing #2.

- **[If you look carefully on the right-hand side of the page, you'll notice that there's a howling sound off in the distance. Do you think this sound can travel a long way?]** Write the children's responses on a piece of paper and save this for later. (I think the howling sound can travel a long way. I know that when I yell, my brother can hear me. I think sound can travel a long distance.) See Science #1.

- **[The wolves are howling off in the distance. Do you think the older wolves are trying to communicate with the young wolf?]** (Yes, I think their howling would be a way for the young wolf to know they're nearby. I think their howling would let the young wolf know they're on their way to rescue him or her.) See Writing #3.

- **[What do you think the wolf pack is thinking at this point?]** Write the children's comments on a piece of paper. (That poor young wolf. He or she has been gone a long time. Why didn't we look back more often to see how he or she was doing?).

- **[Look carefully at the footprints in the snow. What can you say about them?]** (The footprints are leading up the hill. There's a long trail of footprints.) **Today, we're going to make our own footprints on a piece of paper.** See Art #1.

- **[We can tell from the footprints in the snow that there's a lot of snow on the ground. It must be cold. Earlier, we've talked about what happens when it is cold outside For example, our cheeks get pink and our breath shows in the air.]** See Science #2.

- **[We talked about what the young child and the wolf might be thinking. Today, we're going to make stick puppets and tell the class or a friend our story. It can relate to the book, or you can make up your own story.]** (My friend the wolf and I decided to walk in the woods. We both walked a very long way, and we were tired. We decided to rest by a tree. There was a large squirrel scampering in the tree.) See Art #2.

ACTIVITIES

Art

#1. Decorate a cut-out tracing of our feet.

- **Objective.** Responding. Anchor Standard #7. Perceive and analyze artistic work. Perceive. Select and describe daily life experiences of oneself and others.
- **Level of difficulty.** Moderate. (This task may take several days to complete.)
- **Materials needed.** White construction paper, scissors, pencils, paints, paintbrushes, crayons, markers, stickers, dried flowers, and any other art materials you have.
- **Before the activity.** Prepare the materials needed.
- **Begin the activity by saying,** "Earlier, we measured our feet in the math activity to see how long they were." (See Math #2.)
- **Review the children's responses**. None.
- **Introduce the activity.** "Today, we're going to decorate our feet. We measured our feet in the math activity to see how long they were. Now, we're going to decorate them just for fun."
  1. Have the children carefully trace around each foot. A friend can trace around each foot. Trace each foot on a separate piece of white construction paper. Have them carefully cut out their feet and decorate them in any way they choose. Have them write their name on the back of each foot.

2. Have colored pencils, markers, crayons, dried flowers, stickers, and any other art materials you have. Place their decorated footprint on a board.

- **Extension of the activity.** They can write a simple sentence relaying where their feet have traveled. (These feet have been walking in the park. These feet have been running on the field. These feet have been climbing the tree in my backyard.)

#2. Make stick puppets of the young child and the young wolf.

- **Objective.** Creating. Anchor Standard #1. Generate and conceptualize artistic ideas and work. Investigate, Plan, Make. Engage collaboratively in exploration and imaginative play with materials.
- **Level of difficulty.** Moderate. (This task may take several days to complete.)
- **Materials needed.** White construction paper, pencils, crayons, colored pencils, bamboo skewers, paints, paintbrushes, scissors, plastic wrap, and glue.
- **Before the activity.** Place a large piece of white paper on the board. Have a black marker available for writing the children's responses.
- **Begin the activity by saying,** "Earlier, we talked about what the child and the wolf might be thinking or saying." Write the children responses on a piece of paper.
- **Review the children's responses.** (This has been an incredible journey. The young child has walked such a long way. I don't know how far she can continue to walk and carry me. The young wolf has been so cooperative. He/she doesn't wiggle or whine. I know that he or she would like to get down and walk, but it's just too hard for him or her.)
- **Introduce the activity.** "Today, we're going to make stick puppets and tell the class or a friend your story. It can relate to the book, or

we can make up our own story." (My friend the wolf and I decided to walk in the woods. We both walked a very long way, and we were tired. We decided to rest by a tree. There was a large squirrel scampering in the tree.).

1. Give the children a piece of white construction paper and have them draw or paint both figures. Tell them that their drawing should be large enough to be seen in a presentation. Let their pictures dry. When the pictures are completely dry, have them carefully cut a circle around each figure.

2. Distribute two long bamboo skewers or popsicle sticks to each child. Have them turn the colored/painted figure over and make a glue line the length of the figure. Carefully place the bamboo skewers or popsicle sticks into the glue. Make sure they're turned in the correct direction and firmly placed on the glue line. Place another glue line on top of the skewers/sticks and cover with plastic wrap. Place a heavy book on top of the plastic wrap. Make sure the plastic strip is large enough to prevent glue from getting on the book. Let this dry overnight. Remove the book and plastic wrap and place this in a sunny area for another day. This will ensure that the glue is dry.

3. When all the puppets are completed, invite the children to present their own story. It can be like the present story or a story they've chosen to create on their own. Don't require them to present it to the whole class, but perhaps they'd be willing to present their story to a friend. When they've completed their stories, put their puppets on the bulletin board with some of their writing. (See the following writing sections.)

Writing

#1. Imagine what the young child might be thinking in this situation. Have the children write their ideas.

- **Objective.** Knowledge of Language. Use knowledge of language and its conventions when writing, speaking, reading, or listening. Choose words and phrases to convey ideas precisely.
- **Level of difficulty.** Moderate. (This task may take several days to complete.)
- **Materials needed.** Lined paper and pencils.
- **Before the activity.** Place a large piece of white paper on the board. Have a black marker available for writing the children's responses.
- **Begin the activity by saying,** "Earlier, we discussed what we thought the child was thinking."
- **Review the children's responses.** (I wonder if I should be heading in the direction where the wolves are howling? I wonder if I should let the young wolf go his or her own way. I'm getting very tired of walking.)
- **Introduce the activity.** "Today, you're going to write your favorite comment about what the child was thinking." Have the children write their favorite comment(s) on a piece of lined paper or have them write their own sentence(s). Be available to help them sound out the words. Allow them to draw a picture if they'd like. Attach their sentence(s) to their picture.

#2. Imagine what the young wolf might be thinking in this situation. Have the children write their ideas.

- **Objective.** Knowledge of Language. Use knowledge of language and its conventions when writing, speaking, reading, or listening. Choose words and phrases to convey ideas precisely.

- **Level of difficulty.** Moderate. (This task may take several days to complete.)
- **Materials needed.** Lined paper and pencils.
- **Before the activity.** Place a large piece of white paper on the board. Have a black marker available for writing the children's responses.
- **Begin the activity by saying,** "Earlier, we discussed what we thought the young wolf was thinking."
- **Review the children's responses.** (This has been an incredible journey. The young child has walked such a long way. I don't know how far she can continue to walk and carry me.)
- **Introduce the activity.** "Today, you're going to write your favorite comment about what the young wolf was thinking." Have the children write their favorite comment(s) on a piece of lined paper or have them write their own sentence(s). Be available to help them sound out the words. Allow them to draw a picture if they'd like. Attach their sentence(s) to their picture.

#3. Think about and write what the wolf pack might tell the young wolf in this situation.

- **Objective.** Comprehension and Collaboration. Participate in collaborative conversations with diverse partners about topics and texts with peers and adults in small and larger groups. Build on what others say in conversations by linking their comments to the remarks of others.
- **Level of difficulty.** Moderate. (This task may take several days to complete.)
- **Materials needed.** Lined paper and pencils.
- **Before the activity.** Place a large piece of white paper on the board. Have a black marker available for writing the children's responses.

- **Begin the activity by saying,** "Earlier, we wondered if the wolves were trying to communicate with the young wolf because they were howling off in the distance."
- **Review the children's responses.** (Mother Wolf: I know my young wolf is nearby because I can smell him or her. I know he or she couldn't be too far away because we noticed earlier that he or she was still there.)
- **Introduce the activity.** "Today, we're going to think and write about what the wolf pack might tell the young wolf in this situation. If you were a member of the wolf pack, what would you try to tell the young wolf?" Invite two children to practice what the wolf pack and the young wolf might say to each other. Invite them to come to the front of the room and relay the conversation. The children could also write their responses on a piece of paper. (Young wolf, don't get upset. Save your energy. We'll be there before you know it. You've shown great courage. Wait just a little longer.)

Science

#1. Find out how fast sound can travel. Draw sound waves.

- **Objective.** Physical Science. Waves. Light and Sound. Plan and conduct investigations to provide evidence that vibrating materials can make sound and that sound can make materials vibrate.
- **Level of difficulty.** Moderate. (This task may take several days to complete.)
- **Materials needed.** Lined paper, pencils, white construction paper, and crayons or colored pencils.
- **Before the activity.** Place a large piece of white paper on the board. Have a black marker available for writing the children's responses. Go to the internet and type, "How far does sound travel in an hour?" Choose an age-appropriate website for the children. Go to the

internet and type, "Sound waves for kids." Preview the video before showing it to the children.

- **Begin the activity by saying,** "Earlier, we noticed that there was a howling sound off in the distance. We wondered if sound could travel a long way." Write the children's estimates of how far sound might travel.

- **Review the children's responses.** (I think sound can travel fifty miles per hour. I think sound can travel fast. I think sound can travel twenty-five miles per hour.)

- **Introduce the activity.** "Today, we're going to find out if sound can travel a long distance."

1. Go to the internet and type, "How far does sound travel in an hour?" Select the age-appropriate website you chose. Read and discuss this information with the children. "Sound can travel through air at 761 miles per hour!" Have the children write this fact on a piece of paper.

2. There are several videos that the children will enjoy hearing and watching. Preview these videos before you show them to the children. Go to the internet and type, "Videos of Sound Waves for Kids." There's also a video about high-pitched and low-pitched sounds. It demonstrates the different pitches by placing water in bottles. The less water that's in the bottle, the lower the pitch. The fuller the bottle, the higher the pitch. You can also have the children draw various soundwaves.

#2. Observe and record the local weather. Create a daily weather sheet.

- **Objective.** Earth and Space Science. Weather and Climate. Use and share observations of local weather conditions to describe patterns over time.

170

- **Level of difficulty.** Moderate. (This task will take a month to complete.)
- **Materials needed.** Weather sheets (see resource section) for each child and crayons or colored pencils.
- **Before the activity.** Place a large piece of white paper on the board. Have a black marker available for writing the children's responses. Make copies of the weather sheet for each child. (See resource section.) Have pencils and colored pencils available. Go to the internet and type, "Weather symbols for kids." Choose an age-appropriate website for them.
- **Begin the activity by saying,** "Earlier, we talked about how we knew it was cold outside."
- **Review the children's responses.** (Our cheeks get pink and our breath shows in the cold weather.)
- **Introduce the activity.** "This month, we're going to observe and record the weather."
  1. Give each child a blank weather sheet. (See resource section.) Have them put the name of the month at the top of the sheet and write the numbers of the days in the correct location. Go to the internet and type, "Weather symbols for kids." Select the age-appropriate website you chose. Read and discuss the information. Decide as a class which weather symbols they'll use.
  2. Have the children observe and record the weather each day at the same time. They can draw the various symbols (e.g., sun, cloud, wind symbol, raindrop, and snowflake) to indicate the day's weather.
  3. **Extension of the activity.** Have the children compare the local weather with weather throughout the United States. "Is the weather the same in different locations?"

Monday	Tuesday	Wednesday	Thursday	Friday

Monday	Tuesday	Wednesday	Thursday	Friday

Math

#1. Take a survey and record the results to the question, "How far do you think the young child could walk in the snow?"

- **Objective.** Measurement and Data. Represent and Interpret data. Draw a picture graph and a bar graph (with single-unit scale) to represent a data set with up to four categories. Solve simple, put-together, take-apart, and compare problems using information presented in a bar graph.
- **Level of difficulty.** Moderate. (This task may take several days to complete.)
- **Materials needed.** Sticky notes, pencils, graph paper, crayons, and colored pencils.
- **Before the activity.** Place a large piece of white paper on the board, with specific miles written on the bottom of the paper to record the number of miles the young child might be able to walk in the snow (e.g., one mile, two miles, three miles.) Have a black marker available for writing the children's responses. Give each child a sticky note.
- **Begin the activity by saying,** "Earlier, we discussed how far the young child could walk in the snow."
- **Review the children's responses.** (I think the young child can walk one mile in the snow. I think the young child can walk five miles in the snow. I think the child can walk eight miles in the snow.)

172

- **Introduce the activity.** "Today, I'm going to ask you how far you think the young child could walk in the snow."

1. Have the children write how far they think the young child could walk in the snow. Have them write the number on the front of a sticky note and then print their name on the back of the note (e.g., one mile, two miles, three miles.) "Then, we'll graph the results."

2. Put a large piece of paper on the board with sections showing how far the young child could walk in the snow (e.g., one mile, two miles, three miles, four miles).

3. Ask the children to come to the board one at a time. Have them place their note on the number of miles they think the young child could walk in the snow (e.g., one mile, two miles, three miles). When all the sticky notes have been attached, record the results.

4. Write the numbers and names on the board. Here's how this might look:

   One mile—Karen, Joe, Matt

   Two miles—Sarah, Ben, Dillon

   Three miles—Larry, Mary, Shawn

5. Distribute half-inch graph paper to each child. Talk about what is needed to form a graph—a title, numbers, and names. Show the children various graphs and discuss the things that were listed on the graph. Write an example on the board. Have the children create a graph showing their results.

#2. Learn if weight can be distributed over the surface of the snow to prevent sinking.

- **Objective.** Apply scientific knowledge and skills to understand issues and everyday events. Apply understanding of the concept of weight distribution.

- **Level of difficulty.** Moderate. (This task may take several days to complete.)

- **Materials needed.** Ruler, lined paper, white construction paper, and pencils.
- **Before the activity.** Place a large piece of white paper on the board. Have a black marker available for writing the children's responses. Go to the internet and type, "Do snowshoes work?" In addition, go to the internet and type, "How snowshoes work/Children's Science Center." This will lead you to a site with an experiment for the children to do.
- **Begin the activity by saying,** "Earlier, we discussed how weight can be distributed over an area to prevent sinking." Our feet would sink in the snow because the weight isn't distributed over a large area.
- **Review the children's responses.** (I've seen people use snowshoes to walk in the snow. They don't sink. Snowshoes help you when you're walking in the snow. Snowshoes are wider than my feet, so I don't sink into the snow.)
- **Introduce the activity.** "Today, we're going to learn why we don't sink into the snow when we wear snowshoes." (A wider surface area of the snowshoe allows weight to be distributed across the snow.)
1. Go to the internet and type, "Do snowshoes work?" Select the age-appropriate website you chose. Read and discuss the information. Write their responses on a piece of paper.
2. Go the website of the Children's Science Center you pulled up earlier with the experiment for the children to do. Watch and discuss what's relayed on the video.
3. Write their responses on a piece of paper. In the video, the children take a plastic animal and have it "walk" through some flour. Then they cut out round circles and put them on the bottom of the animal's feet. This prevents the animal from sinking into the flour. It's something the children could try in a science center.

Have the children explain to a friend why we don't sink into the snow when we're wearing snowshoes.

- **Extension of the activity.** Today, we're going to trace around the feet of our friend."

1. Have the children choose a partner for this task. Have each child carefully trace around one foot of their friend on a piece of white construction paper. Trace around the other foot on another piece of white construction paper. The friend can then trade places so both of them have their feet traced.

2. Now, introduce and discuss a ruler. Tell the children that one edge of the ruler shows inches, while the other edge shows centimeters. If the children haven't had an opportunity to practice with a ruler, have them measure off a desired measurement. For example, they might draw a line that's four inches long. They might then draw a line that's ten inches long. Then have them do the same for half-inch increments.

3. When you feel the children can accurately measure the inch and half-inch measurements, have them measure the drawings of their own feet. An older student or an adult might help the children with this task. They should round off the measurement to the nearest half-inch length. Emphasize that they need to place the ruler at the furthest portion of their foot and measure the full length of their foot. Have their partner check this measurement.

4. If the two partners agree with the number, carefully write the number on the back of the foot. Be sure both partners measure and record. The teacher may want to make a random check of the children's measurements.

5. When all the measurements have been taken, place a piece of paper with inch and half-inch measurements marked on the bottom of the paper. Place Xs above the correct measurement for each

child. Print the names of the children below each measurement. Determine the largest and smallest foot measurement. (When this activity is completed, allow them to decorate their feet drawings. See art section.) Here is an example of what the paper might look like.

4 in.	4 ½ in.	5 in.	5 ½ in.	6 in.	6 ½ in.	7 in.	7 ½ in.	8 in.	8 ½ in.	9 in.
X	X	X	X	X	X	X	X	X	X	X
	X		X							
Sally	Jim	Mary	Tom	Sue	Ali	Stan	Phil	Eli		
Kerri	Debbi		Jane							

Wolf in the Snow illustration: The young child trying to cross a stream/river on the left-hand side of the page and a screeching owl on the right-hand side of the page

Direct the children's attention to the left-hand side of the page where the young child is trying to cross the stream/river, with an animal growling at her. There's a screeching sound coming from the forest on the right-hand side of the page. Encourage them to answer the following questions in complete sentences.

QUESTIONS

The brackets around the text indicate questions/instructions an adult should read to the children. Examples of how the children may answer the questions are included in parentheses.

- **[What do you see on this page?]**
- **[Today, we're going to talk about a special word. That special word is *determination*. Determination means sticking to something until you finish it. How would you describe the determination of the young child?]** Write the children's comments on a piece of paper and save this for later. (The young child shows determination because she really wants to protect the young wolf. I think the young child shows determination because she is purposely heading for the wolf pack. I think the young wolf is very lucky to have the young child carry it for such a long distance.) Write the children's comments on a piece of paper and save this for later. See Writing #1.
- **[Would you say that the wolf pack has demonstrated determination? Why or why not?]** (Well, they are searching for

the young wolf. They've traveled a long distance. I don't think they'll leave the area without the young wolf.)

- Direct the children to look at the left-hand side of the page. **[What is the young child doing in the top, right-hand picture?]** Write the children's responses on a piece of paper and save this for later (The young child is trying to cross a stream/river while it's snowing. The young child is trying to carefully cross the stream/river by stepping on stones. The young child is trying to balance herself, while carrying the young wolf.) See Science #1.

- **[How is the child helping herself to cross the river?]** (Well, she is trying to balance herself, using her arm to balance, while stepping on the stones. **[Would this help her cross the river? Why or why not?]** (The young child's arm is stretched out, which will help to balance her. I think it will help her cross the stream/river.)

- **[Today, we're going to try to use our arms to balance our bodies while we stand on one foot.]** Discuss how athletes use their arms to balance on a balance beam. Have the children stand on one foot. Tell them they can use their arms to balance their bodies for as long as possible. Now, have them stand on the other foot, doing the same thing. Have them try to balance their body without using their arms. **[Was there a difference in their ability to balance themselves? Why or why not?]**

- Note that the young child doesn't seem to be wearing heavy pants. **[Why do you think it would be a good idea for her to wear heavy pants?]** (Heavy pants would keep warmth close to the body. It's important to stay as warm as possible in the cold; otherwise, it could be very dangerous.)

- **[What is the young child doing on the bottom picture?]** (She is trying to defend herself from an animal.) **[What would you do in this situation?]** Write the children's comments on a piece of paper and save it for later. See Science #3.

178

- **[What kind of animal do you think is growling?]** List all the children's responses on a piece of paper and save this for later. (Well, it has a striped tail and dark circles around the eyes, so maybe it's a raccoon.) **[What do you know about raccoons?]** Place a large piece of paper on the board and list all the children's responses. Save this for later. See Science #2.

- **[What is the young child using to defend herself?]** (She's using a stick to defend herself.)

- **[Why do you think she chose a stick?]** (It was the only thing available.)

- **[Do you think the growling animal wants to be in this situation? Why or why not?]** (Well, I think the animal would prefer to be left in a peaceful forest. It doesn't want to defend itself, but it has no other option. I think it would like to be left alone.)

- **[Do you think the growling animal will attack the child and the young wolf? Why or why not?]**

- **[What would you do in this situation?]** (I'd make loud noises to scare the animal. I'd wave the stick to scare it.)

- Direct the children to look at the right-hand side of the page. Note that there's an owl in the tree. **[What do you know about owls?]** Place a large piece of paper on the board and list all the things they know about owls. Save this paper for later. (Owls have feathers. Owls have large eyes. Owls make a unique sound.) See Science #4.

- **[Let's learn a little more about owls.]** Go to the internet and type, "Owl unit for preschoolers—owls." This will direct you to a link for a preschool site that has some good information relevant for young children, along with craft ideas.

- **[We've learned that owls eat various things in the wild. Today, we're going to examine an owl pellet to see what's inside.]** See Science #5.

179

- Talk about how owls have an ability to rotate their heads. Direct the children to try to rotate their heads from one side of their necks to another. That distance isn't as far as an owl can rotate. Draw a circle on the board. Demonstrate that a circle has 360 degrees. A half circle has 180 degrees. An owl can rotate or swivel its head 270 degrees. See Math #1 and Math #2.
- **[Owls are very unusual creatures.]** Show the children pictures of different types of owls, pointing out the various patterns of the feathers. Have the children draw/paint their favorite owl. Let these pictures dry. Save these pictures for later. See Art #1.
- **[How would you describe the look on the child's face while she's walking below the owl?]** (The child looks very scared and tired. I think she has every right to feel this way, because she just had to defend herself from a growling creature. She looks like she needs to rest. I feel sorry for the child.)

ACTIVITIES

Art

#1. Learn about owls and their feathers. Draw/paint their favorite owl.

- **Objective.** Creating. Anchor Standard #1. Generate and conceptualize artistic ideas and work. Investigate, Plan, Make. Engage in creative art making in response to an artistic problem.
- **Level of difficulty.** Moderate. (This task may take several days to complete.)
- **Materials needed.** White construction paper, pencils, white feathers, glue, paintbrushes, and paints.
- **Before the activity.** Place a large piece of white paper on the board. Have a black marker available for writing the children's

responses. Ask the children if they have any owl feathers. Ask them to bring the feather(s) to class. Show the children different pictures of owls. Have lots of books available for the children to examine. Have them relay any information they know about owls. Write this information on the piece of paper and save it for later. Go to the internet and type, "Show me different owls." Choose a website that's age-appropriate for the children. Various websites have barn owls, elf owls, great gray owls, and spotted owls. Then, go to the internet and type, "Show me an owl feather." Again, choose a website that's age-appropriate for the children.

- **Begin the activity by saying,** "Earlier, we looked at various pictures of owls and discussed some facts about them."
- **Review the children's responses.** (I think the owl is an amazing creature because it can rotate its head so far. I think the owl is great because it can silently soar in the air. The owl feathers help it to blend in with the environment.)
- **Introduce the activity.** "Today, we're going to learn about and observe different owls and their feathers. Then, we'll draw/paint our favorite owl."
  1. If possible, show the children an owl feather. One of the children in class may have one, so invite them to bring it to class. If that's not possible, owl feathers can be purchased on the internet or books from the library can be shown to illustrate various owl feathers. Go to the internet and type, "Show me different owls." Choose a website that's age-appropriate for the children. Read and discuss the information with the children.
  2. Have the children draw/paint their favorite owl. Let these dry. Then have them write down their favorite fact(s) about the owl that they learned from the website. Save this for later.
  3. Go to a second internet website and type, "Show me an owl feather." Again, choose a website that's age-appropriate for the

children. Read and discuss the information with the children. Write any comments the children have regarding owl feathers. (Owl feathers have different patterns. They have assorted colors.) If possible, show a real owl feather and have the children carefully examine it. If an owl feather isn't available, look at various books to discuss the differences.

4. Tell them that they're going to create an "owl feather." This feather will be cut and glued to the owl painting they did earlier. Give each child a white feather. These can be purchased at a craft store. Have the children carefully brush the feather with the paint color of their choice. Owl feather colors can be brown, reddish-brown, tan, and gray. They should choose only one color that appeared on their favorite owl. Let the feathers dry. Have the children carefully cut and glue their brushed feather pieces to their drawing/painting. Let these dry.

5. Place their pictures on the bulletin board, with their favorite owl fact(s) attached. (I think the owl is an amazing creature because it can rotate its head so far. I think the owl is great because it can silently soar in the air.)

Writing

#1. Discuss and write about determination. Draw a picture of a situation in which they expressed their determination.

- **Objective.** Comprehension and Collaboration. Participate in collaborative conversations about topics and texts with diverse partners, including peers and adults, in small and larger groups. Build on what others say in conversations by linking their comments to the remarks of others.

- **Level of difficulty.** Moderate. (This task may take several days to complete.)

- **Materials needed.** Lined paper and pencils, white construction paper, crayons, paintbrushes, and paints.
- **Before the activity.** Place a large piece of white paper on the board. Have a black marker available for writing the children's responses.
- **Begin the activity by saying,** "Earlier, we talked about the young child's determination."
- **Review the children's responses.** (I think the young child shows determination because she really wants to protect the young wolf. I think the young child shows determination because she is purposely heading for the wolf pack. I think that the young wolf is very lucky to have the young child carry him or her for such a long distance. That shows real determination.)
- **Introduce the activity.** "Today, we're going to talk about the young child's determination." Review the children's comments. (I think the young child shows determination because she really wants to protect the young wolf. I think the young child shows determination because she is purposely heading for the wolf pack. I think the young wolf is very lucky to have the young child carry it for such a long distance. That shows real determination.)
  1. "Has there ever been a time in your life when you demonstrated determination?" Write the children's comments on a piece of paper. (I demonstrated determination when I fixed the flat tire on my bike. I demonstrated determination when I completed a large homework packet. I demonstrated determination when I finished all my chores.)
  2. Have the children draw/paint a picture of a time when they showed determination. Let these dry.
  3. Have them write one of the examples of determination on a piece of lined paper and attach it to their drawing/painting. If they'd like to write their own example of determination, allow them to write their own sentence(s). Be available to help them sound out any words.

Science

#1. Learn about balancing skills.

- **Objective.** Physical Science. Forces and Interactions. Pushes and Pulls. Plan and conduct an investigation to compare the effects of different strengths or different directions of pushes and pulls on the motion of an object.
- **Level of difficulty.** Easy.
- **Materials needed.** The game Twister.
- **Before the activity.** Place a large piece of white paper on the board. Have a black marker available for writing the children's responses. Go to the internet and type, "Balancing skills for kids." Choose an age-appropriate website for the children.
- **Begin the activity by saying,** "Earlier, we discussed why it might be dangerous to cross a stream/river in the snow. The child was trying to use her arm to balance herself while stepping on stones going over the stream/river."
- **Review the children's responses.** (Well, the young child and the young wolf could fall into the stream/river. They would get very cold. The young child's clothes would be wet. It would be difficult to get warm.).
- **Introduce the activity.** "Today, we going to discuss why it might be dangerous to cross a stream/river in the snow." Review the children's responses once more. Today, we're also going to learn about balancing skills. Go to the internet and type, "Balancing skills for kids." Choose an age-appropriate website for the children. Read and discuss the information with the children. There are several exercises the children might enjoy trying. The game of Twister is a way for them to practice balancing.

#2. Learn about raccoons.

- **Objective.** Life Science. Structure, Function, and Information Processing. Read texts and use media to determine patterns in behavior of parents and offspring that help offspring survive.
- **Level of difficulty.** Easy.
- **Materials needed.** None.
- **Before the activity.** Place a large piece of white paper on the board. Have a black marker available for writing the children's responses. Go to the internet and type, "Tell me about raccoons." Choose an age-appropriate website for the children.
- **Begin the activity by saying,** "Earlier, we observed that the animal on this page was growling. We noticed it had a striped tail and dark circles around its eyes. We thought it might be a raccoon."
- **Review the children's responses.** (A raccoon has a dark "mask" around its eyes. It has a long, striped tail. Raccoons can climb trees. They move around at night."
- **Introduce the activity.**
  1. "Today, we're going to learn about raccoons." When we looked at the picture, we noticed the animal had a striped tail and dark circles around its eyes. We thought it might be a raccoon. We wrote down all the facts we knew about raccoons. Review the children's comments. (A raccoon has a dark "mask" around its eyes. It has a long, striped tail. They can climb trees. They move around at night.).
  2. Go to the internet and type, "Tell me about raccoons." Select the age-appropriate website you chose. Read and discuss the information with the children. Write down the information they learned about raccoons from the website. Have them tell a friend their favorite fact(s) about raccoons. Were any of their

first responses about raccoons inaccurate? Discuss these inaccuracies.

#3. Learn about raccoons. Learn some safety tips about defending ourselves from a raccoon.

- **Objective.** Life Science. Interdependent Relationships in Ecosystems. Construct an argument supported by evidence for how plants and animals (including humans) can change the environment to meet their needs.
- **Level of difficulty.** Moderate. (This task may take several days to complete.)
- **Materials needed.** Lined paper, pencils, white construction paper, crayons, paintbrushes, and paints.
- **Before the activity.** Place a large piece of white paper on the board. Have a black marker available for writing the children's responses. Go to the internet and type, "Wildlife safety tips—raccoons." Choose an age-appropriate website for the children.
- **Begin the activity by saying,** "Earlier, we observed that the young child was trying to defend herself from the raccoon."
- **Review the children's responses.** (The raccoon looks mad. The raccoon has its mouth open. The raccoon is growling.)
- **Introduce the activity.** "Today, we're going to learn some safety tips about defending ourselves from a raccoon." Go to the internet and type, "Wildlife safety tips—raccoons." Select the age-appropriate website you chose. Read and discuss the information with the children. Write the raccoon facts and safety tips on the paper that's on the bulletin board. Have the children draw a picture of a raccoon and then write their favorite raccoon fact and/or safety tip. Have the children share their raccoon picture and their favorite raccoon safety tip with a friend.

#4. Create a KWL chart (things I *know* about owls, things I *want* to learn about owls, and things I *learned* about owls).

- **Objective.** Life Science. Structure, Function, and Information Processing. Read texts and use media to determine patterns in behavior of parents and offspring that help offspring survive.

- **Level of difficulty.** Moderate. (This task may take several days to complete.)

- **Materials needed.** Markers.

- **Before the activity.** Place a large piece of white paper on the board divided into three sections. Label the paper with the three KWL designations. (An example is shown at the end of this activity.) Have a black marker available for writing the children's responses. Go to the internet and type, "Owls." Choose an age-appropriate website for the children.

- **Begin the activity by saying,** "Earlier, we noticed there was an owl in the tree, and we wrote down some facts about owls."

- **Review the children's responses.** (Owls hunt at night. Owls have good eyesight. Owls have beautiful feathers.)

- **Introduce the activity.** "Today, we're going to make a KWL chart about owls. KWL stands for 'things I *know* about owls,' 'things I *want* to learn about owls,' and 'things I *learned* about owls.'" Remind them again of the owl in the tree and the facts they compiled.

  1. Before reading the research information on the website about owls, have the children tell you some things they'd like to learn about owls. Write these on the KWL chart in the "want to learn" section. (I'd like to know how many baby owls are born at a time. I'd like to know how old they are when they start flying. I'd like to learn about their hearing.)

  2. "Today, we're going to research additional information about owls and add this information to our KWL chart." Go to the internet

187

and type, "Owls." Select the age-appropriate website you chose. Read and discuss the information with the children.

3. Write down the additional facts the children learned on the KWL chart in the "learned" section. (Owls hunt at night. Owls have good eyesight. Owls have beautiful feathers.). Place the chart in a location where the children can add additional information as they discover new facts. Have markers available for the children to use.

Here's an example of a KWL chart on owls:

Things I *Know* about Owls	Things I *Want* to Learn about Owls	Things I *Learned* about Owls
I know that owls have good eyesight.	I want to learn how many baby owls are born at once.	I learned that owls can rotate their heads.

#5. Examine an owl pellet. Sort the contents of the owl pellet.

- **Objective.** Life Science. Interdependent Relationships in Ecosystems. Use observations to describe patterns of what plants and animals (including humans) need to survive.
- **Level of difficulty.** Challenging. (This activity may take several days to complete.)
- **Materials needed.** Owl pellets, trays, paper towels, plastic gloves, glasses, bamboo sticks, and pictures of animal skeletons.
- **Before the activity.** Order owl pellets on the internet in advance of this activity. Place a large piece of white paper on the board. Have a black marker available for writing the children's responses.
- **Begin the activity by saying,** "Earlier, we read and listened to information related to owls."
- **Review the children's responses.** (Owls hunt at night. Owls have good eyesight. Owls have beautiful feathers.)

- **Introduce the activity.** "Today, we're going to examine an owl pellet." You can order owl pellets for each child from the internet. Allow enough time to have them delivered before you start this lesson.

1. Tell the children that they're going to investigate what's inside the pellet, so they need to think and act like scientists and researchers. Discuss how they think scientists act. Create a few simple rules before you start. (Scientists proceed cautiously and carefully. They never play around with the materials they use.) Write these simple rules on a large piece of paper. Emphasize that no inappropriate behavior will be tolerated. Tell them that the materials will be collected if they can't follow the rules.

2. Distribute plastic gloves, glasses, a tray, paper towels, and two-pointed bamboo sticks cut into approximately five- to six-inch pieces, so these sticks can probe the owl pellet. Tell the children to put on their plastic gloves and glasses. Tell them they're not to proceed until they receive further instruction.

3. Give each child an owl pellet. If the owl pellets are wrapped, tell the children to carefully remove the wrapping. Have them place this material on the outside of their tray. Using the pointed bamboo sticks, have them carefully separate the materials inside the pellet. Very quickly, the children will realize that the material is something the owl ate (e.g., a mouse). Have them separate the material into groups (e.g., bones and fur).

4. When the children have completed this process, direct them to discuss what they have in their owl pellet. Have pictures of various skeletons, including a mouse skeleton, as the pellet will probably be filled with mouse material. Talk about the regurgitation process.

Math

#1. Learn how far an owl can rotate its head. Learn about and use a protractor.

- **Objective.** Mathematical Practice Standard. Mathematically proficient students consider the available tools when solving a mathematical problem. These tools might include pencil and paper, concrete models, a ruler, a protractor, a calculator, a spreadsheet. Proficient students are sufficiently familiar with tools appropriate for their grade or course to make sound decisions about when each of these tools might be helpful, recognizing both the insight to be gained and their limitations.

- **Level of difficulty.** Moderate. (This task may take several days to complete.)

- **Materials needed.** Nothing for the younger children. For the older children, have protractors, paper, and pencils available.

- **Before the activity.** Place a large piece of white paper on the board. Have a black marker available for writing the children's responses. Go to the internet and type, "How far can an owl turn its head?" Choose an age-appropriate website for the children. Additionally, go to the internet and type, "International Owl Center." You'll learn lots of interesting information on this website.

- **Begin the activity by saying,** "Earlier, we talked about how far an owl could rotate its head."

- **Review the children's responses.** (I saw an owl turn its head toward the back of its body. I think an owl can turn its head very far. Owls can turn their heads a long way.)

- **Introduce the activity.** Today, we're going to learn how far an owl can rotate (turn) its head.

  1. Go to the internet and type, "How far can an owl turn its head." Choose an age-appropriate website for the children. Read and

discuss the information with the children. Write down some of the interesting facts on a piece of paper.

2. In addition, the International Owl Center has some wonderful information and videos the children will enjoy seeing/watching. Write the facts related to the owl center on a piece of paper. Have the children relay to a friend their favorite fact(s).

- **Extension of the activity.** For the older students, show them a protractor and explain that it measures the number of degrees/angles in a half circle, which is 180 degrees.

  1. Draw a straight line on the board and a half circle connecting both ends of the straight line to the half circle. Divide the half circle into two equal parts, showing two right angles. Show where both right angles would be on the line. (_____|_____) A right angle has 90 degrees. There's a right angle on the right-hand side of the 90-degree location and one on the left-hand side. If I add 90 degrees to 90 degrees, it equals 180 degrees, or a straight line. Show the protractor to the children, emphasizing that the bottom portion of the protractor is a straight line. It has 180 degrees, starting from 0 degrees to 180 degrees.

  2. Show the measurement designations on the outside of the protractor. The number on the outside of the protractor shows single degrees. It goes from 0 degrees, all the way to 180 degrees. The middle of the protractor shows 90 degrees, which is a right angle. If I flip the protractor down on the straight line, it will create a circle. A complete circle has 360 degrees. The children can practice drawing various angles/degrees in the next activity.

#2. Practice drawing angles with a protractor.

- **Objective.** Mathematical Practice Standard. Mathematically proficient students consider the available tools when solving a mathematical problem. These tools might include pencil and paper, concrete models, a ruler, a protractor, a calculator, and a spreadsheet. Proficient students are sufficiently familiar with tools appropriate for their grade or course to make sound decisions about when each of these tools might be helpful, recognizing both the insight to be gained and their limitations.

- **Level of difficulty.** Moderate. (This task could take several days to complete.)
- **Materials needed.** Lined paper, pencils, and protractors.
- **Before the activity.** Place a large piece of white paper on the board. Have a black marker available for demonstrating various angles.
- **Begin the activity by saying,** "Earlier, we learned about a protractor. A protractor measures the number of degrees/angles in a half circle, which is 180 degrees."
- **Introduce the activity.** "Today, we're going to learn about and draw various angles."

1. Review the information they learned in the prior activity. Again, draw a half circle on the board. Draw a straight line at the bottom of the half circle. Divide the half circle into two equal parts, showing two 90-degree angles.

2. Point to the 90-degree angle on the right-hand side of the protractor and one on the left-hand side of the protractor. "If I add 90 degrees to 90 degrees, it equals 180 degrees, or a straight line."

3. Show the protractor to the children, emphasizing that the bottom portion of the protractor is a straight line. The protractor has 180 degrees, starting from 0 degrees and going up to 180 degrees.

4. Show the measurement designations on the outside of the protractor. The numbers on the outside of the protractor show single degrees. It goes from 0 degrees, all the way to 180 degrees. The middle of the protractor shows 90 degrees, which

is a right angle. If I flip the protractor down on the straight line and draw around it, it will create a circle. A complete circle has 360 degrees. Have the children practice drawing various angles on a piece of paper.

Direct the children's attention to the pages where the young child is holding the young wolf, with howling sounds in the distance. Encourage them to answer the following questions in complete sentences.

QUESTIONS

The brackets around the text indicate questions/instructions an adult should read to the children. Examples of how the children may answer the questions are included in parentheses.

- **[What do you see on this page?]**
- **[How do you know that the wolves are getting closer?]** (The word "howl" seems to make it appear as if the wolves are getting closer. That word seems to indicate they're getting closer to the young child and the young wolf.)
- Explain that the person who draws the pictures in a book is called the illustrator. **[How do you think the illustrator could show that the wolves are getting closer?]** (The illustrator prints the word larger and larger. The word "howl" is smaller on the left-hand side of the page. The words get increasingly larger.) See Writing #1.
- **[Do you think the young wolf is getting excited?]** (Well, his or her legs are moving, and his or her head is turned in the direction of the howling.) See Writing #2.
- **[Do you think the young child is excited?]** Write the children's responses on a piece of paper and save this for later. (Well, the young child looks scared. The young child's eyes are opened wide. The young child looks concerned.) See Science #1.

- **[Do you think it would be difficult to carry the young wolf for such a long distance?]** (I think it would be hard to carry that young wolf. When I carry things, it gets more difficult the longer I carry them.) See Science #2.

ACTIVITIES

Writing

#1. Practice an illustrative technique.

- **Objective.** Text Types and Purposes. Write narratives to develop real or imagined experiences or events using effective technique, descriptive details, and clear event sequences. Use concrete words and phrases and sensory details to convey experiences and events precisely.
- **Level of difficulty.** Easy.
- **Materials needed.** White construction paper, crayons, and black markers.
- **Before the activity.** Place a large piece of white paper on the board. Have a black marker available for writing the children's responses.
- **Begin the activity by saying,** "Earlier, we noticed that the illustrator wrote the word "Howl" to make it appear that the wolves were nearby, and the sound was louder."
- **Review the children's responses.** (The word "howl" is written in large letters. It makes it seem like the sound is very loud. I like the way the illustrator wrote the word "howl." It really makes me think the wolves are howling.)
- **Introduce the activity.** "Today, we're going to practice this same illustrative technique." Have the children think of words that could be emphasized in this way (e.g., stop, stay, no, hurry, and wait).

Write these words on a piece of paper for the children to see. Have the children think of a situation where these words could be used (e.g., a parent telling a young child to stop walking across the street, an animal owner telling an animal to wait, or an older sibling telling a younger sibling to hurry). Give the children a piece of white construction paper and have them draw a simple picture to reflect one of these words/situations. Give them a black marker and have them write one of these words to demonstrate this technique (e.g., stop, stay, no, hurry, or wait).

#2. Talk about and discuss ways animals and people show excitement.

- **Objective.** Text Types and Purposes. Write narratives to develop real or imagined experiences or events using effective technique, descriptive details, and clear event sequences. Use concrete words and phrases and sensory details to convey experiences and events precisely.
- **Level of Difficulty.** Easy.
- **Materials needed.** None.
- **Before the activity.** Place a large piece of white paper on the board. Have a black marker available for writing the children's responses.
- **Begin the activity by saying,** "Earlier, we noticed the young wolf looked like he/she was excited. We talked about how the young wolf was moving his/her legs and his/her head was turned in the direction of the howling and we discussed why."
- **Review the children's responses.** (The young wolf knows his/her family is nearby. I think the young wolf is excited about the possibility of seeing his/her family. The young girl is scared. Her eyes look big.)
- **Introduce the activity.** "Today, we're going to talk about and express some ways people and animals show excitement. What are some ways people show they're excited." Write the children's responses on a piece of paper. (People smile. They wave their hands. They

use words to express their excitement.) Have the children show a friend how they show they're excited. (I jump up and down and yell, "Yeeessss!") "What are some ways animals show they're excited?" Write the children's responses on a piece of paper. (Animals show excitement by wagging their tails. They show excitement by barking. Sometimes, they turn in circles.) Have the children tell a friend how their pet/animals show excitement.

Science

#1. Learn about fears.

- **Objective.** Life Science. Interdependent Relationships in Ecosystems, Animals, Plants, and their environment. Communicate solutions that will reduce the impact of humans on the land, water, air, and/or other living things in the local environment.
- **Level of difficulty.** Easy.
- **Materials needed.** None.
- **Before the activity.** Place a large piece of white paper on the board. Have a black marker available for writing the children's responses. Go to the internet and type, "Fear in children." Choose an age-appropriate website for the children.
- **Begin the activity by saying,** "Earlier, we noticed the young child looks excited."
- **Review the children's responses.** (Well, the young child looks scared. The young child's eyes are open wide. The young child looks concerned.).
- **Introduce the activity.** "Today, we're going learn about fear." Ask the children to name some of the things they're afraid of (e.g., snakes, spiders, water, or high places.) Write the children's responses on a piece of paper. "Our body responds in many ways when we're scared or excited." Go to the internet and type, "Fear in children."

Choose an age-appropriate website for the children. Read and discuss the information with the children. There are several videos that explain different childhood fears. Preview these videos before you show them to the children. Have the children show a friend how they show fear. (I show fear when I cover my head in bed. I show fear when I cover my face with my hands. I show fear when I yell.)

#2. Learn about and experiment with lifting and carrying an object for various amounts of time.

- **Objective.** Physical Science. Structure and Properties of Matter. Analyze data obtained from testing different materials to determine which materials have the properties best suited for an intended purpose.
- **Level of difficulty.** Easy.
- **Materials needed.** Two five-pound weights.
- **Before the activity.** Place a large piece of white paper on the board. Have a black marker available for writing the children's responses. Go to the internet and type, "Difficulties for young children lifting things." Choose an age-appropriate website for the children." In addition, go to the internet and type, "Kitchen counter chronicles—simple machines." This will guide you to a link with an experiment on how to move a lion. The kids will enjoy doing this experiment.
- **Begin the activity by saying,** "Earlier, we discussed whether it would be difficult to carry the young wolf."
- **Review the children's responses.** (I think it would be hard to carry the young wolf. When I carry things, it gets more difficult the longer I carry them.).
- **Introduce the activity.** "Today, we're going to learn if it would be difficult for the young girl to carry the young wolf for a long distance."
  1. Go to the internet and type, "Difficulties for young children lifting things." Select the age-appropriate website you chose. There is

an information section about strength training for young children that you might want to review. Read and discuss the information with the children.

2. To demonstrate the difficulty of carrying the young wolf, have the children hold up two five-pound weights for various lengths of time. Extend the length of time to see how their body reacts (e.g., ten minutes, twenty minutes, thirty minutes). You may want to have them do this at home using heavy household items (e.g., two large cans of food). Have a discussion with the children about how they felt at the start of the experiment and how they felt after an extended length of time. (It was easy at the beginning of the experiment, but it got harder to carry the weight over time.)

3. Go to the internet and type, "Kitchen counter chronicles—simple machines." Follow the link that has an experiment on how to move a lion. The kids will enjoy doing this experiment.

Direct the children's attention to the page where the young child is holding the young wolf and an older wolf is approaching them. Encourage them to answer the following questions in complete sentences.

QUESTIONS

The brackets around the text indicate questions/instructions an adult should read to the children. Examples of how the children may answer the questions are included in parentheses.

- **[What do you see on this page?]**
- **[Do you think the older wolf recognizes the young wolf?]** Write the children's responses on a piece of paper and save this for later. (The older wolf recognizes the young wolf. The young wolf is trying to get down onto the snow. I think the older wolf smells its young cub. I think the young wolf smells its mother.) See Science #1.
- **[Do you think wolves have good hearing?]** Write the children's responses on a piece of paper and save this for later. (Wolves have amazing ears. I think they have a good sense of hearing, but I think their sense of smell is better.) See Math #1 and Science #3.
- Point out that there are many footprints in the snow from both the young child and the wolf. **[How many footsteps/footprints would be made in one hundred yards?]** Note that one hundred yards is the length of a football field. Have the children estimate the number of footsteps/footprints in one hundred yards. Write the children's names and estimates on a three-by-five card. Keep this card for later. See Math #2.

- **[How would a mother wolf recognize her young cub?]** Write the children's comments on a piece of paper and save this for later. (I think the mother wolf would be able to identify the smell of the young wolf. I think the young wolf's markings would be identified by the mother wolf.) Note that the sense of smell is an important sense in both animals and humans. **[Why do we need to smell things?]** (The sense of smell could protect animals and humans from dangerous/toxic substances. It might stop an animal from eating things that could harm it.) See Science #2.

- Direct the children to look at the facial expression of the larger wolf. **[How would you describe this expression?]** (The older wolf looks determined. The wolf's head is down, and it's coming directly toward the child and the young wolf. The wolf's ears are folded back on its head.) See Writing / Oral Language #1 and #5.

- Direct the children to look at the facial expression of the young child. **[How would you describe this expression?]** (The child's eyes are very large. The child seems afraid to move.) See Writing / Oral Language #2 and #5.

- Direct the children to look at the expression of the young wolf in the child's arms. **[How would you describe this expression?]** (The young wolf looks excited. The young wolf seems to want to go to the larger wolf.) See Writing / Oral Language #3.

- **[How would you feel if you were in this situation?]** (I think I would be scared. If a large wolf were coming toward me, I wouldn't know how the wolf might react.)

- **[If it were possible for the older wolf to thank the young child for helping the young wolf survive, what do you think the older wolf would say to the child?]** See Writing / Oral Language #4.

ACTIVITIES

Writing / Oral Language

#1. Use adjectives to describe the facial expression of the older wolf.

- **Objective.** Conventions of Standard English. Demonstrate command of the conventions of standard English grammar and usage when writing or speaking. Use frequently occurring adjectives.
- **Level of difficulty.** Easy.
- **Materials needed.** None.
- **Before the activity.** Place a large piece of white paper on the board. Have a black marker available for writing the children's responses.
- **Begin the activity by saying,** "Earlier, we discussed the facial expression of the older wolf."
- **Review the children's responses.** (The older wolf looks determined. The wolf's head is down, and she's coming directly toward the child and the young wolf. The wolf's ears are folded back on her head.)
- **Introduce the activity.** Today, we're going discuss the facial expression of the older wolf (the young wolf's mother). Review the children's responses once more. "The expression on the older wolf's face could be described in a variety of ways. When we describe things, we're using adjectives. Let's see how many words we can find to describe the older wolf's expression." Write as many words/adjectives on a piece of paper as the children can imagine. (The older wolf looks determined. She looks forceful. She looks mad.). Keep this paper up for a few days and have the children add words to the list. Have a marker available for the children to add words to the list.

#2. Use adjectives to describe the facial expression of the young child.

- **Objective.** Conventions of Standard English. Demonstrate command of the conventions of standard English grammar and usage when writing or speaking. Use frequently occurring adjectives.
- **Level of difficulty.** Easy.
- **Materials needed.** None.
- **Before the activity.** Place a large piece of white paper on the board. Have a black marker available for writing the children's responses.
- **Begin the activity by saying,** "Earlier, we talked about the facial expression of the young child."
- **Review the children's responses.** (The child's eyes are large. The child seems afraid to move.)
- **Introduce the activity.** "Today, we're going discuss the facial expression of the young child." Review the children's responses once more. "The expression on the young child could be described in a variety of ways. When we describe things, we're using adjectives. Let's see how many words we can find to describe the young child's expression." Write as many words/adjectives on a piece of paper as the children can imagine. (The young child looks frightened. The young child looks scared. The young child looks overwhelmed.) Keep this paper up for a few days and have the children add words to the list. Have a marker available for the children to add words to the list.

#3. Have the children participate in a short oral presentation.

- **Objective.** Comprehension and Collaboration. Recount or describe key ideas or details from a text read aloud or information presented orally or through other media.
- **Level of difficulty.** Easy.

- **Materials needed.** None.
- **Before the activity.** Have the children form groups of three. One of the children will enact the part of the young wolf, one child will be the young girl, and one child will be the mother wolf.
- **Begin the activity by saying,** "Earlier, we talked about the facial expression and motions of the young wolf and the older wolf."
- **Review the children's responses.** (The young wolf looks excited. The older wolf looks determined.)
- **Introduce the activity.** "Today, we're going to imagine that we're in this situation." Choose several children to be the young wolf, the child, and the older wolf. Allow them to imagine a conversation that might take place. Have them practice this conversation before they present it to the class. Have them come to the front of the room and enact the situation that appears on the page. Have them present what they think might happen. (Young Wolf: "Mom! I'm OK. I've been walking so long. I wondered where everyone went. This child has carried me for a long way. I'm so grateful I had such a good friend." Older Wolf: "Who is that person carrying you? I've traveled a long distance to find you. Are you OK? Should I growl at her? Hurry up and come over here. We're going back to the pack." Young Child: "I'm so glad to see you! I've carried your young wolf a very long way. I know you're concerned.")

#4. Write a thank you note to the young child.

- **Objective.** Conventions of Standard English. Demonstrate command of the conventions of standard English capitalization, punctuation, and spelling when writing. Use commas in greetings and closings of letters.
- **Level of difficulty.** Easy.
- **Materials needed.** Thank you cards/notes and pencils.

- **Before the activity.** Place a large piece of white paper on the board. Have a black marker available for writing the children's responses.
- **Begin the activity by saying,** "Earlier, we talked about the things the older wolf might say or do to thank the child for protecting the young wolf."
- **Review the children's responses.** (Dear young child, how can I thank you for helping my young wolf? I don't think he or she would have survived in the snow without your help. You must be exhausted! I will always be grateful to you for having the courage to help him or her. Sincerely, Mother Wolf).
- **Introduce the activity.** Today, we're going to write a thank you note from the mother wolf to the young child. Write the children's comments on a piece of paper. When the children have decided which statement they want to relay, give them a thank you card. The children will write their message on the card. (Dear young child, how can I think you for helping my young wolf? I don't think he or she would have survived in the snow without your help. You must be exhausted! I will always be grateful to you for having the courage to help him or her. Sincerely, Mother Wolf). If the children want to write their own sentence(s), be available to help them sound out the words.

#5. Describe the expression on the faces of the young child, the young wolf, and the older wolf/mother. Use adjectives to describe their expressions.

- **Objective.** Text Types and Purposes. Write informative/explanatory texts to examine a topic and convey ideas and information clearly. Develop the topic with facts, definitions, concrete details, quotations, or other information and examples related to the topic.
- **Level of difficulty.** Moderate. (This task may take several days to complete.)

- **Materials needed.** White construction paper, pencils, crayons, colored pencils, paintbrushes, and paints.
- **Before the activity.** Place a large piece of white paper on the board. Have a black marker available for writing the children's responses.
- **Begin the activity by saying,** "Earlier, we talked about the expressions of the young child, the young wolf, and the older wolf."
- **Review the children's responses.** (The young child looks scared, terrified, shocked, and uncertain. The young wolf looks excited, anxious, agitated, and eager. The older wolf looks determined, forceful, and mad.)
- **Introduce the activity.** "Today, we're going to draw/paint each character and write adjectives below each one." Have the children draw or paint the young child, the young wolf, and the older wolf. On a separate piece of paper, have the children write adjectives that describe their expressions. (The young child looks scared, terrified, shocked, and uncertain. The young wolf looks excited, anxious, agitated, and eager. The older wolf looks determined, forceful, and mad.) Have the children glue or staple the adjectives below or around the pictures.

Science

#1. Discover if animals can recognize their own kind.

- **Objective.** Life Science. Structure, Function, and Information Processing. Make observations to construct an evidence-based account that young plants and animals are like, but not exactly like, their parents.
- **Level of difficulty.** Moderate. (This task may take several days to complete.)
- **Materials needed.** Lined paper and pencils.

- **Before the activity.** Place a large piece of white paper on the board. Have a black marker available for writing the children's responses. Go to the internet and type, "Can animals recognize their own offspring?" Choose an age-appropriate website for the children. Go to the internet and type, "Smell experiments for kids." Preview the website before you show it to the children.
- **Begin the activity by saying,** "Earlier, we discussed whether animals were able to recognize their own kind."
- **Review the children's responses.** (I think a mother can recognize her baby. A mother also knows the smell of her young baby. I think animals do have the ability to recognize their young.)
- **Introduce the activity.** "Today, we're going to find out whether animals are able to recognize their own kind." Go to the internet and type, "Can animals recognize their own offspring?" Select the age-appropriate website you chose. Read and discuss this information with the children. Write the important facts on a piece of paper. "Most mothers can smell their young. However, they use their other senses to recognize their young as well." Review the various senses that might be used. Have the children write their favorite fact on a piece of lined paper. If the children want to write their own sentence(s), be available to help them sound out the words. There are some interesting videos the children might enjoy seeing. Go to the internet and type, "Smell experiments for kids." This website has several experiments the children might enjoy doing. Preview the website before you show it to them.

#2. Set up a smell center in the classroom.

- **Objective.** Life Science. Structure, Function, and Information Processing. Use materials to design a solution to a human problem by mimicking how plants, and/or animals use their external parts to help them survive, grow, and meet their needs.

- **Level of difficulty.** Moderate. (This task may take several days to complete.)
- **Materials needed.** Small jars, lemon juice, rose petals, onion, and garlic.
- **Before the activity.** Place a large piece of white paper on the board. Have a black marker available for writing the children's responses. Go to the internet and type, "Tell me about a wolf's sense of smell." Choose an age-appropriate website for the children.
- **Begin the activity by saying,** "Earlier, we discussed how we thought the mother wolf could recognize her young cub."
- **Review the children's responses.** (A wolf has a very good sense of smell. It can recognize its young. A wolf's sense of smell protects it from other animals.)
- **Introduce the activity.** "Today, we're going review whether a mother wolf can recognize her young cub by the sense of smell. The sense of smell is important for both animals and humans." Go to the internet and type, "Tell me about a wolf's sense of smell." Select the age-appropriate website you chose. Read and discuss the information with the children. Write the facts they learned on a piece of paper. Have the children relay one fact they learned to a friend.
- **Extension of the activity.** Set up a smell center in the science center. Fill small jars with various things the children can smell and identify. Put numbers on the jars so they can identify the item in the jar with the master "smell list" (e.g., lemon juice, rose petals, onion, and garlic).

#3. Review the information related to a wolf's sense of hearing.

- **Objective.** Life Science. Structure, Function, and Information Processing. Use materials to design a solution to a human problem by mimicking how plants and/or animals use their external parts to help them survive, grow, and meet their needs.

- **Level of difficulty.** Easy.
- **Materials needed.** None.
- **Before the activity.** Place a large piece of white paper on the board. Have a black marker available for writing the children's responses. Go to the internet and type, "Do wolves have good hearing?" Choose an age-appropriate website for the children.
- **Begin the activity by saying,** "Earlier, we discussed whether wolves have good hearing."
- **Review the children's responses.** (Wolves have very good hearing. Wolves rely on their hearing to locate their prey. I think wolves have better hearing than humans.)
- **Introduce the activity.** "Today, we're going to review information related to a wolf's hearing." Go to the internet and type, "Do wolves have good hearing?" Select the age-appropriate website you chose. Read and discuss the information with the children. Have them relay their favorite fact(s) to a friend.

Math

#1. Learn about wolves' ears and how far they can rotate them.

- **Objective.** Mathematical Practice Standard. Mathematically proficient students consider the available tools when solving a mathematical problem. These tools might include pencil and paper, concrete models, a ruler, a protractor, a calculator, or a spreadsheet. Proficient students are sufficiently familiar with tools appropriate for their grade or course to make sound decisions about when each of these tools might be helpful, recognizing both the insight to be gained and their limitations.

- **Level of difficulty.** Moderate. (This task may take several days to complete.)
- **Materials needed.** Protractor, paper, colored pencils, ruler, and circle page for each child. (Copy the backside of the clock pattern in the resource section so the numbers don't appear.)
- **Before the activity.** Place a large piece of white paper on the board. Have a black marker available for writing the children's responses. Go to the internet and type, "Tell me about a wolf's ears." Choose an age-appropriate website for the children.
- **Begin the activity by saying,** "Earlier, we wondered about a wolf's ears and whether wolves have good hearing."
- **Review the children's responses.** (I think wolves have amazing ears. I think they have a good sense of hearing, but I think their sense of smell is better. I think a wolf's ears are very important. Their ears tell us important information about how the wolf is feeling. They're able to hear other predators in the area.)
- **Introduce the activity.** "Today, we're going to learn about a wolf's hearing and their ears." Go to the internet and type, "Tell me about a wolf's ears." Select the age-appropriate website you chose. Read and discuss the information with the children. Write some of the facts on a piece of paper. "We discovered that wolves have an amazing sense of hearing. They also have amazing ears. They can move their ears in many directions. They can move them sideways, backward, downward, and forward."
- **Extension of the activity.**
"We've learned that wolves have a great sense of hearing. They also have amazing ears. They can move their ears in many directions. They can move them sideways, backward, downward, and forward. Wolves can move their ears 180 degrees."
1. For the older children, show them 180 degrees on a protractor. Draw a large circle on the board. Draw a horizontal line through

the middle of the circle. Explain to the children that a circle has 360 degrees. Half of the circle would represent 180 degrees. (Use the line drawn in the middle of the circle to indicate half or 180 degrees.)

2. Give the children the circle page that was copied earlier and have them use colored pencils to mark the 180 degrees shown on the semicircle. Have the children verify that there are 180 degrees in this half circle.

3. To extend the lesson further, you may want them to use a ruler and pencil and create various angles. Explain to them that an angle is a space between two intersecting lines. You could also go to the internet and type, "Define an angle." Choose an age-appropriate website for the children. Read and discuss the information with the children. Have them place their protractor on this straight line and mark off various angles (e.g., 23°, 47°, or 86°) on the outside of the protractor. Have them draw a straight line from the center point on the straight line to various points on the outside of the protractor.

#2. Count the number of steps it takes to walk one hundred yards.

- **Objective.** Measurement and Data. Measure and estimate lengths in standard units. Measure the length of an object by selecting and using appropriate tools such as rulers, yardsticks, meter sticks, and measuring tapes.

- **Level of difficulty.** Challenging. (This task may take several days to complete.)

- **Materials needed.** A yardstick, tape measure, measuring wheel, or Google Earth, which you'll use to measure off one hundred yards (i.e., the length of a football field).

- **Before the activity.** Invite an adult or older student to help the children count the number of steps it takes them to reach one hundred yards. Place a large piece of white paper on the board. Have a black marker available for writing the children's responses. Measure off one hundred yards.

- **Begin the activity by saying,** "Earlier, we estimated how many footsteps/footprints might be made in one hundred yards."

- **Review the children's responses.** (I think that will be a lot of footsteps! I think it will take 200 steps to reach one hundred yards. I think it will take 500 steps to walk one hundred yards.)

- **Introduce the activity.** "Today, we're going to find out how many footsteps it takes to reach one hundred yards."

1. Prior to the lesson, measure off one hundred yards. Have the children review the class estimates of how many footsteps it would take to walk one hundred yards. Have the children write down their personal estimate on a three-by-five card. (I think it will take 245 footsteps to walk one hundred yards.) Make sure they have their name written on the card. Collect these cards for later.

2. Show the children the starting location and the ending location of the one hundred yards. One at a time, have them walk the one hundred yards with an older student or adult to help them count the number of footsteps it takes to reach this distance. Have the adult or older student record the number of steps on the front of the three-by-five card, marking that number as "walk #1." Make sure they have their name of the card. They may want to do the walk a couple of times to make sure the number is accurate. Have the adult or older student record the number of footsteps it takes for the second walk on the back of the card (labeled "walk #2"). Emphasize to the children that the number may vary slightly due to the distance of each step. Make sure the number of footsteps is written on the front and back of each three-by-five card.

3. Distribute their original estimates of how many footsteps it would take to walk one hundred yards. Discuss the differences between the estimates and how many steps it actually took them to walk the distance. "What did you learn from the experience?" (My estimated number of footsteps wasn't even close! I didn't think it took that many footsteps to walk that distance.)

QUESTIONS

The brackets around the text indicate questions/instructions an adult should read to the children. Examples of how the children may answer the questions are included in parentheses.

- **[What do you see on these pages?]**
- The two large pictures of the young child and the older wolf are inside large circles. They look like picture frames. Today, we're going to create a picture frame for these two characters. See Art #1.
- **[How would you describe the look on the young child's face? Today, we're going to learn about similes.]** Explain that a simile is a comparison between two things that uses the words "like," "as," and, "than." Write a few comparisons on a piece of paper and have the children complete the sentence(s) with as many descriptive words as they can think of for the above question (e.g., surprised, anxious, afraid, or scared). Write these descriptive words on a piece of paper. Keep the paper up for several days and allow the children to add words to the list.
- **[How would you describe the look of the older wolf?]** Direct the children to see how many adjectives or descriptive words they can think of (e.g., determined, focused, calm, or alert). Write these

descriptive words on a piece of paper. Keep the paper up for several days and allow the children to add words to the list.

- **[How would you describe the weather conditions on this page?]** (Well, it's snowing, so it must be cold. It's snowing hard.)

- **[How do wolves stay warm in the snow?]** Write the children's responses on a piece of paper and save this for later. (They stay close to each other. They find protection.) See Science #1.

- **[Do you think the young wolf will be happy to see his or her mother?]** Write the children's responses on a piece of paper and save this for later. (I think the young wolf will be happy to see his or her mother. I think the young wolf can hardly wait to get back to the pack.) Tell the children that today, they're going to create some similes. See Writing #1.

ACTIVITIES

Art

#1. Draw/paint pictures of the young child holding the young wolf and the older wolf. Create two picture frames for the drawings/ paintings.

- **Objective.** Creating. Anchor Standard #2. Organize and develop artistic ideas and work. Investigate. Explore uses of materials and tools to create works of art or design.

- **Level of difficulty.** Moderate. (This task may take several days to complete.)

- **Materials needed.** White construction paper, paints, paintbrushes, crayons, colored pencils, scissors, cardboard, and glue. Materials to decorate the frames (e.g., pine needles, stickers, pieces of an actual pine cone, cotton, or fur).

215

- **Before the activity.** Prepare the materials.
- **Begin the activity by saying,** "Earlier, we looked at the two large pictures on this page."
- **Introduce the activity.** "Today, we're going to draw/paint both the young child holding the young wolf, as well as the older wolf. Then we'll create picture frames for both drawings/paintings."
  1. Give the children two circular pieces of construction paper for their drawing/painting. Have them draw or paint these two characters. Let the paintings dry.
  2. Now, we're going to make picture frames for the drawings/paintings. You can lightly trace these two circular forms (see resource section) onto a heavy piece of poster board or cardboard. Carefully measure two or three inches away from the original circular form and draw the outside circle around the form. Cut around the outer circle.
  3. You can decorate the frames in whatever way you choose. Allow the children to glue various items onto the frames (e.g., pine needles, stickers, and/or pieces of an actual pine cone or cotton or fur). When the frames are dry, place the pictures the children drew/painted earlier of the young child holding the young wolf, as well as the older wolf in the center of the frames. Have them glue the paintings in place and let them dry. Display these on the bulletin board.

Writing

#1. Create similes about the young wolf being happy.

- **Objective.** Vocabulary Acquisition and Use. Demonstrate understanding of figurative language, word relationships, and nuances in word meanings. Explain the meaning of simple similes and metaphors (e.g., "as pretty as a picture") in context.

- **Level of difficulty.** Moderate. (This task may take several days to complete.)
- **Materials needed.** Lined paper, pencils, white construction paper, crayons, paintbrushes, paints, and colored pencils.
- **Before the activity.** Place a large piece of white paper on the board. Have a black marker available for writing the children's responses. Write the children's similes on the paper.
- **Begin the activity by saying,** "Earlier, we talked about similes. A simile is a comparison between two unlike things that uses the words 'than,' 'like,' or 'as.'"
- **Review the children's responses.** (The tree is as tall as a __. The cat is like a soft __. The snow is as white as___. The squirrel is faster than a___. The car is as fast as___.)
- **Introduce the activity.** "Today, we're going to try to create some similes about the young wolf being happy." Write the children's responses on a piece of paper. Start by saying, "The young wolf is as happy as ..." and let the children fill in the blank (a child in a candy store, a cat on a soft pillow, a bird eating seeds, a baby goat jumping in the grass). See how many comparisons the children can think of. Have them write their favorite simile on a piece of lined paper. They might enjoy drawing a picture of this simile.
- **Extension of the activity.** The same activity could be done for the mother / older wolf being happy. Write the children's responses on a piece of paper. "The mother wolf is as happy as ..." (a dog with a bone, a hippo in mud, a child with a new toy). See how many comparisons the children can think of. Have them write their favorite simile on a piece of lined paper. They might enjoy drawing a picture of this simile.

Science

#1. Have the children learn how wolves keep dry/warm in the snow.

- **Objective.** Life Science. Structure, Function, and Information Processing. Use materials to design a solution to a human problem by mimicking how plants and/or animals use their external parts to help them survive, grow, and meet their needs.
- **Level of difficulty.** Moderate. (This task may take several days to complete.)
- **Materials needed.** Lined paper and pencils.
- **Before the activity.** Place a large piece of white paper on the board. Have a black marker available for writing the children's responses. Go to the internet and type, "How do wolves keep warm?" Choose an age-appropriate website for the children.
- **Begin the activity by saying,** "Earlier, we talked about how we thought the wolves keep dry/warm in the snow."
- **Review the children's responses.** (They stay close to each other. They find protection.)
- **Introduce the activity.** "Today, we're going to find out how wolves keep dry/warm in the snow."
  1. Write down the children's comments about how the wolves keep warm. Review the comments once more. (They stay close to each other. They find protection.)
  2. Go to the internet and type, "How do wolves keep warm?" Select the age-appropriate website you chose. Read and discuss this information with the children.
  3. Have the children write their favorite fact on a piece of lined paper. This site also has a word search that the children will enjoy. They may enjoy stapling their fact sheet to the bottom of the picture of the older wolf. (See Art #1.)

Wolf in the Snow **illustration: Page with three panels**

Direct the children's attention to the left-hand side of the page, where you see three panels. The top panel shows the older wolf approaching the young child and the young wolf. The second panel shows the young wolf approaching the older wolf, and the third panel shows the older wolf carrying the young wolf off by his or her neck. Encourage them to answer the following questions in complete sentences.

QUESTIONS

The brackets around the text indicate questions/instructions an adult should read to the children. Examples of how the children may answer the questions are included in parentheses.

- **[What do you see on this page?]** Write the children's comments on a piece of paper and save this for later. See Art #1.

- Have the children look at the top panel on the left-hand side of the page. **[How would you describe what's happening on this panel?]** Write the children's comments on a piece of paper and save this for later. (Well, the young child is facing a large wolf, who's growling. The young child looks scared.)

- Have the children look at the second panel on the left-hand side of the page. Have them describe what they see. (Well, the young wolf is trying to reach the older wolf. I think the young wolf must know the older wolf.). **[Do you think the young wolf is scared? Do you think the older wolf recognizes the young wolf?]** Write the children's comments on a piece of paper and save this for later. See Art #2.

- Have the children look at the third panel on the left-hand side of the page. Have them describe what they see. Write the children's responses on a piece of paper and save this for later (The older wolf is carrying the young wolf off in the opposite direction. The older wolf is carrying the young wolf by the neck. The young wolf doesn't seem to be upset. The young child looks tired.) See Art #3.

- **[Do you think the older wolf is happy? What do you think she's thinking?]** Write the children's comments on a piece of paper and save this for later. (I think that's my young cub. I'll be so relieved when I get him or her back to the pack.) **[Do you think the young wolf is happy? What do you think the young wolf is thinking?]** Write the children's comments on a piece of paper and save this for later. (Yippie, I get to go back with the pack, but I'll miss the young child.) **[Do you think the young child is happy? What do you think the young child is thinking?]** Write the children's comments on a piece of paper and save this for later. (I'm so glad the older wolf found the young wolf. I know the young wolf will be glad to be back with the pack. I'm happy for them.). See Writing #1, #2, or #3.
- **[Do you think the young child dropped the young wolf? Or do you think the young wolf jumped down by itself? Why or why not?]**
- **[What do you think the young child is thinking?]** Write the children's comments on a piece of paper and save this for later. (The young child knows the approaching wolf is the young wolf's mother. I think the young child wonders what will happen to her.) See Art #1 and Writing #1.
- **[What do you think the young wolf is thinking?]** Write the children's comments on a piece of paper and save this for later. (Hooray! I see Mom! She's really come to get me. I sure have missed her.) See Art #1 and Writing #2.
- **[What do you think the older wolf is thinking?]** Write the children's comments on a piece of paper and save this for later (I think that's

my young cub. I think I'll take the young wolf back to the pack.). See Art #1 and Writing #3.

- Have the children look carefully at the middle picture. **[How would you describe the middle panel?]** Write the children's comments on a piece of paper and save this for later. (Well, the young wolf is trying to reach the older wolf. I think the young wolf must know the older wolf.) See Art #2.

- **[Do you think the young wolf is afraid of the older wolf? Why or why not?]** Write the children's comments on a piece of paper and save this for later. (Well, it looks like the young wolf is eager to reach the older wolf. The young wolf knows she's his or her mother.)

- Have the children look carefully at the bottom panel. **[How would you describe the bottom panel?]** Write the children's comments on a piece of paper and save this for later. (Well, the older wolf is carrying the young wolf away.) See Art #3.

- **[How does the older wolf know the young wolf is her cub?]** Write the children's comments on a piece of paper and save this for later. (Well, the older wolf must recognize the young wolf by his or her scent.

- **[How do you think the older wolf feels about finding the young wolf?]** Write the children's comments on a piece of paper and save this for later.

- Point out that the mother wolf is carrying the young wolf around its neck. **[Do you think it hurts the young wolf to be carried by its neck? What other animals carry their young in this manner?]** Write the children's responses on a piece of paper.

ACTIVITIES

Art

#1. Create three panel pictures of this page.

- **Objective.** Responding. Anchor Standard #8. Interpret intent and meaning in artistic work. Analyze. Interpret art by identifying the mood suggested by a work of art and describing relevant subject matter characteristics of form.
- **Level of difficulty.** Moderate. (This task may take several days to complete.)
- **Materials needed.** White construction paper, cut in half lengthwise. Cut enough construction paper for each child to have three strips of paper. Cut enough poster board for each child to have three strips. Cut the poster board larger than the white construction paper. Have pencils, paintbrushes, paints, crayons, colored pencils, and glue available.
- **Before the activity.** Prepare the materials.
- **Begin the activity by saying,** "Earlier, we talked about what was happening on all three panels on the left-hand side of the page."
- **Review the children's responses.** "We'll remember first what we thought about the first panel." (Well, the young child is facing a large wolf, who's growling. The young child looks scared.) "Next, we'll review what we thought about the second panel." (Well, the young wolf is trying to reach the older wolf. I think the young wolf must know the older wolf.). "Now, we'll remember our thoughts on the third panel." (The older wolf is carrying the young wolf off in the opposite direction. She's carrying the young wolf by the neck. The young wolf doesn't seem to be upset. The young child looks tired.).
- **Introduce the activity.** "Today, we're going to recreate the three panel pictures on the left-hand side of the page." Give the children

three strips of construction paper. Have them print their name on the back of each strip. Have them paint or draw the three panels. Let these dry and then glue them to strips of poster board. Save these panels for later.

#2. Have the children create a path for the young wolf to reach its mother.

- **Objective.** Responding. Anchor Standard #8. Interpret intent and meaning in artistic work. Analyze. Interpret art by identifying the mood suggested by a work of art and describing relevant subject matter and characteristics of form.
- **Level of difficulty.** Moderate. (This task may take several days to complete.)
- **Materials needed.** Six-inch wide strips of poster board, small squares of poster board to draw the young wolf, glue, paintbrushes, paints, crayons, colored pencils, popsicle sticks, scissors, and rulers.
- **Before the activity.** Place a large piece of white paper on the board. Have a black marker available for writing the children's responses.
- **Begin the activity by saying,** "Earlier, we looked at the second panel and described what we saw." We imagined what the young wolf and mother wolf might be thinking/saying. Review the children's responses.
- **Review the children's responses.** (Young Wolf: "Is that really you, Mom? I've walked and walked until I thought I'd drop." Mother Wolf: "Are you OK, little wolf? The family has been looking for you everywhere!")
- **Introduce the activity.** "Today, we're going to create a path for the young wolf to reach the older wolf."
1. Have the children look carefully at the second panel. Give them a long strip of poster board. With a ruler, have them trace a line in the center of the poster board. Leave room for them to draw

the young child on the left-hand side of the paper strip and the older wolf on the right-hand side of the paper strip.

2. Have them carefully cut on this line. Give each child a popsicle stick. Have the children draw or paint the young wolf on a separate piece of poster board and let this dry. Have the children cut a circle around the young wolf and glue this to the popsicle stick. Let this dry.

3. Have them insert the popsicle stick into the cut area, moving the young wolf toward the older wolf. Allow the children to verbalize what they think both wolves might be thinking/saying to a friend. (Young Wolf: "Is that really you, Mom? I've walked and walked until I thought I'd drop." Mother Wolf: "Are you OK, little wolf? The family has been looking for you everywhere!")

#3. Have the children create a path for the mother wolf to carry off the young wolf.

- **Objective.** Connecting. Anchor Standard #10. Synthesize and relate knowledge and personal experiences to make art. Synthesizing. Develop a work of art based on observations of surroundings.
- **Level of difficulty.** Moderate. (This task may take several days to complete.)
- **Materials needed.** Six-inch wide strips of poster board, small squares of poster board to draw the mother/young wolf, glue, paints, paintbrushes, crayons, colored pencils, popsicle sticks, scissors, and rulers.
- **Before the activity.** Place a large piece of white paper on the board. Have a black marker available for writing the children's responses.
- **Begin the activity by saying,** "Earlier, we looked at the third panel and described what we saw." We imagined what the young wolf and mother wolf might be thinking/saying.

224

- **Review the children's responses.** (The older wolf is carrying the young wolf off in the opposite direction. The young child looks tired. Young Wolf: "I'm so happy to be going back to the pack." Mother Wolf: "I'm so relieved to find my little wolf!" Young Child: "I'm happy for the young wolf.")
- **Introduce the activity.** "Today, we're going to create a path for the older wolf to carry off the young wolf."

1. Have the children look carefully at the third panel. Give them a long strip of poster board. Have the children use a ruler to trace a line in the center of the poster board, leaving room to draw the young child on the left-hand side of the paper strip.

2. Have them carefully cut on this line. Give each child a popsicle stick. Have the children draw or paint the mother wolf carrying off the young wolf on a separate piece of poster board and let this dry. Have the children cut a circle around the mother wolf and the young wolf and glue this to the popsicle stick. Let this dry.

3. Have them insert the popsicle stick into the cut area, moving the mother wolf and young wolf away from the young child. Allow the children to verbalize what they think both wolves might be thinking/saying to a friend. (Young Wolf: "I'll miss that young child! "Mom, I'm so glad to see you! I've walked and walked until I thought I'd drop." Mother Wolf: "Are you OK, little wolf? The family has been looking for you everywhere!")

Writing

#1. Have the children write what the young child might be thinking in this situation.

- **Objective.** Vocabulary Acquisition and Use. Use words and phrases acquired through conversations, reading, and being read to when responding to texts, including using adjectives and adverbs to describe. (When other kids are happy, that makes me happy).

- **Level of difficulty.** Moderate. (This task may take several days to complete.)
- **Materials needed.** Lined paper and pencils.
- **Before the activity.** Place a large piece of white paper on the board. Have a black marker available for writing the children's responses.
- **Begin the activity by saying,** "Earlier, we discussed what we thought the young child might be thinking."
- **Review the children's responses.** (The young child knows the approaching wolf is the young wolf's mother. I think the young child wonders what will happen to her.)
- **Introduce the activity.** "Today, we're going to write what we think the young child might be thinking/saying as the mother wolf approaches her." Review the children's comments once more. Have the children write their favorite sentence(s) on a piece of lined paper. If they'd like to write their own sentence, be available to help them sound out and write the words. Have them attach this sentence/paragraph to their first panel drawing/painting.

#2. Have the children write what the young wolf might be thinking in this situation.

- **Objective.** Vocabulary Acquisition and Use. Use words and phrases acquired through conversations, reading, and being read to when responding to texts, including using adjectives and adverbs to describe. (When other kids are happy, that makes me happy).
- **Level of difficulty.** Moderate. (This task may take several days to complete.)
- **Materials needed.** Lined paper and pencils.
- **Before the activity.** Place a large piece of white paper on the board. Have a black marker available for writing the children's responses.

- **Begin the activity by saying,** "Earlier, we discussed what we thought the young wolf was thinking."
- **Review the children's responses.** (Hooray! I see Mom! She's really come to get me. I sure have missed her.)
- **Introduce the activity.** "Today, we're going to write what we think the young wolf might be thinking/saying as the mother wolf approaches her." Review the children's comments. (The young wolf knows the approaching wolf is his or her mother. I think the young wolf wonders what will happen to him or her.). Have the children write their favorite sentence(s) on a piece of lined paper. If they'd like to write their own sentence, be available to help them sound out and write the words. Have them attach this sentence/paragraph to their second panel drawing/painting.

#3. Have the children write what the older wolf, the mother wolf might be thinking in this situation.

- **Objective.** Vocabulary Acquisition and Use. Use words and phrases acquired through conversations, reading, and being read to when responding to texts, including using adjectives and adverbs to describe. (When other kids are happy that makes me happy.)
- **Level of difficulty.** Moderate. (This task may take several days to complete.)
- **Materials needed.** Lined paper and pencils.
- **Before the activity.** Place a large piece of white paper on the board. Have a black marker available for writing the children's responses.
- **Begin the activity by saying,** "Earlier, we discussed what we thought the older wolf / mother was thinking."
- **Review the children's responses.** (That's my baby cub. I'm going to take him or her home. The wolf pack will be glad to see him or her.)

- **Introduce the activity.** "Today, we're going to write what we think the older wolf / mother might be thinking/saying as she carries her young wolf back to the pack." Review the children's comments once more). Have the children write their favorite sentence(s) on a piece of lined paper. If they'd like to write their own sentence(s), be available to help them sound out the words. Have them attach this sentence/paragraph to their third panel drawing/painting.

Wolf in the Snow illustration: Young child sweating in the snow

Direct the children's attention to the right-hand side of the page, where the young child has her hands in the snow and sweat is dripping down her face. Encourage them to answer the following questions in complete sentences.

QUESTIONS

The brackets around the text indicate questions/instructions an adult should read to the children. Examples of how the children may answer the questions are included in parentheses.

- **[What do you see on this page?]**
- **[How would you describe the young child?]** Write the children's comments on a piece of paper and save it for later. (Well, the young child looks exhausted. The young child looks so tired that she fell into the snow.) See Writing #1.
- **[What do you notice coming from the young child's mouth covering?]** Write the children's comments on a piece of paper and save it for later. (Well, it looks like fog. It must be the child's breath.) See Science #1.
- **[Do you know what causes this "clouded breath"?]** Write the children's comments on a piece of paper and save this for later. See Science #1.
- **[What do we call the drops coming off the young child's face?]** Write the children's responses on a piece of paper and save this for later. (Well, the young child is sweating. Moisture is dripping off her face.) See Science #2.

- **[Why do you think the wolves didn't follow the young child?]** Write the children's comments on a piece of paper and save this for later. (Well, they know the young wolf is safe.).

ACTIVITIES

Writing

1. Discuss and write about a time when the children were very tired.

- **Objective.** Writing Standards. Text Type and Purposes. Write narratives in which they recount a well-elaborated event or short sequence of events, include details to describe actions, thoughts, and feelings; use temporal words to signal event order; and provide a sense of closure.
- **Level of difficulty.** Moderate. (This task may take several days to complete.)
- **Materials needed.** White construction paper, crayons, paints, paintbrushes, lined paper, and pencils.
- **Before the activity.** Place a large piece of white paper on the board. Have a black marker available for writing the children's responses.
- **Begin the activity by saying,** "Earlier, we described how the young child looked."
- **Review the children's responses.** (Well, the young child looks exhausted. The young child looks so tired that she fell into the snow).
- **Introduce the activity.** "Today, we're going to describe the young child and talk about a time when we were very tired."
  1. Review the children's comments about how the young child looks. (Well, the young child looks exhausted. The young child looks so tired that she fell into the snow.)

2. "Have you ever been that tired?" Invite the children to come to the front of the room and explain when they felt this way. Don't require them to speak but ask for volunteers. (I remember after a soccer game I thought I would fall to the ground. I went for a hike with my family, and I was very exhausted!)

3. Have the children draw a picture of a time when they felt this tired. Have them write one or two sentence(s) on a piece of lined paper about their experience. Be available to help them sound out the words.

Science

#1. Discover why our breath looks like "fog" when we breath in freezing air.

- **Objective.** Earth and Space Science. Weather and Climate. Use and share observations of local weather conditions to describe patterns over time.

- **Level of difficulty.** Moderate. (This task may take several days to complete.)

- **Materials needed.** White construction paper, crayons, and colored pencils. If you choose to do the "fog in a jar" experiment described below, preview the website prior to the activity. The website gives the exact items needed to complete the experiment.

- **Before the activity.** Place a large piece of white paper on the board. Have a black marker available for writing the children's responses. Go to the internet and type, "Water vapor." Choose an age-appropriate website for the children. Go to the internet and type, "Weather Experiment: Fog in a Jar." Choose an age-appropriate website for the children.

- **Begin the activity by saying,** "Earlier, we noticed the young child had 'clouded breath' coming out of her mouth. We wondered what caused this to happen."
- **Review the children's responses.** (I think it's warm breath coming out of the young child's mouth.)
- **Introduce the activity.** "Today, we're going to find out what caused the 'clouded breath' of the young child."

1. Review the children's comments. (Warm breath coming out of the young child's mouth caused this to happen.). Go to the internet and type, "Water vapor." Select the age-appropriate website you chose. Read and discuss this information with the children.

2. Have them draw a picture and explain to a friend what happens when they see water vapor coming out of their friend's mouth.

3. Pull up the website with the 'fog in a jar' experiment you found earlier. This experiment demonstrates what happens when warm air mixes with the cold air. Demonstrate this experiment for the children. The children could do this experiment in small groups.

#2. Learn why our body *sweats* when we get hot.

- **Objective.** Life Science. Interdependent Relationships in Ecosystems, Animals, Plants, and their Environment. Communicate solutions that will reduce the impact of humans on the land, water, air, and/or other living things in the local environment.
- **Level of difficulty.** Easy.
- **Materials needed.** None.
- **Before the activity.** Place a large piece of white paper on the board. Have a black marker available for writing the children's responses. Go to the internet and type, "Why do we sweat for kids." Choose an age-appropriate website for the children.

- **Begin the activity by saying,** "Earlier, we noticed moisture was dripping off the child's face." Why does this happen? Write the children's responses on a piece of paper.
- **Review the children's responses.** (The child has been walking for a long distance, which causes her body to sweat.)
- **Introduce the activity.** "Today, we're going to find out why our body sweats when we get hot."
    1. Review the children's comments. (The child has been walking for a long distance, which causes her body to sweat.)
    2. Go to the internet and type, "Why do we sweat for kids." Select the age-appropriate website you chose. There are several videos that explain the sweating process. Have the children watch a video and then discuss the information.
    3. Have the children tell a friend about a time when they were hot, tired, and sweating.
- **Extension of the activity.** There's also an experiment on plants losing water. Go to the internet and type, "Do plants sweat?" Have the children watch the video and then discuss the information with them. Perhaps, you could do the experiment with them.

QUESTIONS

The brackets around the text indicate questions/instructions an adult should read to the children. Examples of how the children may answer the questions are included in parentheses.

- **[What do you see on this page?]** (The young child is walking away from the wolves because she knows the wolves will take care of the young wolf. The young wolf is surrounded by the wolf pack.) **[What do you think the young child is thinking?]** Write the children's comments on a piece of paper and save this for later. (I'm so glad the young wolf is safe. The wolf pack recognizes the young wolf. I wish I were with my family. I hope I get home soon.) See Writing #1.

- **[How many wolves do you see?]** (Well, there are five wolves.) See Math #1.

- **[In what direction is the young child heading?]** (Well, if the top of the page is north, then the young child is heading east.) See Science #1.

- **[Why do you think the wolves don't follow the young child?]** (Well, they know the young wolf is safe.)

- Direct the children to look carefully at the wolves. **[Who's turned toward the young child?]** (Well, it looks like the dark wolf, the mother wolf is turned toward the child.)

- **[Why do you think the mother wolf doesn't go after the young child?]** Write the children's responses on a piece of paper and save this for later. See Art #1.

- Note that the young child must be thinking all sorts of thoughts on her way home. **[If the child could wish for anything, what do you think the child would wish for?]** Write the children's responses on a piece of paper and save this for later. (I wish I could be home in front of a nice, warm fire. I wish I could take the young wolf home with me.) See Writing #2.

ACTIVITIES

Art

#1. Create stick puppets of the "mother" wolf and the young child.

- **Objective.** Connecting. Anchor Standard #10. Synthesize and relate knowledge and personal experiences to make art. Synthesize. Develop a work of art based on observations of surroundings.

- **Level of difficulty.** Moderate. (This task may take several days to complete.)

- **Materials needed.** Poster board, pencils, crayons, colored pencils, paints, paintbrushes, bamboo sticks, glue, and scissors.

- **Before the activity.** Place a large piece of white paper on the board. Have a black marker available for writing the children's responses.

- **Begin the activity by saying,** "Earlier, we discussed why we thought the darker wolf, the mother wolf didn't go after the young child.

- **Review the children's responses.** (I think the mother wolf knows that the young child helped her cub. I think the mother wolf just wanted to get her wolf cub back to the pack.)
- **Introduce the activity.** "Today, we're going to make stick puppets for both the mother wolf and the young child."
  1. "We discussed why we thought the darker wolf, the mother wolf didn't go after the young child." Review the children's responses. (I think the mother wolf knows the young child helped her cub. I think the mother wolf just wanted to get her wolf cub back to the pack.)
  2. Have the children sketch both characters onto a piece of poster board and then have them color/paint them. Let them dry. Cut a circle around both figures.
  3. Using long, thin bamboo sticks, glue these sticks to the back of the figures. Allow them to dry. Have the children conduct a conversation between the mother wolf and the young child. (Young Child: "I hope the young wolf is happy to be back with his or her family." Mother Wolf: "You certainly took good care of my young cub!")

Writing

#1. Discuss what the young child is thinking as she walks away from the wolves.

- **Objective.** Writing Standards. Text Types and Purposes. Write opinion pieces on topics or tests supporting a point of view with reasons. Introduce the topic or text they are writing about, state an opinion, and create an organizational structure that lists reasons.
- **Level of difficulty.** Moderate. (This task may take several days to complete.)
- **Materials needed.** Lined paper and pencils.

- **Before the activity.** Place a large piece of white paper on the board. Have a black marker available for writing the children's responses.

- **Begin the activity by saying,** "Earlier, we noticed the young child was walking away from the wolves. The young child glanced back at the wolves and knew the wolves would take good care of the young wolf. We discussed what the young child might be thinking."

- **Review the children's responses.** (I'm so glad the young wolf is safe. The wolf pack recognizes him or her. I wish I was with my family. I hope I get home soon.)

- **Introduce the activity.** "Today, we're going to continue to imagine what the young child is thinking as she walks away from the wolves."

  1. "What do you think the young child is thinking?" Write down and review the children's responses. (I'm so glad that the young wolf is safe. The wolf pack recognizes the young wolf. I wish I were with my family. I hope I get home soon.)

  2. Have the children write their favorite comment(s) on a piece of lined paper and share it with a friend.

#2. Discuss what the young child might be thinking/wishing for as she's walking home.

- **Objective.** Reading Standards for Literature. Key Ideas and Details. Describe how characters in a story respond to major events and challenges.

- **Level of difficulty.** Moderate. (This task may take several days to complete.)

- **Materials needed.** Long pieces of lined paper and pencils.

- **Before the activity.** Place a large piece of white paper on the board. Have a black marker available for writing the children's responses.

- **Begin the activity by saying,** "Earlier, we thought the young child might be thinking all sorts of thoughts on her way home. What do you think she might be thinking/wishing for?"

- **Review the children's responses.** (I wish I could be home in front of a nice, warm fire. I wish I could take the young wolf home with me. I wish I had a big cup of hot chocolate!)
- **Introduce the activity.** "Today, we're going to discuss what the young child might be thinking as she walks home."
  1. Review what the young child might be thinking as she walks in the opposite direction. (I wish I could be home in front of a nice, warm fire. I wish I could take the young wolf home with me. I wish I had a big cup of hot chocolate right now!)
  2. We'll also make a list of things she might wish for. Write the children's responses on a piece of paper. (I wish I had warmer pants on. I wish I had something to eat. I wish I could be sitting in front of the warm fire.) Give the children long pieces of paper where the children can write a list of wishes. Have the children share their list with a friend.

Science

#1. Verify that the child is heading east.

- **Objective.** Earth and Space Science. Space Systems. Patterns and Cycles. Use observations of the sun, moon, and stars to describe patterns that can be predicted.
- **Level of difficulty.** Easy.
- **Materials needed.** Place a copy of a compass rose onto a projector, so the children can easily see the various directions on it. If you don't have a projector, enlarge the compass rose on a copy machine (see resource section) and glue it onto a piece of poster board. It should be large enough for the children to see.
- **Before the activity.** Place a large piece of white paper on the board. Have a black marker available for writing the children's responses.

- **Begin the activity by saying,** "Earlier, we noticed the young child was heading east. How do we know for sure that she's heading in this direction?"
- **Review the children's responses.** (Well, I can see the markings on the compass rose. There's N for north, S for south, E for east, and W for west. She's heading east.)
- **Introduce the activity.** "Today, we're going to determine that the child was heading east. "How do we know?" Allow the children to express how they know the young child is heading east. An atlas might display a compass rose that you can show the children. You might want to take the children outside and give them oral directions. (Walk north to the fence. Now turn west and walk to the slide. Turn east and walk to the playground area. Now turn south and walk to the end of the grass area.)

Math

#1. Write number sentences that equal 5.

- **Objective.** Operations and Algebraic Thinking. Decompose numbers less than or equal to 10 into pairs in more than one way, by using objects or drawings and record each decomposition by a drawing or equation (e.g., $5 = 2 + 3$ and $5 = 4 + 1$).
- **Level of difficulty.** Moderate. (This task may take several days to complete.)
- **Materials needed.** Strips of poster board, scissors, glue, hole punch, colored paper, dots, stickers, pom-poms, and other craft supplies that can be glued and counted on paper. (For example, 1 sticker + 4 stickers = 5 stickers.)
- **Before the activity.** Place a large piece of white paper on the board. Have a black marker available for writing the children's responses.

- **Begin the activity by saying,** "Earlier, we counted the number of wolves we saw on this page. We said there were 4 older wolves and 1 younger wolf for a total of 5 wolves on the page."
- **Review the children's responses.** (I see 5 wolves on the page.)
- **Introduce the activity.** "Today, we're going to find different ways to show the 5 wolves shown on this page."

1. "How could we show this in a number sentence?" Write the children's responses on the paper. Eventually, they'll discover various numerical combinations that would equal five (e.g., 0 + 5 = 5, 1 + 4 = 5, 2 + 3 = 5, 3 + 2 = 5, 4 + 1 = 5, and 5 + 0 = 5).

2. "Does the answer change when the numbers are in different positions?" No, the two numbers will still equal 5. Have the children draw dot combinations to demonstrate the various numerical combinations. You could have the children use a hole punch to punch out small dots, and then, they could glue the dots onto individual strips of paper. You could also use stickers, pom-poms, or other craft materials.

Wolf in the Snow illustration: Child on top of hill, breathing hard

Direct the children's attention to the left-hand side of the page where the young child is on top of the hill, and she is breathing hard. On the right-hand side of the page, the child is making huffing sounds and trips on her knee. Encourage them to answer the following questions in complete sentences.

QUESTIONS

The brackets around the text indicate questions/instructions an adult should read to the children. Examples of how the children may answer the questions are included in parentheses.

- **[What do you see on this page?]**
- **[What time of day is it?]** (Well, the sky is dark, so it must be night.)
- **[Are there places where it can be dark during the day?]** (Yes, there are places where the sun doesn't shine for periods of time. Alaska is one of those places.) See Art #1 and Science #1 and #3.
- **[How many hours do you think the young child has been walking?]** (Well, the sky is dark, so it's late. If the young child started walking home from school when the sun was shining, that means she has been walking many hours.) See Math #1.
- Tell the children to look carefully at the child on the left-hand side of the page. **[What is coming out of the young child's face covering?]** Write the children's comments on a piece of paper and save this for later. (It looks like fog. White stuff is coming out of her face covering.) See Science #2.

- **[Is the child getting closer to home?]** (Well, the child is closer to the two lights, so she must be heading in the direction of people. She has traveled a long distance.) See Writing #2.
- **[Who do you think is barking?]** (The young child's dog is barking. I think the dog is with the adult, trying to find the young child. It could be a search and rescue dog from a surrounding community.) See Writing #3.
- **[Could the two barking sounds off in the distance be wolves? Why or why not?]** (I don't think the two barking sounds in the background are wolves, because wolves usually make a howling sound. I think it must be a dog barking because dogs bark and wolves howl.) See Science #4.
- **[Do you think the young child knows someone is looking for her? Why or why not?]** Write the children's responses on a piece of paper and save this for later. (Well, if the young child looks off into the distance, she will see two lights. She may also hear barking sounds off in the distance.) Ask the children to think of ways the young child could let those looking for her know where she was. Write the children's responses on a piece of paper and save this for later. See Writing #4.
- **[How do we know the child is getting tired?]** (It looks like the child is sitting on her knees on the left-hand side of the page. The words "huff....huff" on the right-hand side of the page let us know she is getting tired. Finally, the young child falls on her knees, so she must be very tired.) See Writing #5.
- **[What other words or phrases could we use to indicate that the child is getting tired?]** Write the children's responses on a piece of paper and save this for later. (Yikes. Whew. Oh my goodness. I'm so tired). See Writing #6.
- **[Is the child getting closer to home?]** (Well, the child is getting closer to the two lights that appear in the sky, so she must have

traveled a long distance.) **[Would there be any way for the young child to know if she was getting close to home?]** Write the children's responses on a piece of paper and save this for later. (Well, she would recognize certain things in the area like mountains, hills, and canyons.) See Science #5.

- **[What is happening to the child on the bottom right-hand side of the page?]** (The child is falling on her knee.) See Science #6.
- Have the children note that the young child has her eyes closed. **[Why do you think she has her eyes closed?]** (Well, she's probably so tired she can't keep her eyes open.) See Writing #7.

ACTIVITIES

Art

#1. Discover if there are places where it stays dark during the day. Make sunrise pictures.

- **Objective.** Responding. Anchor Standard #7. Perceive and analyze artistic work. Perceive. Perceive and describe aesthetic characteristics of one's natural world and constructed environments.
- **Level of difficulty.** Moderate. (This task may take several days to complete.)
- **Materials needed.** White construction paper; paintbrushes; and orange, yellow, red, pink, and purple paint.
- **Before the activity.** Place a large piece of white paper on the board. Have a black marker available for writing the children's responses. Go to the internet and type, "Show me sunrises." Choose an age-appropriate website for the children.
- **Begin the activity by saying,** "Earlier, we wondered if there were places in the world where it stayed dark during the day."

- **Review the children's responses.** (I lived in Alaska, and during the winter, it was very dark. During the summer, the sun was up in the sky until 10:00 p.m.)
- **Introduce the activity.** "Today, we're going to find out if there are places in the world where it stays dark during the day."

1. Go to the internet and type, "Tell me about the polar night." Choose an age-appropriate website for the children. Review the information on the website you selected. "We discovered that parts of the world experience darkness during the day. It's cause for celebration when the sun does appear."

2. Today, we're going to create sunrise pictures. Go to the internet and type, "Show me sunrises." Select the age-appropriate website you chose. Have the children look at the various pictures of sunrises.

3. Give the children a large piece of white construction paper. Have them spread orange, yellow, purple, and pink paint onto the paper. Use one color at a time. They can use paintbrushes or their fingers to spread the paint on the paper. The colors should blend together. Let the paintings dry.

4. Have the children cut out pictures from magazines or cut out black silhouetted shapes to add to their pictures (e.g., trees, animals, rocks, or hills).

#2. Make a picture puzzle.

- **Objective.** Responding. Anchor Standard #7. Perceive. Select and describe works of art that illustrate daily life experiences of self and others.
- **Level of difficulty.** Easy.
- **Materials needed.** Sketch paper and crayons, paint and paintbrushes, or colored pencils.

- **Before the activity.** Place a large piece of white paper on the board. Have a black marker available for writing the children's responses.
- **Begin the activity by saying,** "Earlier, we talked about how the young child had walked a very long way. She started walking home from school when the sun was shining, and now it's dark."
- **Review the children's responses.** (Well, the young girl has walked so far, she must be tired. I know that if I walked that far, I'd be super tired.)
- **Introduce the activity.** "Today, we're going to draw a picture of the young child falling in the snow." If the children want to draw another picture, allow them to draw whatever they choose.

1. Give the children a five-by-eight-inch card to draw their picture. The children should cover the entire card, pressing the crayons heavily into the card. This card should be heavy enough to cut later for the puzzle pieces.
2. When the children have drawn their picture, have them turn the five-by-eight-inch card over and draw three lines through the back of the puzzle. Each line should start at an edge and continue to the opposite edge. It shouldn't be too complicated.
3. Have the children carefully cut along the lines and have them put their "puzzle" together. Give each child a plastic zipper bag to put their "puzzle" inside. Write their name on the front of the plastic bag with a permanent marker. Allow them to exchange their "puzzle" with a friend.

Writing / Oral Language

#1. Write about a time when they were so tired they couldn't keep their eyes open.

- **Objective.** Writing Standards. Text Types and Purposes. Write informative/explanatory texts to examine a topic and convey ideas and information clearly. Develop the topic with facts, definitions, and details.

- **Level of difficulty.** Moderate. (This task may take several days to complete.)
- **Materials needed.** White construction paper, crayons, colored pencils, paints, paintbrushes, lined paper, and pencils.
- **Before the activity.** Place a large piece of white paper on the board. Have a black marker available for writing the children's responses.
- **Begin the activity by saying,** "Earlier, we discussed why we thought the young child was closing her eyes. Have you ever been so tired you simply couldn't keep your eyes open?"
- **Review the children's responses.** (I was so tired after hiking that I fell fast asleep in the car. I was so tired after running a 5K race that I could hardly wait to get home to fall asleep.)
- **Introduce the activity.** "Today, we're going to talk and write about a time when you were so tired you couldn't keep your eyes open."
  1. Review the children's comments. (I was so tired after hiking that I fell fast asleep in the car. I was so tired after running a 5K race that I could hardly wait to get home to fall asleep.)
  2. Have the children draw a picture of how/when this happened to them and have them write a sentence or short paragraph about the event. (I was so tired after hiking, that I fell fast asleep in the car. I was so tired after running a 5K race that I could hardly wait to get home to fall asleep.)

#2. Discuss and write what their home means to them.

- **Objective.** Writing Standards. Research to Build and Present Knowledge. Recall information from experiences or gather information from print and digital sources; take brief notes on sources and sort evidence into provided categories.

- **Level of difficulty.** Moderate. (This task may take several days to complete.)
- **Materials needed.** Lined paper and pencils.
- **Before the activity.** Place a large piece of white paper on the board. Have a black marker available for writing the children's responses. Ask the children what their home means to them. Write their comments on the paper.
- **Begin the activity by saying,** "Earlier, we wondered if the young child was getting closer to her home. I bet she really appreciates her home. She must be eager to get home to a warm fireplace."
- **Review the children's responses.** (Home is where I feel safe. Home is where I learn. Home is where my dog lives.)
- **Introduce the activity.** "Today, we're going to write a few sentences about what our home means to us."
  1. "We saw two lights off in the background, and a dog was barking. We know the young child has been traveling a long distance, so we can guess the young child might be getting closer to her home. The thought of getting home must be a strong thought in the young child's mind. Today, we're going to write some sentences about what home means too us." (Home is where I feel safe. Home is where I learn. Home is where my dog lives.)
  2. Give the children pieces of lined paper and have them write their favorite sentence(s). If they'd like to create their own sentence(s), be available to help them sound out the words. Allow the children to draw a picture of what their home means to them.

#3. Discuss the actions/thoughts of the dog.

- **Objective.** Writing Standards. Text Types and Purposes. Write opinion pieces on topics or texts, supporting a point of view with reasons. Introduce the topic or text they are writing about, state an opinion, and create an organizational structure that lists reasons.

- **Level of difficulty.** Easy.
- **Materials needed.** None.
- **Before the activity.** Place a large piece of white paper on the board. Have a black marker available for writing the children's responses.
- **Begin the activity by saying,** "Earlier, we thought the young child's dog might be barking."
- **Review the children's responses.** (The young child's dog is barking. I think the dog is with the adult, trying to find the young child. It could also be a search and rescue dog from a surrounding community.)
- **Introduce the activity.** "Today, we're going to discuss the actions/ thoughts of the dog."

1. "The dog is with the adult, so perhaps they're trying to find the young child." Review the children's responses. (I think the young child's dog is barking. I think the dog is with the adult, trying to find the young child. It could also be a search and rescue dog from a surrounding community.)

2. "If the dog could talk, what words of encouragement do you think it would relay to the young child?" (Dog: Hang in there! I know you've been walking a long, long way. We're on our way to get you. Walk a little way and then rest.) Have the children relay to a friend the words of encouragement they think the dog might relay to the child. Have them write their favorite words of encouragement on a piece of lined paper and read it to the class.

#4. Discuss how you could signal someone for help.

- **Objective.** Language Standards. Vocabulary Acquisition and Use. Use words and phrases acquired through conversations, reading, and being read to when responding to texts.
- **Level of difficulty.** Easy.
- **Materials needed.** None.

- **Before the activity.** Place a large piece of white paper on the board. Have a black marker available for writing the children's responses. Go to the internet and type, "Ways to signal for help." Choose an age-appropriate website for the children.
- **Begin the activity by saying,** "Earlier, we wondered if the child knows someone is looking for her. We wondered what she could do to let them know where she was."
- **Review the children's responses.** (Well, if the young child looks off into the distance, she will see two lights. She may also hear the barking. She could make a whistling sound to let them know she was nearby. She could also yell to them.)
- **Introduce the activity.** "Today, we're going to discuss whether the child knows that someone is looking for her."
  1. Review the children's comments. (Well, if the young child looks off into the distance, she'll see two lights. She may also hear the barking sounds.)
  2. "How could you alert the person/dog you were nearby?" Go to the internet and type, "Ways to signal for help." Select the age-appropriate website you chose. "What would you do if you were in this situation?" (I'd use my phone if I had it with me. I'd bang on a tree trunk with a heavy branch so it would send sounds throughout the forest. I'd make clapping sounds.) "Today, you're going to tell a friend how you'd try to signal someone in this situation."

#5. Examine the page and text to determine any clues that let us know if the child is getting tired.

- **Objective.** Reading Standards for Literature. Key Ideas and Details. Describe how characters in a story respond to major events and challenges.
- **Level of difficulty.** Easy.

- **Materials needed.** None.
- **Before the activity.** Place a large piece of white paper on the board. Have a black marker available for writing the children's responses.
- **Begin the activity by saying,** "Earlier, we wondered what clues would help us figure out if the young child was getting tired."
- **Review the children's responses.** (It looks like the child is sitting on her knees on the left-hand side of the page. The words "huff … huff" on the right-hand side of the page let us know she's getting tired. Finally, the young child falls on her knees, so she must be very tired.)
- **Introduce the activity.** "Today, we're going to look at the page to see if we can find clues that let us know if the child is getting tired."
  1. Review the children's comments. (It looks like the child is sitting on her knees on the left-hand side of the page. The words "huff … huff" on the right-hand side of the page let us know that she is getting tired. Finally, the young child falls on her knees, so she must be very tired.).
  2. "Today, you're going to tell a friend about a time when you were very tired." (I was very tired when my family went hiking and we walked a very long way. I was huffing like the young child. When we finished our hike, it took me a few minutes to stop breathing hard.)

#6. Select words that could express the young child's exhaustion/ tiredness.

- **Objective.** Language Standards. Vocabulary Acquisition and Use. Demonstrate understanding of word relationships and nuances in word meanings. Identify real-life connections between words and their use. (For example, describe foods that are spicy or juicy.)
- **Level of difficulty.** Easy.

- **Materials needed.** White construction paper, lined paper, pencils, crayons, and colored pencils (optional).
- **Before the activity.** Place a large piece of white paper on the board. Have a black marker available for writing the children's responses.
- **Begin the activity by saying,** "Earlier, we wondered what other words could be used to indicate that the young child was getting tired."
- **Review the children's responses.** (Yikes. Whew. Oh my goodness. I'm so tired!)
- **Introduce the activity.** "Today, we're going to think of words that would let the reader know the young child was very tired." Review the children's comments once more. Keep this paper on the board so the children can add other words to the list. Perhaps they'd like to draw a picture and write their favorite word(s) to show that the young child was tired.

#7. Engage in an oral expression experience.

- **Objective.** Speaking and Listening Standards. Presentation of Knowledge and Ideas. Report on a topic or text, tell a story, or recount an experience with appropriate facts and relevant, descriptive details, speaking clearly at an understandable pace.
- **Level of difficulty.** Easy.
- **Before the activity.** Place a large piece of white paper on the board. Have a black marker available for writing the children's responses.
- **Begin the activity by saying,** "Earlier, we noticed that the young child had her eyes closed. We thought the child was so tired that she couldn't keep them open. Has there ever been a time when you were that tired?"
- **Review the children's responses.** (I was so tired when I finished my swimming lesson that I sat on the edge of the pool and rested.

I was so tired when I finished my soccer practice that I wanted to go to sleep.)

- **Introduce the activity.** "Today, we're going tell each other about a time when we were so tired it was difficult for us to keep our eyes open." (I was so tired when I finished our family hike that I wanted to sit on the side of the trail for an hour. I was exhausted when I completed the 5K run at school, and I wanted to fall on the grass).

    1. The picture gives us hints that the child was so tired she couldn't keep her eyes open. Review the children's comments. (The young child has her eyes closed. We thought the child was so tired she couldn't keep them open.)

    2. "Have you ever been that tired?" Invite the children to share a time when they were that tired. Ask one or two of the children to come to the front of the class and tell their classmates about the experience. (I was so tired when I finished my swimming lesson that I sat on the edge of the pool and rested. I was so tired when I finished my soccer practice that I wanted to go to sleep.) This should be on a voluntary basis. Do not require that each child share an experience in front of the class. Perhaps they'd feel more comfortable sharing their experience with a friend.

Science

#1. Learn about places where it stays dark during the day.

- **Objective.** Earth and Space Science. Space Systems. Patterns and Cycles. Make observations at different times of the year to relate the amount of daylight to the time of year.
- **Level of difficulty.** Challenging. (This task may take several days to complete.)

- **Materials needed.** Flour, salt, water, tortillas, and maps of the areas that experience the polar night (e.g., Alaska, Sweden, Finland, and Lapland).
- **Before the activity.** Place a large piece of white paper on the board. Have a black marker available for writing the children's responses about places that experience the polar night. Go to the internet and type, "Tell me about the polar night." Choose an age-appropriate website for the children. Go to the internet and type, "Polar arts and crafts." Again, choose an age-appropriate website for the children. Directions for making dough and tortilla maps can be found by searching the internet for "how to make a salt map" and "how to make a tortilla map."
- **Begin the activity by saying,** "Earlier, we wondered if there were places in the world where it stayed dark during the day."
- **Review the children's responses.** (Yes, there are places where the sun doesn't shine for periods of time. I used to live in Alaska, and the sun didn't shine during the day.)
- **Introduce the activity.** "Today, we're going to find out if there are places in the world where it stays dark during the day."
  1. "Do you know of any places where it stays dark during the day?" Write the children's responses on a piece of paper. (Yes, there are places where the sun doesn't shine for periods of time. Alaska is one of those places. Sweden, Finland, and Lapland also experience this.)
  2. Go to the internet and type, "Tell me about the polar night." Select the age-appropriate website you chose. Read and discuss this information with the children. Look at a map to show parts of the world where this occurs.
  3. Go to the internet and type, "Polar arts and crafts." Select the age-appropriate website you chose. This site has several projects the children will enjoy creating.

253

4. They can make a salt or tortilla map of the Arctic region. Go to the internet and type, "How to make a salt map." In addition, go to the internet and type, "How to make a tortilla map." These should allow you to pull up websites that will give you directions on how to make the dough, as well as creating the map.

#2. Understand/review why we see our breath when it's cold outside.

- **Objective.** Earth and Space Science. Weather and Climate. Use and share observations of local weather conditions to describe patterns over time.
- **Level of difficulty.** Easy.
- **Materials needed.** None.
- **Before the activity.** Place a large piece of white paper on the board. Have a black marker available for writing the children's responses. Go to the internet and type, "Why do you see your breath when it's cold?" Choose an age-appropriate website for the children.
- **Begin the activity by saying,** "Earlier, we noticed the young child had something coming out of her face covering."
- **Review the children's responses.** (It looks like fog. White stuff is coming out of her face covering.)
- **Introduce the activity.** "Today, we're going to review what causes 'fog' to come out of the young child's face covering or out of our mouths."

1. Ask the children to list things they remember from their prior experience with this topic. (I remember that "fog" forms when hot air comes in contact with cold air. I remember that it was called condensation.) Go to the internet and type, "Why do you see your breath when it's cold?" Select the age-appropriate website you chose. Review this information with the children. There are some videos on the internet that the children might enjoy watching. Preview the videos before you show them to the children.

254

#3. Learn how some animals are suited to live in very cold areas.

- **Objective.** Engineering Design. Life Science. Interdependent Relationships in Ecosystems. Construct an argument with evidence that, in a particular habitat, some organisms can survive well, some survive less well, and some cannot survive at all.
- **Level of difficulty.** Easy.
- **Materials needed.** Lard, plastic gloves, large pot, ice, and water (optional task).
- **Before the activity.** Place a large piece of white paper on the board. Have a black marker available for writing the children's responses. Go to the internet and type, "How do arctic animals stay warm?" Choose an age-appropriate website for the children. You could also go to the internet and type, "How do animals stay warm in the winter?" Choose an age-appropriate website for the children.
- **Begin the activity by saying,** "Earlier, we talked about how cold weather can pose problems for people." (We can get very cold. We need to wear special clothing. We need to take precautions when we're in the snow.) Cold weather poses many problems for people living in cold areas; however, some arctic animals seem to thrive in cold weather and cold water.
- **Review the children's responses.** (I think animals have thick fur that helps to protect them. I think animals have a lot of fat on their bodies that helps them.)
- **Introduce the activity.** "Today, we're going to learn about how some arctic animals adapt and thrive in cold weather and cold water."
  1. Go to the internet and type, "How do arctic animals stay warm in icy water?" Select the age-appropriate website you chose. Read and discuss this information with the children.

2. There is an experiment on the website that demonstrates how the blubber of an animal insulates it from cold water. In the experiment, the children put lard onto a plastic glove and then plunge their hand into icy water. Have the children do this experiment if you've decided to include it. The lard insulates against the cold.

3. There are several videos the children might enjoy watching. Preview these videos before you show them to the children.

4. "Animals that live in places other than the arctic region also adapt to the cold weather." Go to the internet and type, "How do animals stay warm in the winter?" Select the age-appropriate website you chose. Read and discuss this information with the children. There are several videos the children might enjoy watching. Preview these videos before you show them to the children.

#4. Discover whether wolves bark or howl.

- **Objective.** Engineering Design. Life Science. Interdependent Relationships in Ecosystems. Construct an argument that some animals form groups that help members survive.

- **Level of difficulty.** Easy.

- **Materials needed.** None.

- **Before the activity.** Log onto the internet and type, "Wolves howling." Choose an age-appropriate website for the children.

- **Begin the activity by saying,** "Earlier, we discussed why we thought it was a dog barking in the distance and not wolves."

- **Review the children's responses.** (I don't think the two barking sounds in the background are wolves, because wolves usually make a howling sound. I think it must be a dog barking because wolves make a howling sound.)

- **Introduce the activity.** "Today, we're going to watch a video that shows some wolves howling." Go to the internet and type, "Wolves howling." Select the age-appropriate website you chose. Let the children listen to the wolves howling. Talk about the difference between a bark and a howl. Take the children outside and let them howl like a wolf.

#5. Learn about different landforms.

- **Objective.** Engineering Design. Life Science. Interdependent Relationships in Ecosystems. Make a claim about the merit of a solution to a problem caused when the environment changes and the types of plants and animals that live there may change.
- **Level of difficulty.** Moderate. (This task may take several days to complete.)
- **Materials needed.** White construction paper, pencils, crayons, and colored pencils.
- **Before the activity.** Place a large piece of white paper on the board. Have a black marker available for writing the children's responses. Go to the internet and type, "Tell me about landforms." Choose an age-appropriate website for the children.
- **Begin the activity by saying,** "Earlier, we wondered if the young child was getting closer to home."
- **Review the children's responses.** (Well, she would recognize certain things, such as mountains, hills, or canyons.)
- **Introduce the activity.** "Today, we're going to speculate about whether the young girl knows she's getting closer to her home. How would she know?" Review the children's comments. (Well, perhaps she would recognize certain things, such as mountains, hills, or canyons.) Today, we're going to learn about landforms. Go to the internet and type, "Tell me about landforms." Select the age-appropriate website you chose. Read and discuss the information with them. Have them draw their favorite landform (e.g., a canyon, a mountain, or a hill).

#6. Learn about our knees.

- **Objective.** Engineering Design. Physical Science. Forces and Interactions. Plan and investigate to provide evidence of the effects of balanced and unbalanced forces on the movement of an object.
- **Level of difficulty.** Easy.
- **Materials needed.** None.
- **Before the activity.** Place a large piece of white paper on the board. Have a black marker available for writing the children's responses. Go to the internet and type, "The knee for kids." Choose an age-appropriate website for the children.
- **Begin the activity by saying,** "Earlier, we noticed that the young girl fell on her knee."
- **Review the children's responses.** (The knee bone is hard. The knee bone sticks out. I can see my knee bone when I look at my leg.)
- **Introduce the activity.** "Today, we're going to learn some information about our knees."
  1. "What do you know about your knee?" Write down the children's comments. (I can feel that my knee bone is hard. The knee bone sticks out. I can see my knee bone when I look at my leg.). "Today, we're going to learn more about our knee."
  2. Go to the internet and type, "The knee for kids." Select the age-appropriate website you chose. Read and discuss the information with the children. Have them memorize the names of the bones.
- **Extension of the activity.** You could sing the song, "Head, Shoulders, Knees, and Toes," just for fun. In addition, Shel Silverstein has a poem about knees that the children might enjoy hearing. It's called "Stop Thief!"

Math

#1. Estimate how long the young child has been walking. Practice telling time on a clock.

- **Objective.** Measurement and Data. Work with time and money. Tell and write time from analog and digital clocks to the nearest five minutes, using "a.m." and "p.m."
- **Level of difficulty.** Moderate. (This task may take several days to complete.)
- **Materials needed.** Poster board, clock (see resource section), scissors, brads, and glue.
- **Before the activity.** Place a large piece of white paper on the board. Have a black marker available for writing the children's responses. Prepare all the materials.
- **Begin the activity by saying,** "Earlier, we wondered how many hours the young child had been walking."
- **Review the children's responses.** (Well, the sky is dark, so it's late. If the young child started walking home from school when the sun was shining, that means she has been walking many hours.)
- **Introduce the activity.** "Today, we're going to guess how long the young girl has been walking."
    1. Have the children relay how long they think the young girl has been walking. (I think she's been walking for three hours. I think she's been walking for four hours.)
    2. "We're going to make clocks to determine how many hours the young child might have been walking." (See resource section.) Give the children the clock and clock's hands page. Have them glue this page to a piece of heavy poster board and let this dry.
    3. Have the children carefully cut around the clock and clock's hands. Tell them to carefully poke a hole with their pencil in the center of the clock. There's a dot at this location. Have them

do the same thing for the clock's hands. Give each child a long brad and have them put the brad through the clock's hands. The minute hand should be on the top. Have them put the brad through the center of the clock and fold the flaps back on the back side of the clock. Have them write their name on the back side of the clock.

- **Extension of the activity.** Give examples of various times that the young child might leave school. You might ask, "If the young child left school at 2:00 p.m., how many hours would it take until the sky gets dark?" This, of course, depends on the area, but give examples that would apply for the local location. Allow the children to practice with each other, giving different start and ending times. Here are a few examples:

- If the young child left school at 1:30 p.m., and it gets dark at 6:00 p.m., how many hours and minutes have elapsed? (It's been four and a half hours.)

- If the young child left her house at 8:00 a.m., and it gets dark at 5:30 p.m., how many hours and minutes have elapsed? (It's been nine and a half hours.)

Wolf in the Snow illustration: Wolves moving toward the child

Direct the children's attention to the page where the wolves are moving toward the child. Encourage them to answer the following questions in complete sentences.

QUESTIONS

The brackets around the text indicate questions/instructions an adult should read to the children. Examples of how the children may answer the questions are included in parentheses.

- **[What do you see on this page?]**
- Have the children note how the wolves are approaching the young child who's curled up in an opening in the forest. **[What do you think is going to happen?]** (I think the wolves will scare the young child. I think the wolves will protect the young child.) Write the children's comments on a piece of paper and save this for later. See Art #2 and Writing #1.
- **[Has the young wolf been able to keep up with the pack?]** (Well, the young wolf is in the middle of the pack. He or she's not trailing behind the other wolves, so he or she must be rested enough to keep up with the other members of the pack.) See Science #1.
- **[Is this the original wolf pack that was looking for the young wolf? How do you know?]** (Well, the young wolf wouldn't be willing to join this pack if he or she wasn't familiar with the other wolves.) Write the children's comments on a piece of paper and save this for later. See Science #2.
- Note that the young child is surrounded by trees. **[Is this good protection for the young child?]** (The child found a spot that was

surrounded by trees. The trees gave her some protection from the wind and snow. It was a good decision to go to this location.) Write the children's comments on a piece of paper and save it for later. See Science #3.

- Point out that the young child seems close enough to hear the barking sounds and see the two lights off in the distance. **[Do you think she hears the barking? Do you think she sees the two lights?]** Write down the children's responses on a piece of paper and save this for later. (The young child might hear the barking sounds off in the distance. However, if she's soundly asleep, she might not hear the barking. If the young child is sleeping, the young child wouldn't see the two lights.) See Science #4 and #5.

- **[How far can sound travel?]** Write the children's estimates on a piece of paper and save it for later. (I think sound can travel a long way. I think sound can travel one hundred yards.). See Science #4.

- **[How far away can the light be seen?]** Write the children's responses on a piece of paper and save it for later. (I think the light can be seen for a long distance. I remember seeing the light from my dad's flashlight on a camping trip from a long distance away.) See Science #5.

- **[What are some dangers of falling asleep in the snow?]** Write the children's comments on a piece of paper and save this for later. (Falling asleep in the snow could be dangerous. An animal could attack the young child. The cold could cause frostbite.) See Science #6.

- **[Do you think the wolves are simply traveling in this direction, or do you think they're following the child? Why or why not?]** (I think the wolves are traveling toward the child to make sure she is safe. I think the wolves want to make sure the young child is found by someone.)

- **[Do you think the young wolf wants to help the young child?]** Write the children's comments on a piece of paper and save it for later. (Young Wolf: "The young child looks so cold. I want to help her.") See Art #1 and Writing #2.

- **[What do you think the people who are searching for the young child are thinking?]** (I wonder if she found shelter. I wonder if she is safe. I wonder if she is injured.) See Writing #3.

- **[How far do you think the young wolf can travel in a day?]** Write the children's comments on a piece of paper and save it for later. (The older wolves are used to walking/running long distances to track down their prey. The young wolf can't walk/run as far as the older wolves.) See Science #1 and Math #1.

- **[How are people rescued in various situations?]** (The fire department rescues people in buildings. The police rescue people in flooding situations. The coast guard rescues people in boats.) Write the children's comments on a piece of paper and save it for later. See Science #7.

ACTIVITIES

Art

#1. Create a mural showing the wolves approaching the young child in the trees.

- **Objective.** Creating. Anchor Standard #1. Generate and conceptualize artistic ideas and work. Investigate, Plan, Make. Brainstorm collaboratively multiple approaches to an art or design problem.

- **Level of difficulty.** Moderate. (This task may take several days to complete.)

- **Materials needed.** A large piece of paper for the children to create a mural, paints, paintbrushes, and pencils.
- **Before the activity.** Prepare the materials.
- **Introduce the activity by saying,** "Earlier, we discussed whether the young wolf wants to help the young child."
- **Review the children's responses.** (Young Wolf: "That young child looks so cold. I hope she wakes up.")
- **Introduce the activity.** "Today, we're going to create a group mural showing the wolves approaching the young child in the trees." Get a large piece of butcher paper and allow the children to pencil in their portion of the drawing. Once they're satisfied with their drawing, allow them to paint the mural. This can be done one or two children at a time. Have paints available for them to use. You might want to put down a piece of paper to protect the floor. Have the children put on old shirts when they paint the mural.

#2. Make a small figure of the young child.

- **Objective.** Connecting. Anchor Standard #10. Synthesize and relate knowledge and personal experiences to make art. Synthesize. Create art that tells a story about a life experience.
- **Level of difficulty.** Moderate. (This task may take several days to complete.)
- **Materials needed.** Squares of red and white felt, polyester fiberfill, fabric glue, and markers.
- **Before the activity.** Place a large piece of white paper on the board. Have a black marker available for writing the children's responses. Prepare the materials.
- **Introduce the activity.** "Earlier, we wondered how the young child could get some protection from the weather conditions and the wind. What do you think?" Write the children's responses on a piece of paper and save this for later.

- **Review the children's responses.** (I think the trees would give the young child some protection. Wind travels through the trees, so I don't think they'd give much protection.)
- **Introduce the activity.** "Today, we're going to create a small figure of the young child. This figure will be placed inside a coffee container, and we'll use a hair dryer to see if the outside of the can gives the figure some protection." Direct the children to cut out two coat sections (the front and back sections) for the young child. (See resource section. Reduce the image on a copy machine.) Then guide them through the remainder of the steps: Cut out a small circular "face" from the white felt. Make a face on the white felt using markers. Glue the front coat section to the back coat section, leaving the bottom portion open. Let this dry. Carefully fill the coat with small pieces of polyester fiberfill. When the figure is filled, gently glue the bottom portions together. Let this dry. Glue on the face.

Writing

#1. Engage in a writing experience.

- **Objective.** Writing Standards. Text Types and Purposes. Write opinion pieces on topics or texts, supporting a point of view with reasons. Introduce the topic or text they are writing about, state an opinion, and create an organizational structure that lists reasons.
- **Level of difficulty.** Moderate. (This task may take several days to complete.)
- **Materials needed.** Lined paper, pencils, white construction paper, crayons, paints, paintbrushes, and colored pencils.
- **Before the activity.** Place a large piece of white paper on the board. Have a black marker available for writing the children's responses.

- **Begin the activity by saying,** "Earlier, we noticed the wolves were approaching the young child in the forest. We discussed what we thought might happen."
- **Review the children's responses.** (I think the wolves will scare the young child. I think the wolves will protect the young child.)
- **Introduce the activity.** "Today, you're going to choose one of the wolves and write what you think that wolf might be thinking/saying."
  1. Write the children's comments on a piece of paper. (Dark wolf in the background: "I wonder if this young child is wearing enough clothes to keep her warm." Young Wolf: "I know how tired the young child is, because she carried me a long distance." Wolf in the front: "This young child is very kind. She helped the youngest member of our pack.")
  2. Have the children write their favorite comment(s) on a piece of lined paper. If they want to write their own sentence, be available to help them sound out the correct spelling of the words. The children might enjoy recreating this picture. Give them a piece of white construction paper, crayons, colored pencils, or paints to complete their drawing. Attach their comments to the drawing.

#2. Imagine and write about whether the young wolf would like to help the young child.

- **Objective.** Writing Standards. Text Types and Purposes. Write opinion pieces on topics or texts, supporting a point of view with reasons. Introduce the topic or text they are writing about, state an opinion, and create an organizational structure that lists reasons.
- **Level of difficulty.** Moderate. (This task may take several days to complete.)
- **Materials needed.** Lined paper and pencils.
- **Before the activity.** Place a large piece of white paper on the board. Have a black marker available for writing the children's responses.

- **Begin the activity by saying,** "Earlier, we discussed whether we thought the young wolf wanted to help the young child." Write the children's comments.

- **Review the children's responses.** (She's probably so tired she can't walk any further. I think it would be dangerous for her to fall asleep in the snow. That young child looks so cold.)

- **Introduce the activity.** "Today, we're going to write one comment the young wolf might want to express." Write the children's comments on a piece of paper. (That young child looks so cold. I want to help her. If I stand near her and howl, she'll wake up!) Have the children write their favorite comment(s) on a piece of lined paper. If they'd like to write their own sentence(s), be available to help them sound out the words. Put the children's comments around the group mural painted earlier. (See Art #1.)

#3. Imagine and write what the adult and dog searching for the young child might be thinking.

- **Objective.** Writing Standards. Text Types and Purposes. Write opinion pieces on topics or texts, supporting a point of view with reasons. Introduce the topic or text they are writing about, state an opinion, and create an organizational structure that lists reasons.

- **Level of difficulty.** Moderate. (This task may take several days to complete.)

- **Materials needed.** Lined paper and pencils.

- **Before the activity.** Place a large piece of white paper on the board. Have a black marker available for writing the children's responses.

- **Begin the activity by saying,** "Earlier, we discussed what the adult and dog who were searching for the young child might be thinking." Write down the children's comments.

- **Review the children's responses.** (Adult: "The young child has been gone an awfully long time. I really hope she found shelter."

Dog: "My best friend is out in the snow all by herself. I can hardly wait to have her come home. I want to sit on the rug with her.")

- **Introduce the activity.** "Today, we're going to create some conversation bubbles to relay their comments" (see resource section). (Adult: "The young child has been gone a long time. I really hope she found shelter." Dog: "My best friend is out in the snow all by herself. I can hardly wait to have her come home. I want to sit on the rug with her.") Have the children write their favorite comment(s) on a conversation bubble. If they'd like to write their own sentence(s), be available to help them sound out the words. Put the children's comments on the bulletin board.

Science

#1. Learn how far wolves can travel in a day.

- **Objective.** Life Science. Structure, Function, and Information Processing. Read texts and use media to determine patterns in behavior of parents and offspring that help offspring survive.
- **Level of difficulty.** Easy.
- **Materials needed.** Lined paper and pencils.
- **Before the activity.** Place a large piece of white paper on the board. Have a black marker available for writing the children's responses. Go to the internet and type, "How far can wolves travel in a day?" Choose an age-appropriate website for the children. Read and discuss this information with the children.
- **Begin the activity by saying,** "Earlier, we discussed whether the young wolf was able to keep up with the pack."
- **Review the children's responses.** (I think the young wolf will have trouble keeping up with the pack because he or she's so much smaller. The young wolf hasn't developed the stamina the older wolves have developed.)

- **Introduce the activity.** "Today, we're going learn how far wolves can travel in a day. We're also going to discuss why the young wolf had difficulty keeping up with the wolf pack."

  1. "Why do you think it would be more difficult for the young wolf to keep up?" (Well, he/ she's much smaller than the other wolves. He or she has been walking a long way. The young wolf hasn't developed the stamina the older wolves have developed.) Write the children's comments on a piece of paper. Review their comments.

  2. Go to the internet and type, "How far can wolves travel in a day"? Select the age-appropriate website you chose. Read and discuss this information with the children. Have the children write one fact they learned from the website on a piece of lined paper.

#2. Learn how to identify wolves by their size and markings.

- **Objective.** Life Science. Structure, Function, and Information Processing. Read texts and use media to determine patterns in behavior of parents and offspring that help offspring survive.
- **Level of difficulty.** Easy.
- **Materials needed.** Lined paper and pencils.
- **Before the activity.** Place a large piece of white paper on the board. Have a black marker available for writing the children's responses. Go to the internet and type, "How to recognize various wolves by their size and markings." Choose an age-appropriate website for the children.
- **Begin the activity by saying,** "Earlier, we discussed whether this was the original wolf pack that we saw earlier in the book."
- **Review the children's responses.** (Well, the young wolf wouldn't be willing to join this pack if he or she wasn't familiar with the other wolves. I think this is the same pack that was looking for the young wolf.)

- **Introduce the activity.** "Today, we're going to discuss whether this was the original wolf pack we saw earlier in the book."
  1. "How could you determine if this was the same pack?" (Well, the young wolf wouldn't be willing to join this pack if he or she wasn't familiar with the other wolves. I think this is the pack that was looking for the young wolf.) Write the children's comments on a piece of paper. (I think this is the same wolf pack because the size of the wolves is similar. I think this is the same wolf pack because the markings on the wolves are similar.)
  2. Go to the internet and type, "How to recognize various wolves by their size and markings." Select the age-appropriate website you chose. Read and discuss this information with them. Have the children write their favorite comment or their favorite fact about wolf markings.

#3. Determine whether the trees provided some protection for the young child.

- **Objective.** Engineering Design. Earth and Space Science. Weather and Climate. Make a claim about the merit of a design solution that reduces the impacts of a weather-related hazard.
- **Level of Difficulty.** Easy.
- **Materials Needed.** Small figure of the young child (see Art #2), large coffee can, hair dryer, cardboard, glue, and heavy books.
- **Before the activity.** Place a large piece of white paper on the board. Have a black marker available for writing the children's responses. Go to the internet and type, "Trees as protection in the forest." Choose an age-appropriate website for the children.
- **Begin the activity by saying,** "Earlier, we observed that the young child was surrounded by trees." Do you think these trees provided protection for the young child?

270

- **Review the children's responses.** (The child found a spot that was surrounded by trees. The trees gave her some protection from the wind and snow. It was a good decision to go to this location.)
- **Introduce the activity.** "Today, we're going to discuss whether the trees provided some protection for the young child."

1. "Do you think these trees provided protection for the young child?" Write down and review the children's comments. (The child found a spot that was surrounded by trees. The trees gave her some protection from the wind and snow. I think it was a good decision to go to this location.) Go to the internet and type, "Trees as protection in the forest." Select the age-appropriate website you chose. Read and discuss this information with them.

2. To demonstrate the protective ability of the trees, glue the closed end of a large coffee container to a heavy piece of cardboard. Let this dry. Place several heavy books at the ends of the cardboard to hold it down. Place the small figure of the child they made earlier inside the coffee container (see Art #2). Leave the lid off so the children can observe what happens to the sock figure inside the coffee container.

3. Using a blow dryer or small fan, blow directly in front of the coffee can. Have the children observe the reaction of the wind on the small figure inside the container. Ask the children if the figure moved inside the container. "Was there a little movement or a lot of movement? What could you say about the protection of the trees?" (Well, the trees gave the young child some protection.) Have the children tell a friend what they observed inside the container.

#4. Discuss whether the young child can hear the barking sounds of the dog. Discover how far sound travels.

- **Objective.** Physical Science. Waves. Light and Sound. Plan and conduct investigations to provide evidence that vibrating materials can make sound and that sound can make materials vibrate.
- **Level of difficulty.** Moderate. (This task may take several days to complete.)
- **Materials needed.** Lined paper and pencils.
- **Before the activity.** Place a large piece of white paper on the board. Have a black marker available for writing the children's responses. Go to the internet and type, "How far does sound travel?" Choose an age-appropriate website for the children.
- **Begin the activity by saying,** "Earlier, we observed that the young child is close enough to hear the barking sounds of the dog. We wondered if the child might hear these sounds off in the distance."
- **Review the children's responses.** (If the young child was sound asleep, she might not hear the barking. If the young child was merely resting, she might hear the dog barking in the distance.)
- **Introduce the activity.** "Today, we're going to discuss whether we think the young child can hear the barking sounds of the dog."
  1. "We wondered if the child might hear these sounds off in the distance." Write down and review the children's comments. (If the young child was sound asleep, she might not hear the barking. If the young child was merely resting, she might hear the dog barking in the distance.)
  2. Go to the internet and type, "How far does sound travel?" Select the age-appropriate website you chose. Read and discuss this information with the children. Have them write one sentence about the speed of sound.

272

#5. Learn how far light travels.

- **Objective.** Physical Science. Waves. Light and Sound. Make observations to construct an evidence-based account that objects in darkness can be seen only when illuminated.
- **Level of difficulty.** Moderate. (This task may take several days to complete.)
- **Materials needed.** Lined paper and pencils.
- **Before the activity.** Place a large piece of white paper on the board. Have a black marker available for writing the children's responses. Go to the internet and type, "How far can light travel?" Choose an age-appropriate website for the children.
- **Begin the activity by saying,** "Earlier, we discussed how far we thought light could travel."
- **Review the children's responses.** (I think the light can travel twenty yards. I think light can travel far.)
- **Introduce the activity.** "Today, we're going to find out how far light travels." Write down and review the children's comments. Go to the internet and type, "How far can light travel?" Select the age-appropriate website you chose. Read and discuss this information with them. Have them write one sentence that relays how far light can travel.

#6. Discuss and learn the dangers of falling asleep in the snow.

- **Objective.** Life Science. Interdependent Relationships in Ecosystems, Animals, Plants, and their Environment. Make a claim about the merit of a solution to a problem caused when the environment changes and the types of plants and animals that live there may change.
- **Level of difficulty.** Easy.
- **Materials needed.** None.

- **Before the activity.** Place a large piece of white paper on the board. Have a black marker available for writing the children's responses. Go to the internet and type, "What are the dangers of falling asleep in the snow?" Choose an age-appropriate website for the children. Go to the internet and type, "What are the dangers of frostbite?" Choose an age-appropriate website for the children.
- **Begin the activity by saying,** "Earlier, we discussed the possible dangers of falling asleep in the snow."
- **Review the children's responses.** (Falling asleep in the snow is dangerous. An animal could attack the young child. The cold could cause frostbite.)
- **Introduce the activity.** "Today, we're going to find out about the dangers of falling asleep in the snow." Go to the internet and type, "What are the dangers of falling asleep in the snow?" Select the age-appropriate website you chose. Read and discuss this information with the children. Go to the internet and type, "What are the dangers of frostbite?" Select the age-appropriate website you chose. Read and discuss this information with the children. Have them relay to a friend one important fact they learned from the website.

#7. Learn about search and rescue operations.

- **Objective.** Life Science. Interdependent Relationships in Ecosystems, Animals, Plants, and their Environment. Make a claim about the merit of a solution to a problem caused when the environment changes and the types of plants and animals that live there may change.
- **Level of Difficulty.** Moderate. (This task may take several days to complete.)
- **Materials Needed.** Lined paper and pencils.
- **Before the activity.** Place a large piece of white paper on the board. Have a black marker available for writing the children's responses.

Go to the internet and type, "Search and rescue." Choose an age-appropriate website for the children.

- **Begin the activity by saying,** "Earlier, we discussed how people are rescued in various situations."

- **Review the children's responses.** (The fire department rescues people in buildings. The police rescue people in flooding situations. The coast guard rescues people in boats.)

- **Introduce the activity.** "Today, we're going to learn about search and rescue operations."

  1. Write and review what the children know about these three groups.

  2. Go to the internet and type, "Search and rescue." Select the age-appropriate website you chose. Read and discuss this information with the children. Have them write one fact they learned from the website.

- **Extension of the activity.** As an additional educational experience, invite a search and rescue team from your local area to visit the children.

Math

#1. Determine how long it takes the children to walk one mile. Compare this to how far a wolf can travel in a day.

- **Objective.** Measurement and Data. Represent and interpret data. Draw a picture graph and a bar graph (with single-unit scale) to represent a data set with up to four categories. Solve simple, put-together, take-apart, and compare problems using information presented in a bar graph.

- **Level of difficulty.** Moderate. (This task may take several days to complete.)

- **Materials needed.** Measuring instruments or Google Earth, three-by-five-inch cards for each child, pencils, and a stopwatch.
- **Before the activity.** Place a large piece of white paper on the board. Have a black marker available for writing the children's responses. Go to the internet and type, "How far can wolves travel in a day?" Choose an age-appropriate website for the children.
- **Begin the activity by saying,** "Earlier, we discussed how far we thought the young wolf could travel in a day."
- **Review the children's responses.** (I think the young wolf could travel five miles a day. I think the young wolf could travel ten miles a day.)
- **Introduce the activity.** "Today, we're going to see how long it takes us to walk one mile."
  1. Write and review the children's estimates. Take the children out to a field area and use a meter stick or similar measuring device to measure one mile. One meter is three feet and three inches. A mile is 5,280 feet.
  2. Once you've measured off the distance, allow each child to walk one mile. Have an older child or adult use a stopwatch to time each child. Write the child's name and time on a three-by-five-inch card and save these for later.
  3. Based on this information, calculate how many miles they could travel in a designated time period. (For example, if Kelly could travel 1 mile in x minutes, she could travel 2 miles in x minutes.) Discuss how this compares to how far a wolf can travel in a day. "A wolf can travel 30 to 45 miles in a day, or an average of 37.5 miles a day."

Wolf in the Snow illustration: Wolves surrounding the young child

Direct the children's attention to the page where you see the wolves surrounding the young child. Encourage them to answer the following questions in complete sentences.

QUESTIONS

The brackets around the text indicate questions/instructions an adult should read to the children. Examples of how the children may answer the questions are included in parentheses.

- **[What do you see on this page?]**
- **[Why do you think the wolves followed and surrounded the young child?]** Write the children's responses on a piece of paper and save this for later. (The wolves followed the young child because they smelled her. They followed her because they wanted to make sure she was safe). See Science #1 and Math #1.
- **[Who is closest to the young child?]** (It looks like the young wolf is the closest.) **[Why do you think the young wolf came so close to the young child?]** Write the children's comments on a piece of paper and save this for later. (The young wolf had been carried a long way by the young child, so he or she feels safe being near her.) See Writing #1.
- **[Do you think the wolves are protecting the young child? Why or why not?]** Write the children's comments on a piece of paper and save this for later. (Young Wolf: "This young child carried me an awfully long distance. I want to make sure she is safely found." Other Wolves: "If we surround the young child, it will generate some heat.") See Art #1.

- **[Would you describe the wolf pack's actions as unusual?]** (The wolves surrounding the young child to protect her would be considered unusual. Most wolves surround their prey to attack it.)
- Have the children look at the young wolf on the bottom panel of the left-hand side of the page. **[Do you think the young wolf will lick the young child? Why do you think he or she might do that?]** Write the children's comments on a piece of paper and save this for later. (The young wolf wants the young child to wake up. The young wolf wants the young child to know that he or she is nearby.) See Science #3.
- **[Do you think the young wolf's presence and body heat will wake the child? Why or why not?]** See Science #2.
- Have the children look at how the young child is rolled up in a ball. **[Why do you think she did that?]** Write the children's comments on a piece of paper and save this for later. (She wants to keep the warm air close to her body for warmth.) See Writing #2.
- **[What is our normal temperature?]** Write the children's comments on a piece of paper and save this for later. Using a digital thermometer, take the children's temperature. Write each child's name and individual temperature on a card. Tell them their temperatures will vary from person to person and will also vary according to what physical exercise they've done. See Science #4 and Math #2.
- **[How can we tell from looking at the picture that the young child is cold?]** (There's "fog" coming out of the young child's face covering. There are squiggly lines above the child indicating that she is shivering.) See Art #2 and Writing #3.
- Direct the children to look at the right-hand side of the page. **[What are the wolves doing?]** (They're howling.)
- **[How many wolves are howling?]** (It looks like four wolves are howling.)

278

- Note that one wolf is not howling but has his or her face turned toward the barking. **[Would you say this wolf was observant? Why or why not?]**
- **[Do you think the young child will wake up with all the howling? Why or why not?]**
- Note that it appears the barking is getting closer. **[Do you think the wolves will run away if they see the dog?]**
- **[Do you think the people approaching the young child, as well as the wolves, will be concerned? Why or why not?]**
- **[What two sounds are shown on this page?]** (Howling and barking sounds. HOOOWWL and bark. See Writing #4 and #5.

ACTIVITIES

Art

#1. Create a diorama showing the young child in the snow, surrounded by the wolves.

- **Objective.** Presenting. Anchor Standard #5. Develop and refine artistic technique and work for presentation. Analyze. Distinguish between different materials or artistic techniques for preparing artwork for presentation.
- **Level of difficulty.** Challenging. (This task may take several days to complete.)
- **Materials needed.** Shoebox with a lid, pencils, poster board, scissors, paints, paintbrushes, crayons, colored pencils, glue, clay, trees (see resource section), floral foam, wolves, red and white felt, polyester fiberfill, markers, and cotton balls.
- **Before the activity.** Place a large piece of white paper on the board. Have a black marker available for writing the children's responses.

- **Begin the activity by saying,** "Earlier, we discussed whether we thought the young wolf was protecting the young child."
- **Review the children's responses.** (Young Wolf: "This young child carried me a long distance. I want to make sure she is found. If we surround the young child, it will generate some heat.")
- **Introduce the activity.** "Today, we're going to create a diorama showing the young child lying in the snow, with the wolves surrounding her." Write and review the children's comments about whether the wolves were trying to protect the young child.

1. Ask the children to bring in a shoebox with a lid. Have them write their names on the bottom of their boxes. Have them decide where they want to cut out the peephole. Have them draw a small circle at this location and, with the help of an older student or adult, poke the hole in the chosen area. Then have the children carefully cut out a small hole. Have them put the lid on their shoebox, allowing them to look inside their diorama. Tell them that they should frequently look inside the shoebox to see if the young child, wolves, and trees are in view.

2. Have the children paint the inside of their shoebox to resemble a forest area. Let this dry.

3. Have the children make the figure of the young child. Give them two small pieces of red felt. Have them draw the coat onto a piece of paper before they cut it out, to make sure it's the right size. Have them place the paper pattern onto the red felt and carefully cut it out. Have the children glue the outside edges together, leaving the bottom portion open. Let dry. Fill the figure with polyester fiberfill and glue the bottom edge. Let that dry. Cut out a small circular face from the white felt and draw her face with markers. Glue the face to the top of the coat. Let that dry. Glue the figure of the young child in the center of the shoebox. Let it dry.

4. Have the children draw the five wolves on pieces of posterboard. Have them color, paint, or use colored pencils to shade each wolf. Carefully cut a circle around each wolf. Glue each wolf into some clay or floral foam, so they'll stand up. Let that dry. Glue the wolves around the young child and let these dry.

5. Give the children the trees from the resource section. Have the children cut a circle around the trees. Have them glue the trees onto some poster board to make them stronger. Let these dry. Carefully cut around each tree. Have the children color, paint, or use colored pencils to shade the trees. Each matching set of trees will have one tree with a line drawn in the center. Have the children cut along this line. It will be cut close to the top. The cut portion will slide over the top of the second tree. Glue these two tree portions into the floral foam. Drip glue down the center of the trees. The children might have to gently press the trees until they're stuck together. Let dry. Have them glue the trees that are stuck in the floral foam around the young child and wolves.

6. Give each child several cotton balls. Have them gently pull these apart and glue them to the bottom of the shoebox. When the entire bottom portion is covered, let the cotton balls dry. Put the lid on the top of the shoebox and allow the children to peek into their peephole. They may want to carefully exchange shoeboxes with their friend so they can see what their friend created. Place the dioramas near the children's comments about whether the wolves were protecting the young child or not.

#2. Use an illustrative technique to show that the young child was cold in the snow.

- **Objective.** Creating. Anchor Standard #3. Refine and complete artistic work. Reflect, refine, and continue. Elaborate visual information by adding details in a piece of artwork to enhance emerging meaning.

- **Level of difficulty.** Moderate. (This task may take several days to complete.)
- **Materials needed.** White construction paper, pencils, paints, paintbrushes, crayons, and colored pencils.
- **Before the activity.** Prepare the materials.
- **Begin the activity by saying,** "Earlier, we observed and discussed how the illustrator showed that the young child was cold."
- **Review the children's responses.** (The illustrator used squiggly lines around the young child to show that she was shivering.)
- **Introduce the activity.** "Today, we're going to use an illustrative technique to show that the young child was cold in the snow. We noticed that there were squiggly lines draw around the child on the bottom panel of the page. We're going to draw the young child and use this illustrative technique to show that the young child is cold in the snow."

Writing

#1. Reenact a scene in the book showing the young child lying in the snow, with the young wolf close to her.

- **Objective.** Speaking and Listening. Presentation of Knowledge and Ideas. Tell a story or recount an experience with appropriate facts and relevant descriptive details, speaking audibly in coherent sentences.
- **Level of Difficulty.** Easy.
- **Materials Needed.** None.
- **Before the activity.** Place a large piece of white paper on the board. Have a black marker available for writing the children's responses.

- **Begin the activity by saying,** "Earlier, we discussed why we thought the young wolf came so close to the young child." Write and review the children's comments.

- **Review the children's responses.** (The young wolf had been carried a long way by the young child, so he or she felt safe being near her. The young wolf knew that the young girl was his or her friend.)

- **Introduce the activity.** "Today, we're going to reenact a scene from the book showing the young child lying in the snow, with the young wolf close to her. We'll pretend that one of you is the child lying in the snow, while the other one will pretend to be the young wolf standing near her. The 'young wolf' will explain to the audience why he or she decided to come close to the young child."

1. Have one child roll up and lay on the floor. Have another child, the "young wolf" stand close to the child on the floor and explain why the wolf chose to come so close. (Young Wolf: "I'm right next to you. Wake up! It's very cold out here. You should try to walk a little further. Don't be afraid. My family is surrounding you. We'll protect you until someone comes." Young Wolf: "I'll lick your face to keep you warm. My body heat will help to protect you.")

#2. Discuss why the young child is curled up in a ball in the forest.

- **Objective.** Speaking and Listening Standards. Comprehension and Collaboration. Recount or describe key ideas or details from a text read aloud or information presented orally or through other media.

- **Level of difficulty.** Moderate. (This task may take several days to complete.)

- **Materials needed.** Lined paper and pencils.

- **Before the activity.** Place a large piece of white paper on the board. Have a black marker available for writing the children's responses.

- **Begin the activity by saying,** "Earlier, we discussed why the young child might be curled up into a ball." Write and review the children's comments.
- **Review the children's responses.** (She wants to keep the warm air close to her body for warmth.)
- **Introduce the activity.** "Today, we're going to discuss why the young child is curled up in a ball in the forest." Write and review the children's comments. (It's very cold outside, so the young girl is trying to keep warm. She's curled up to keep the warm air near her body.) "What would you do differently if you were in this situation?" (I would dig down near a tree for more protection. I would pull off some pine branches to sleep on. I would try to create a snow barrier to protect me from the wind.) Have the children choose their favorite sentence(s) and write it on a piece of lined paper.

#3. Discuss and draw an illustrative technique that's developed on this page.

- **Objective.** Reading Standards for Literature. Integration of Knowledge and Ideas. Use information gained from the illustrations and words in a print or digital text to demonstrate understanding of its characters, setting, or plot.
- **Level of difficulty.** Moderate. (This task may take several days to complete.)
- **Materials needed.** White construction paper, pencils, crayons, paints, paintbrushes, colored pencils, and lined paper.
- **Before the activity.** Place a large piece of white paper on the board. Have a black marker available for writing down the children's responses.
- **Begin the activity by saying,** "Earlier, we looked at the picture on the bottom left-hand side of the page and said we thought the young child was cold. We noticed that there was 'fog' coming from

the young child's face. We also noticed that the illustrator had drawn squiggly lines surrounding the body indicating that she was cold and shivering."

- **Review the children's responses.** (The squiggly lines really are effective. It makes it seem like the young child is really shivering. The "fog" coming out of her mouth looks real.)

- **Introduce the activity.** "Today, we're going to pretend that we're the illustrator of this page and draw the squiggly lines and 'fog' around the child." Have the children draw a picture of the young child lying in the snow, with the "fog" and squiggly lines around the child. Then have them write one sentence about how the "fog" and the squiggly lines make the drawing come to life. (I think the squiggly lines really make a difference. It makes it seem like the young child is really shivering. The "fog" coming out of her mouth looks real.)

#4. Create an acrostic poem, using the words "howl" and "bark."

- **Objective.** Reading Standards. Range of Reading and Level of Text Complexity. Actively engage in group reading activities with purposes and understanding.

- **Level of difficulty.** Moderate to challenging. (This task may take several days to complete.)

- **Materials needed.** White construction paper, pencils, crayons, paints, paintbrushes, colored pencils, and lined paper.

- **Before the activity.** Place a large piece of white paper on the board. Have a black marker available for writing the children's responses.

- **Begin the activity by saying,** "Earlier, we discussed that we knew at least two sounds could be heard on the right-hand side of the page." Write and review the children's comments.

- **Review the children's responses.** (A howling sound and a barking sound).

- **Introduce the activity.** "Today, we're going to create two class acrostic poems with the words 'howl' and 'bark.' In an acrostic poem, the first letter of each new line spells out the word (in this case, howl and bark)." Here is an example of what the completed poems may look like:

H O O O W W L
Horrible weather
Often occurs in this area.
Opening the sky to snow.
Only the strongest can survive,
Winter.
When the temperatures go down,
Low.

B A R K
Barking in the background,
Around every tree.
Rushing toward the child,
Keeping their fingers crossed.

Have the children think of things that could be written for each letter. Then have them copy the final class acrostic poem onto a piece of lined paper. If the children would like to try to create their own poems, be available to help them sound out the words. Allow them to draw a picture that depicts their final poem.

#5. Create an acrostic poem, using sounds that might be heard in the forest.

- **Objective.** Reading Standards. Range of Reading and Level of Text Complexity. Actively engage in group reading activities with purpose and understanding.
- **Level of difficulty.** Moderate to challenging. (This task may take several days to complete.)
- **Materials needed.** White construction paper, pencils, crayons, paints, paintbrushes, colored pencils, and lined paper.

- **Before the activity.** Place a large piece of white paper on the board. Have a black marker available for writing the children's responses.
- **Begin the activity by saying,** "Earlier, we created a class acrostic poem using the words 'howl' and 'bark.' Today, we're going to make a list of sounds we might hear in the forest and then write an acrostic poem."
- **Review the children's responses.** (An owl hoots, an elk bugles, a squirrel screams, a fox yelps, and crunching can be heard in the forest.)
- **Introduce the activity.** "Today, we're going to make a list of the sounds we might hear in the forest and create a class acrostic poem."
  1. Write and review the children's responses on a piece of paper. (An owl hoots, an elk bugles, a squirrel screams, a fox yelps, and crunching can be heard in the forest.) Keep this paper in a location where they can add additional forest sounds.
  2. "In an acrostic poem, the first letters of each new line spell out the word (e.g., hoot, screams, yelps, or crunch)."
  3. Have the children think of things that could be written that begin with each letter of the word(s) they chose to use for the poem(s). Then have them copy the final class acrostic poem onto a piece of lined paper. If the children would like to try to create their own poems, be available to help them sound out the words. Allow them to draw a picture that depicts their final poem.

Here are two examples of acrostic poems using forest sounds:

C R U N C H	H O O T
Crushing leaves,	Horned owl,
Rippling on the ground.	Only just arrived.
Under a light snowfall,	Over the night sky,
Newly fallen,	Thinking of mice!
Crisp winds.	
Howling.	

Science

#1. Discuss why the wolves followed and surrounded the young child. Learn how the wolves knew where to find her.

- **Objective.** Life Science. Interdependent Relationships in Ecosystems, Animals, Plants, and their Environment. Use a model to represent the relationship between the needs of different plants and animals (including humans) and the places they live.
- **Level of difficulty.** Easy.
- **Materials needed.** None.
- **Before the activity.** Place a large piece of white paper on the board. Have a black marker available for writing the children's responses. Go to the internet and type, "How do wolves track?" Choose an age-appropriate website for the children.
- **Begin the activity by saying,** "Earlier, we discussed why the wolves followed and surrounded the young child."
- **Review the children's responses.** (The wolves found the young child because they smelled her. They found her because they wanted to make sure she was safe.)
- **Introduce the activity.** "Today, we're going to discuss whether a wolf or a person has a better sense of smell. We'll also discuss why we think the wolves followed and surrounded the young child. Finally, we'll discuss how the wolves knew where to find her."
  1. "Raise your hand if you think wolves have a better sense of smell than humans." Write the number of children who raised their hand on the board. Tell the children they can only make one choice—either the wolves or the humans have a better sense of smell. "Raise your hand if you think people have a better sense of smell." Write the number of children who raised their hand on the board. Keep these two numbers for the math activity below. Combined, the numbers should equal the total

number of children in class. Go to the internet and type, "Does a wolf or a human have a better sense of smell?" Choose an age-appropriate website for the children. Read and discuss the information with them. "A wolf has a sense of smell that is one hundred times greater than a human's sense of smell." (See Math #1.)

2. "We also wondered why the wolves followed and surrounded the young child. Write and review the children's comments." (The wolves found the young child because they smelled her, and they wanted to make sure she was safe.)

3. "We're also going to discuss how the wolves knew where to find the young child." Go to the internet and type, "How do wolves track?" Select the age-appropriate website you chose. Read and discuss this information with them. "Wolves have a great sense of smell, so they were able to follow the scent of the young child. They could also smell her footprints."

#2. Discuss whether the wolf's presence would wake the young child. Learn about shivering in wintry weather.

- **Objective.** Life Science. Interdependent Relationships in Ecosystems, Animals, Plants, and their Environment. Use a model to represent the relationship between the needs of different plants and animals (including humans) and the places they live.
- **Level of difficulty.** Easy.
- **Materials needed.** None.
- **Before the activity.** Place a large piece of white paper on the board. Have a black marker available for writing the children's responses. Go to the internet and type, "What causes shivering?" Choose an age-appropriate website for the children.
- **Begin the activity by saying,** "Earlier, we discussed whether the wolf's presence would wake the young child."

- **Review the children's responses.** (The young child is so tired she doesn't know the wolf is nearby. I think she might wake up if the young wolf continues to lick her face.)
- **Introduce the activity.** "Today, we're going to discuss whether the wolf's presence would wake the young child."

    1. Write and review the children's responses. (I think the young child is so tired she doesn't know the wolf is nearby. I think she might wake up if the young wolf licks her face.) "We thought the young child must be cold, because she is rolled up in a ball trying to keep warm." (There's snow on the ground. There's "fog" coming out of her mouth. She's lying directly on the snow.) "You can see her breath in the picture. There are squiggly lines near the young child, indicating that she is shivering."

    2. Go to the internet and type, "What causes shivering?" Select the age-appropriate website you chose. Read and discuss the information with the children. "The muscles respond to the wintry weather." Have the children relay their favorite fact to a friend.

#3. Discuss why the young wolf might lick the young child's face. Learn about the body temperature of a wolf.

- **Objective.** Life Science. Interdependent Relationships in Ecosystems, Animals, Plants, and their Environment. Use observations to describe patterns of what plants and animals (including humans) need to survive.
- **Level of difficulty.** Easy.
- **Materials needed.** None.
- **Before the activity.** Place a large piece of white paper on the board. Have a black marker available for writing the children's responses. Go to the internet and type, "Body temperature of a wolf." Choose an age-appropriate website for the children.

- **Begin the activity by saying,** "Earlier, we discussed why we thought the young wolf might lick the young child."
- **Review the children's responses.** (The young wolf wants the young child to wake up. The young wolf wants the young child to know he or she is nearby.)
- **Introduce the activity.** "Today, we're going to discuss why the young wolf might lick the young child's face." Write and review the children's comments. "We'll also learn about the body temperature of a wolf."
  1. "Do you think the warmth of the young wolf's tongue would wake the young child?" Write the children's responses on a piece of paper. Go to the internet and type, "Body temperature of a wolf." Select the age-appropriate website you chose. Read and discuss this information with the children. "The average body temperature of a wolf is ninety-eight point six degrees (98.6°F.)."
  2. Have the children gently feel their own tongues with their fingers. Does their tongue feel warm? If they were in a very cold area, do you think the young wolf's tongue would feel warm? Have the children relay to a friend whether they think the wolf's tongue would be warm on her face.

#4. Learn about the normal body temperature for humans.

- **Objective.** Life Science. Interdependent Relationships in Ecosystems, Animals, Plants, and their Environment. Use observations to describe patterns of what plants and animals (including humans) need to survive.
- **Level of difficulty.** Moderate. (This task may take several days to complete.)
- **Materials needed.** Three-by-five-inch cards, pencils, and a digital thermometer.
- **Before the activity.** Place a large piece of white paper on the board. Have a black marker available for writing the children's responses.

Go to the internet and type, "What is the normal body temperature for a human?" Choose an age-appropriate website for the children.

- **Begin the activity by saying,** "Earlier, we talked about the body temperature of the wolf. We learned the average body temperature of a wolf is ninety-eight point six degrees (98.6°F). Today, we'll learn about our body temperature."
- **Review the children's responses.** (I think our body temperature is ninety degrees [90°F]. I think our body temperature is one hundred degrees [100°F].)
- **Introduce the activity.** "Today, we'll learn about what the normal body temperature for humans is."

1. "Does anyone know what the normal body temperature is?" Write and review the children's responses. Tell the children that their individual body temperature may differ from their friends.
2. Go to the internet and type, "What is the normal body temperature for a human?" Choose an age-appropriate website for the children. Read and discuss the information with them.
3. Bring in a digital thermometer that can be used to measure each child's temperature. Make sure you use a thermometer sheath for each reading. Write each child's name and temperature on a three-by-five-inch card. Save these cards for the math lesson to follow. "We learned that the normal body temperature for a human is 98.6°F." (See Math #2.)

Math

#1. Discuss, review, and graph the results of this question. Do wolves or people have a better sense of smell?

- **Objective.** Measurement and Data. Represent and interpret data. Draw a picture graph and a bar graph (with single-unit scale) to represent a data set with up to four categories. Solve simple,

292

put-together, take-apart, and compare problems using information presented in a bar graph.

- **Level of difficulty.** Moderate. (This task may take several days to complete.)
- **Materials needed.** Graph paper, crayons, and pencils.
- **Before the activity.** Prepare the materials.
- **Begin the activity by saying,** "Earlier, we discussed why we thought the wolves followed and surrounded the young child." (The wolves followed the young child because they smelled her, and they wanted to make sure that she was safe.) "We also read and discussed how wolves use their sense of smell to track. Then we voted whether wolves or people could smell better."
- **Review the children's responses.** Six students thought the wolf had a better sense of smell. Three students thought that people had a better sense of smell.
- **Introduce the activity.** "Today, we're going to make a bar graph of our vote."
  1. Show various bar graphs and discuss what is shown on each graph. "The bar graph that we'll make will show that 6 children thought that the wolves could smell better, while 3 children thought that people could smell better."
  2. The bar graph should be labeled at the top. "Who can smell better, a wolf or a human?" Our voting results showed that 6 children thought that the wolves could smell better, while 3 children thought that people could smell better." Explain that the graph should have the number of people who voted listed on the left-hand side of the graph, and finally, it should have "Human" and "Wolf" written at the bottom of the graph.
  3. Give each child a piece of half-inch graph paper. Have them complete the bar graph.

  Here is an example of what their graphs should look like:

Who can smell better, a wolf or a human?

```
6 _____X_____
5 _____X_____
4 _____X_____
3 _____X_____X_____
2 _____X_____X_____
1 _____X_____X_____
0 _____
                Human              Wolf
```

#2. Verify a similar body temperature.

- **Objective.** Measurement and Data. Describe and compare measurable attributes. Describe measurable attributes of objects, such as length or weight. Describe several measurable attributes of a single object.

- **Level of difficulty.** Easy.

- **Materials needed.** None.

- **Before the activity.** Distribute the three-by-five-inch cards with the children's names and body temperatures written on them.

- **Begin the activity by saying,** "Earlier, we took our temperatures with a digital thermometer. You printed your name and temperature on the card. We discovered that our temperature may be slightly different from our friends.

- **Introduce the activity.** "Today, you're going to find people who have the same temperature as yours." Have the children hold up their card, circling the room to find other children who have the same temperature. Hopefully, every child will find a matching temperature/ group. Have them sit down in their group and discuss why they think their temperature isn't the same as other children's temperatures. (Body temperature varies depending on what people have done earlier, before their temperature is taken.)

> ### *Wolf in the Snow* illustration: An adult and dog approaching the young child with a flashlight
>
> Direct the children's attention to the page where the adult and dog are approaching the young child with a flashlight. Encourage them to answer the following questions in complete sentences.

QUESTIONS

The brackets around the text indicate questions/instructions an adult should read to the children. Examples of how the children may answer the questions are included in parentheses.

- **[What do you see on this page?]**
- **[Did the wolves move away from the young child as the light approached?]** (The wolves moved to the top of the hill.) See Art #1 and #2.
- **[How would you describe the child sitting in the snow?]** Write the children's responses on a piece of paper and save this for later. (The child looks very tired. The child looks scared. The child looks afraid.) See Writing #1.
- **[Do you think the child can stand up?]** Write the children's comments on a piece of paper and save this for later. See Science #1.
- **[Why does the child have her eyes covered?]** Write the children's responses on a piece of paper and save this for later. (The bright light bothered the young child. I don't think the young child could see who was coming, because the light was so bright.) See Science #2 and #4.
- **[What happens when a bright light is shined in your eyes?]** Write the children's comments on a piece of paper and save this for later. See Science #3 and #5.

- **[Do you think the dog will reach the young child first? Why or why not?]** Give each child a sticky note and have them print their name on one side. On the other side, have them write the word "dog" or "adult." Put a piece of paper on the board, with the words "dog" and "adult" on opposite sides of the paper. Have the children place their sticky note on the side of their choice. Tally the results (e.g., dog—8 votes, adult—2 votes). See Math #1.

- **[What kind of dog do you think it is?]** Write the children's responses on a piece of paper and save this for later. See Science #6.

- Have the children look at the right-hand side of the page. **[Do you think the adult had to help the young child stand up? Why wouldn't the child be able to stand up?]** (The child is tired. The child has been sleeping in one position for a long time. The child's muscles are sore.)

- **[How is a wolf suited to live in cold weather?]** Write the children's responses on a piece of paper and save this for later. See Science #7.

- **[Why do you think wolves need to have a good sense of smell?]** Write the children's responses on a piece of paper and save this for later. See Science #8.

- **[Where are the wolves in this picture?]** (The wolves are at the top of the hill.) **[Why do you think they moved away from the young child?]** (The wolves didn't want to be too close to the adult and dog. The wolves thought the adult would want some time alone with the child.) Review some basic information about wolves. See Science #7 and #8.

- Note that the young wolf and the darker wolf in the center of the group aren't howling. **[Why do you think they're quiet?]** Write the children's comments on a piece of paper and save this for later. (The darker wolf is greeting the young wolf. The darker wolf wants to sniff the young wolf.) See Writing #2.

- **[Do you think the young child knows that the wolves surrounded her and were howling? Why or why not?]** (The young child might have been so exhausted she fell asleep and didn't hear the wolves howling. The young child may have heard them howling but was so tired she didn't care.)

- **[How do you think the adult feels at this moment?]** Write the children's comments on a piece of paper and save this for later. (I'm so happy we found you! We've been looking for you a long time. The dog did an amazing job. What a relief.) See Writing #3.

- **[How do you think the young child feels at this moment?]** Write the children's comments on a piece of paper and save this for later. (Wow! I'm so happy they found me. I was so cold and tired. My feet are sore.) See Writing #4.

- **[Do you think the dog is glad to see the young child? Why or why not?]** Write the children's comments on a piece of paper. (Oh boy, there she is! I've been looking for her for a long time. Now, we can go home by the fire.)

- **[Do you think the wolves will stay where they are until the young child is taken away? Why or why not?]** Write the children's comments on a piece of paper. (I think the wolves will stay where they are so the adult and dog can reach her first. I think the wolves will stay on the hill because they know that she'd like to see her family.) See Art #1.

- **[Do you think the young child will approach the wolves? Why or why not?]** Write the children's comments on a piece of paper. (I think she's very tired. She might need to rest. I think she would like to go up the hill to thank them.)

- Note that the family will certainly be glad to have the young child back home. **[Do you think they'll do anything special for the child? Why or why not?]** Write the children's comments on a piece of paper. (The family might have a special celebration. They might cook a special dinner for her. They might do some special outdoor activity together.)

- **[How could the young child thank the adult?]** Write down the children's comments on a piece of paper and save this for later. See Writing #4.

- **[How could the young child thank the wolves?]** Write down the children's comments on a piece of paper and save this for later. See Writing #4.

- **[How could the young child thank the dog?]** Write down the children's comments on a piece of paper and save this for later. See Writing #4.

- **[What do you think the young wolf and the older wolf in the center of the page are thinking?]** (Young Wolf: "The young child took such loving care of me while we were walking in the woods. I know I wasn't easy to carry." Older Wolf: "I'm sure the young child's family will be very happy to have her home. I'm certainly happy to have you back with the pack.") Write down the children's comments on a piece of paper and have them copy their favorite sentence(s).

- **[What do you think the other wolves are thinking?]** Write down the children's comments on a piece of paper and have them copy their favorite sentence(s). (Wolf One: "Mother wolf wasn't about to let her young cub be taken from the pack. She certainly had determination!" Wolf Two: "The young child carefully carried the young wolf for a long distance. She must have wanted to protect the young wolf." Wolf Three: "It's good to know the young child is back with her family. I bet she's happy.")

ACTIVITIES

Art

#1. Make wolf paw prints, using a potato.

- **Objective.** Creating. Anchor Standard #2. Organize and develop artistic ideas and work. Investigate. Create personally satisfying artwork using a variety of materials, tools, and equipment for a variety of artistic processes.

- **Level of difficulty.** Moderate. (This task may take several days to complete.)

- **Materials needed.** Potatoes, paw print (see resource section), knife, black marker, spoon to scoop out potato, gray/black paint, paper plates for the paint, paper towels, white construction paper, crayons, pencils, and colored pencils.

- **Before the activity.** Prepare all the materials. Make a copy of the paw print (see resource section). Cut a potato in half so the middle portion is exposed. Cut out the paw print and place it in the center of the cut potato. Using small pins to secure the paw print onto the exposed potato, trace around it with a black marker. Remove the paw print and small pins. Using a knife, carefully cut around the paw print. Scoop around the paw print with the spoon, creating a raised section on the potato. Only an adult should do this. Make as many potato paw print stamps as needed.

- **Begin the activity by saying,** "Earlier, we discussed how the wolves had moved away from the child. They're at the top of the hill."

- **Review the children's responses.** (I think the wolves will stay where they are so the adult and dog can reach her first. I think the wolves will stay on the hill because they know she'd like to see her family.)

- **Introduce the activity.** "Today, we're going to create some wolf prints going up the hill to each wolf." Give each child a piece of white construction paper. Have them draw a picture of the adult, dog, and young child at the bottom of the paper. Have them draw the five wolves and the forest at the top of the hill. Using the potato stamp made earlier, allow one child at a time to dip the potato into a grayish/black paint mixture and gently blot it onto a paper towel. Have them press it onto their picture, making a trail to each wolf on the hill.

#2. Create five wolves on bamboo sticks that can be moved by the children.

- **Objective.** Presenting. Anchor Standard #5. Develop and refine artistic techniques and work for presentation. Analyze. Ask and answer questions such as where, when, why, and how artwork should be prepared for presentation or preservation.
- **Level of difficulty.** Moderate. (This task may take several days to complete.)
- **Materials needed.** Five bamboo sticks for each child (these can be purchased in most markets), poster board, white construction paper, crayons, paints, paintbrushes, colored pencils, glue, rulers, and plastic wrap.
- **Before the activity.** Prepare the materials.
- **Begin the activity by saying,** "Earlier, we discussed how the wolves had moved away from the child. They're at the top of the hill."
- **Review the children's responses.** (I think the wolves will stay where they are so the adult and dog can reach the young child first. I think the wolves will stay on the hill because they know she'd like to see her family.)
- **Introduce the activity.** "Today, we going to create five moving wolves."

300

1. Give each child five bamboo sticks and a piece of white poster board. Have the children draw/paint each of the five wolves onto the poster board. Let these dry.

2. Guide the children through these steps: First, draw and cut a circle around each wolf. On the back side of the circle, put a glue line down the middle. Place a bamboo stick into this glue line, putting some additional glue on top of the bamboo stick. Place a piece of plastic wrap over the glue line and cover it with a heavy object. Allow this to dry, and then peel off the plastic wrap. Do this same process for the other four wolves.

3. Give each child a piece of white construction paper. Have them draw a picture of the young child, the dog, and the adult at the bottom of their paper. Then have them draw the wolves and the forest area at the top of the paper.

4. Have the children draw paw prints going down the hill from the wolves toward the child. Now, draw a straight line with a ruler from each wolf to the young child. Make sure the lines don't merge into each other.

5. Have the children carefully cut on the straight lines. The children can now insert their bamboo stick(s) into the "path." This will allow the children to move the bamboo stick(s) forward and backward from the group. Allow them to verbalize what the wolves might be saying/thinking.

Writing

#1. Describe how the young child might be feeling and looking sitting in the snow. Use various adjectives.

- **Objective.** Language Standards. Conventions of Standard English. Demonstrate command of the conventions of standard English grammar and usage when writing or speaking. Use frequently occurring adjectives.

- **Level of difficulty.** Easy.
- **Materials needed.** None.
- **Before the activity.** Place a large piece of white paper on the board. Have a black marker available for writing the children's responses.
- **Begin the activity by saying,** "Earlier, we described the young child sitting in the snow."
- **Review the children's responses.** (The child looks tired. The child looks scared. The child looks afraid.)
- **Introduce the activity.** "Today, we're going to write down some adjectives about how the young child might be feeling/looking." Have the children use descriptive words to describe how they think the young child feels and looks. (The young child feels exhausted. The young child is cold. The young child looks stunned. I think the young child looks surprised.) Leave this paper up for a few days so the children can add adjectives to the list. Have the children write their favorite words or a sentence(s). Have them share their favorite words/sentence(s) about the young child with the class.

#2. Have the children write conversation bubbles about what the wolves on the hill might be thinking/saying.

- **Objective.** Writing Standards. Text Types and Purposes. Write opinion pieces on topics or texts, supporting a point of view with reasons. Introduce the topic or text they are writing about, state an opinion, and create an organizational structure that lists reasons.
- **Level of difficulty.** Moderate. (This task may take several days to complete.)
- **Materials needed.** Conversation bubbles (see resource section), scissors, and pencils.

- **Before the activity.** Place a large piece of white paper on the board. Have a black marker available for writing the children's responses.
- **Begin the activity by saying,** "Earlier, we discussed why we thought the young wolf and the dark wolf on the right-hand side of the page weren't howling." Write and review the children's comments.
- **Review the children's responses.** (Dark Wolf: "Well, we know the young child will be safe now." Young Wolf: "I'm so glad she's going home. Howling Wolf: "Well, now we can get back to finding our dinner!" Second Howling Wolf: "I hope the young wolf will keep up with us from now on!" Third Howling Wolf: "I'm ready to get back to the den, I'm hungry!")
- **Introduce the activity.** "Today, we're going to create conversation bubbles describing what the wolves might be saying/thinking." (See resource section.) (Dark Wolf: "Well, we know the young child will be safe now." Young Wolf: "I'm so glad she's going home. Howling Wolf: "Well, now we can get back to finding our dinner!" Second Howling Wolf: "I hope the young wolf will keep up with us from now on!" Third Howling Wolf: "I'm ready to get back to the den, I'm hungry!") Have the children share their conversation bubble(s) with a friend.

#3. Create and write in a journal.

- **Objective.** Writing Standards. Range of Writing. Write routinely over extended periods (time for research, reflection, and revision) and shorter periods (a single sitting or a day or two) for a range of discipline-specific tasks, purposes, and audiences.
- **Level of difficulty.** Moderate. (This task may take several days to complete.)
- **Materials needed.** Individual journals and pencils. Go to a dollar store and buy enough journals for the class. If that's too expensive, create some journals. (Cut some lined paper to a specified dimension.

Cut some colored construction paper larger than the lined paper. Staple the lined paper and the colored construction paper together.)

- **Before the activity.** Place a large piece of white paper on the board. Have a black marker available for writing the children's responses.
- **Begin the activity by saying,** "Earlier, we discussed how the adult in the picture might feel finding the young child."
- **Review the children's responses.** (Today is the best day of my life! I can't express the joy I felt when I saw you sitting in the snow.)
- **Introduce the activity.** "Today, we're going to write what the adult might be feeling and thinking. We're going to use a journal. A journal allows people to write important events and thoughts in a small book." Show an example of a journal. Tell the children they're going to imagine they're the adult in this story, and they're going to write in the journal. (Today is the best day of my life! I can't express the joy I felt when I saw you sitting in the snow.) You can easily make a small journal by stapling several pieces of lined paper inside two pieces of construction paper. Allow the children to decorate their journals.
- **Extension of the activity.** The children might enjoy creating a more elaborate journal. You could create a cloth-covered journal or simply let the children decorate their construction paper journals with stickers, craft items, or drawings. Go to the internet and type, "How to create a cloth-covered journal." Choose an age-appropriate website for the children. Read and discuss the information with the children. There are several videos the children will enjoy hearing and watching. Perhaps an adult or older student would like to help with this project.

#4. Write a thank you card to the adult, the dog, or the wolves.

- **Objective.** Writing Standards. Production and Distribution of Writing. With guidance and support from adults, produce writing in which the development and organization are appropriate to the task and purpose.

- **Level of difficulty.** Moderate. (This task may take several days to complete.)
- **Materials needed.** Thank you cards, pencils, colored construction paper, crayons, colored pencils, glue, scissors, and craft items to glue to the front of the card (optional).
- **Before the activity.** Place a large piece of white paper on the board. Have a black marker available for writing the children's responses.
- **Begin the activity by saying,** "Earlier, we discussed how the child might feel about the adult and the dog rescuing her."
- **Review the children's responses.** (Wow! I'm so happy they found me. I was so cold and tired. My feet are sore.)
- **Introduce the activity.** "Today, we're going to create and write a special thank you card for either the adult, the dog, or the wolves." Have a supply of special thank you cards available, or let the children create their own cards. They could create heart-shaped cards, paw print cards, flashlight-shaped cards, or tree-shaped cards.

1. Have the children practice writing special messages to the adult, the dog, or the wolves. (Dear Little Wolf, I know you were the one who let your family know I tried to help you! You, in turn, had your family help me! Thank you so much. I'll always be looking for you when I walk home from school! Dear Mother Wolf, you, certainly were persistent in searching for your young wolf! I'm glad you found him or her. That must have made you happy.)
2. When they've decided what they want to say, let the children write their message(s) on the thank you card. Be available to help them sound out the words.

Science

#1. Learn about our muscles.

- **Objective.** Life Science. Interdependent Relationships in Ecosystems, Animals, Plants, and their Environment. Use observations to describe patterns of what plants and animals (including humans) need to survive.
- **Level of difficulty.** Easy.
- **Materials needed.** None.
- **Before the activity.** Place a large piece of white paper on the board. Have a black marker available for writing the children's responses. Go to the internet and type, "Tell me about human muscles." Choose an age-appropriate website for the children. In addition, go to the internet and type, "How to explain muscle cramps to children." Choose an age-appropriate website for the children. Finally, go to the internet and type, "How does hydration affect muscles?" Choose an age-appropriate website for the children.
- **Begin the activity by saying,** "Earlier, we discussed whether we thought the adult had to help the young child stand up."
- **Review the children's responses.** (Well, the young girl has been in the snow for a long time. She's also walked a very long way. Her muscles must be sore.)
- **Introduce the activity.** "Today, we're going to learn about our muscles."
    1. "Standing up requires that we use our muscles. We wondered whether the young child would have difficulty standing up after being in the snow for so long." Go to the internet and type, "Tell me about human muscles." Select the age-appropriate website you chose. Read and discuss the information with the children. Challenge them to learn the names of several muscles.

2. "When we sit in one position for a long time, our muscles begin to cramp. "Does anyone know what the word 'cramp' means?]" Allow the children to give their explanations. Go to the internet and type, "How to explain muscle cramps to children." Select the age-appropriate website you chose. Read and discuss the information with them. "A muscle cramp means that the muscles contract. Contract means that the muscle tightens and shortens."

3. Finally, you might want to talk about hydration and muscle cramping. Go to the internet and type, "How does hydration affect muscles?" Select the age-appropriate website you chose. Read and discuss this information with the children. "Has anyone ever experienced a cramp?" Allow them to relay the incident to a friend.

#2. Learn what happens when a bright light is shone by another person into our eyes.

- **Objective.** Engineering Design. Life Science. Structure, Function, and Information Processing. Construct an argument that plants and animals have internal and external structures that function to support survival, growth, and reproduction.
- **Level of difficulty.** Easy.
- **Materials needed.** None.
- **Before the activity.** Place a large piece of white paper on the board. Have a black marker available for writing the children's responses. Go to the internet and type, "What happens to the eyes when a bright light is shone into them?" Choose an age-appropriate website for the children.
- **Begin the activity by saying,** "Earlier, we discussed why the young child was covering her eyes."

- **Review the children's responses.** (The bright light bothered the young child. I don't think the young child could see who was coming, because the bright light was shone into her eyes.)
- **Introduce the activity.** "Today, we're going to find out what happens to our eyes when a bright light is shone into our eyes." Go to the internet and type, "What happens to the eyes when a bright light is shone into them?" Select the age-appropriate website you chose. Read and discuss the information with them. Have the children tell a friend what happens to our eyes when a bright light is shone into them.

#3. Draw and label the eye. Observe the differences between eyes.

- **Objective.** Engineering Design. Life Science. Structure, Function, and Information Processing. Construct an argument that plants and animals have internal and external structures that function to support survival, growth, and reproduction.
- **Level of Difficulty.** Moderate. (This task may take several days to complete.)
- **Materials Needed.** White construction paper, crayons, colored pencils, and pencils.
- **Before the activity.** Place a large piece of white paper on the board. Have a black marker available for writing the children's responses.
- **Begin the activity by saying,** "Earlier, we went to the internet and learned what happens when a bright light is shone into the eyes." Review what they learned from the prior task regarding what happens when a bright light is shone into their eyes. "What happens to your eyes when a bright light is shone into them?"
- **Review the children's responses.** (I can't see when a bright light is shone into my eyes. It makes me want to close my eyes.)
- **Introduce the activity.** "Today, we're going to learn more about the eye." Show a picture of the eye. You may want to go to the internet

and find a picture that can be displayed. Type, "Show me a diagram of the eye." Choose an age-appropriate website for the children. Have them draw and label the eye. Then have them choose a partner and examine each other's eyes. "How are your eyes the same? How are your eyes different?" Allow the children to relay what they observed.

#4. Observe what happens to the pupil of the eye when the eyes are shut for several minutes.

- **Objective.** Engineering Design. Life Science. Structure, Function, and Information Processing. Construct an argument that plants and animals have internal and external structures that function to support survival, growth, and reproduction.
- **Level of difficulty.** Easy.
- **Materials needed.** A picture of the eye. Go to the internet and type, "Show me a diagram of the eye." Choose an age-appropriate website for the children.
- **Before the activity.** Place a large piece of white paper on the board. Have a black marker available for writing the children's responses.
- **Begin the activity by saying,** "Earlier, we discussed why the young child was covering her eyes." Write and review the children's responses.
- **Review the children's responses.** (The bright light made it hard for her to see. She was covering her eyes because the light was very bright.)
- **Introduce the activity.** "Today, we're going to do an experiment with our eyes."
1. "Earlier, we thought the bright light might be bothering the young child We've learned some important things about our eyes." Show a picture of the eye. Allow the children to relay the things they remember about the eye. Quickly, have the children choose

a partner and sit down facing them. One of them will close their eyes for two minutes and then open them, while the other child observes what happens to the eyes.

2. Number the children off, assigning one in each of the partner groups the number 1 and the other one the number 2. Choose which one will close their eyes first. (For example, the 1's will close their eyes first, and the 2's will observe.) Reverse this when the time comes. Tell the observers they must carefully observe their friend's pupil. Show this portion of the eye on the picture they saw earlier. They will need to observe the pupil carefully to see what happens. Tell the children who are closing their eyes that, if they don't keep their eyes completely closed for two minutes, the experiment won't work.

3. Ask them if they're ready to start. When you see that they're ready, tell the 1's to close their eyes. At the end of the two minutes, tell them to open their eyes. The observers should be intently looking at their friend's eye. Ask the observers what they observed. The pupil(s) got smaller. You may have to conduct the experiment several times for the children to adequately observe the results. Reverse the process when you feel the first group has observed the process.

4. Ask them to explain why this happened.

#5. Learn that light moves in a straight line. Create a kaleidoscope.

- **Objective.** Engineering Design. Physical Science. Waves. Waves and Information. Develop a model of waves to describe patterns in terms of amplitude and wavelength and that waves can cause objects to move (including diagrams, analogies, and physical models to illustrate wavelength and amplitude of waves).

- **Level of difficulty.** Challenging. (This task may take several days to complete.)

- **Materials needed.** The website you choose in the next step will guide you to the specific materials you'll need.
- **Before the activity.** Place a large piece of white paper on the board. Have a black marker available for writing the children's responses. Go to the internet and type, "How to make a kaleidoscope." Choose an age-appropriate website for the children.
- **Begin the activity by saying,** "Earlier, we discovered what happens when a bright light is shone into our eyes." Write and review the children's responses. (The pupils get smaller. When we close our eyes for two minutes and we open our eyes, the pupils get smaller.)
- **Review the children's responses.** (I know that, when a bright light is shone into my eyes, it makes me want to cover them. I can't see when a bright light is shone into my eyes.)
- **Introduce the activity.** "Today, we're going to learn some more information about light."
  1. Explain to the children that light moves in a straight line. When the light hits something, it changes direction. That's how a kaleidoscope works. There are several fun projects related to light that can be found on the internet.
  2. NASA has a lesson showing how to make a kaleidoscope. Go to the internet and type, "How to make a kaleidoscope." Select the age-appropriate website you chose. This site has information and directions on how to make a simple kaleidoscope.

#6. Observe and predict what type of dog is in the story.

- **Objective.** Life Science. Structure, Function, and Information Processing. Read texts and use media to determine patterns in behavior of parents and offspring that help offspring survive.
- **Level of difficulty.** Easy.
- **Materials needed.** Books about different types of dogs, baskets, and dog beds.

- **Before the activity.** Place a large piece of white paper on the board. Have a black marker available for writing the children's responses.
- **Begin the activity by saying,** "Earlier, we discussed what type of dog was in the picture."
- **Review the children's responses.** (I think it's a beagle. I think it's a basset hound. I think it's a bloodhound.)
- **Introduce the activity.** "Today, we're going discuss what type of dog we think is in the story."
  1. Write and review the children's comments. (I think it's a beagle. I think it's a basset hound. I think it's a bloodhound.) Have books available in baskets about distinct types of dogs. You might want to place dog beds in a library area, allowing the children to sit and read in these comfortable beds.
  2. Place a piece of paper on a bulletin board so the children can write down what type of dog they think is in the picture. After several days, review the types of dogs that were listed and relay the numbers (e.g. beagle—4, basset—3, hound—2, bloodhound—1). Have the children relay why they thought the dog they chose was the type of dog in the picture. (I chose a hound because it is a medium-sized dog. It has rounded ears. It has marking on the top of its body.) Determine which dog received the most votes.

#7. Discuss the ability of wolves to live in very wintry weather.

- **Objective.** Engineering Design. Life Science. Inheritance and Variation of Traits. Construct an argument that some animals form groups that help members survive.
- **Level of difficulty.** Easy.
- **Materials needed.** Thermometer (see resource section), markers, and a fan.

- **Before the activity.** Place a large piece of white paper on the board. Have a black marker available for writing the children's responses. Go to the internet and type, "Tell me about a wolf's coat." Choose an age-appropriate website for the children.
- **Begin the activity by saying,** "Earlier, we discussed the ability of the wolf to live in cold weather."
- **Review the children's responses.** (A wolf can live in a very cold area because it has very thick fur. Wolves can find protected areas to keep them warm. They come close together to keep warm.)
- **Introduce the activity.** "Today, we're going to find out why the wolf is able to live in such cold weather."
  1. Note that wolves are well-suited to live in cold weather because of their very thick fur. Go to the internet and type, "Tell me about a wolf's coat." Select the age-appropriate website you chose. Read and discuss this information with the children. "The fur is very thick to keep the wolf warm. The tail is also thick, and wolves use their tail to protect their face. When a wolf is lying down, it will wrap its thick tail around its face. The tail will keep the face protected for weather conditions that are as cold as negative sixty degrees Fahrenheit (-60°F.). The freezing point of water is thirty-two degrees Fahrenheit (32°F.), so you can see how cold the weather would be."
  2. Show the children a large picture of a thermometer (see resource section). Draw a line at the -60°F. location. Discuss the number of degrees from that point to the freezing point of water, at 32°F.
- **Extension of the activity.** "A wolf's tail also helps it to keep insects off its face and body. It's like a large fan moving around it's body." You could demonstrate this air movement by placing a fan in front of the children. Have them discuss what happens with the fan is turned on. "Do you think the insects could fly against this fan?" (Probably not!)

#8. Learn about a wolf's sense of smell. Experiment with smelling various substances and determining how far away we can smell that substance.

- **Objective.** Life Science. Structure, Function, and Information Processing. Read texts and use media to determine patterns in behavior of parents and offspring that help offspring survive.
- **Level of difficulty.** Easy.
- **Materials needed.** Various substances for the children to smell (e.g., onion, garlic, coffee, lemon, and orange).
- **Before the activity.** Place a large piece of white paper on the board. Have a black marker available for writing the children's responses. Go to the internet and type, "Tell me about a wolf's sense of smell." Choose an age-appropriate website for the children.
- **Begin the activity by saying,** "Earlier, we learned that wolves have an amazing sense of smell." Write and review the children's responses.
- **Review the children's responses.** (I think a wolf can smell things we can't. I think a wolf has a good sense of smell because it needs to find food. A wolf's sense of smell helps to protect it.)
- **Introduce the activity.** "Today, we're going to learn about a wolf's sense of smell. We'll also learn a little about our sense of smell."
  1. "Wolves have an amazing sense of smell." Go to the internet and type, "Tell me about a wolf's sense of smell." Select the age-appropriate website you chose. Read and discuss this information with the children. "Wolves can smell their prey over a mile away. Their sense of smell is much better than ours. A wolf's sense of smell is approximately one hundred times better than a human's sense of smell."
  2. "Why do you think the wolf has such a good sense of smell?" Write the children's responses on a piece of paper. (The wolf

314

relies on its sense of smell to track down food!) Try some smell experiments with the children and discuss this information with them. Take them outside and have them sit in a straight line. Have an adult or older child stand in front of them. Cut an onion or a piece of garlic in half and move it along the line so the children can smell it. Tell them that the adult or student will move backward, away from them (approximately five feet each time), and they're to raise their hand if they can smell the onion/garlic. When they're unable to smell the onion/garlic, have them stand up. You might want to talk about how the wind direction might affect this outcome. "If the wind is blowing in a different direction, you might not be able to smell the onion/garlic as well as if it's blowing directly at you."

3. "Do you think the wind direction would make a difference when a wolf is hunting?" Write the children's responses on a piece of paper. "What did we discover about smelling the onion/garlic outside?" (Well, the further away we were from the onion/garlic, the more difficult it was to smell it. The same thing happens to the wolf. The further away it is from its prey, the more difficult it would be for it to smell it. The wind blowing in various directions would also influence the wolf's ability to smell.)

Math

#1. Survey and graph the results of the following question: Who will reach the young child first? Will it be the adult or the dog?

- **Objective.** Measurement and Data. Represent and interpret data. Draw a picture graph and a bar graph (with single-unit scale) to represent a data set with up to four categories. Solve simple, put-together, take-apart, and compare problems using information presented in a bar graph.

- **Level of difficulty.** Moderate. (This task may take several days to complete.)
- **Materials needed.** Graph paper, crayons, markers, and pencils.
- **Before the activity.** Place a large piece of white paper on the board. Have a black marker available for writing the children's responses.
- **Begin the activity by saying,** "Earlier, we voted as to who would reach the young child first. Would it be the adult or the dog?"
- **Review the children's responses.** (We voted 2 votes for the adult and 8 votes for the dog.)
- **Introduce the activity.** "Today, we're going to review and graph the results of our vote. We wondered who would reach the young child first. Would it be the adult or the dog? We wrote down our choices on sticky notes and placed them on the paper. The adult received 2 votes, and the dog received 8 votes. Today, we're going to create a graph showing the results. The graph will record the 'Adult Votes' and the 'Dog Votes.'" Here's an example of the graph:

Who will reach the young child first?

N	10											
U	9											
M	8								X			
B	7								X			
E	6								X			
R	5								X			
of	4								X			
K	3								X			
I	2			X					X			
D	1			X					X			
S	0	1	2	3	4	5	6	7	8	9	10	
		Adult							Dog			

1. Give the children some half-inch graph paper and have them write in the numbers 0 through 10 near the bottom of the graph paper (the horizontal line). The numbers should be small enough to fit in the area. (See the example included here.)

2. Have the children write "Number of Kids" on the left-hand side of the graph. Then have them write in the numbers 0 through 10 on the left-hand side of the page (the vertical line). The numbers should be small enough to fit in the area.

3. Have the children write the words "Adult" and "Dog" under the correct numbers (2 and 8) at the bottom of the horizontal line.

4. Next, have the children record the number of "Adult" votes at the correct location on the graph. (Place the X above the number 2.) The X's should be moving upward to record the 2 adult votes. Do this same process for the "Dog" votes. Explain to the children that this method allows us to quickly see the results of our vote. Have the children write the title of the graph at the top of the graph—"Who will reach the young child first?"

5. Have the children take two different-colored crayons and color in the votes (i.e., use one color for the "Adult" votes and another color for the "Dog" votes).

Wolf in the Snow **illustration: The adult and dog going down the hill**

Direct the children's attention to the left-hand side of the page, where you see the adult holding the young child, and the dog going down the hill. Encourage them to answer the following questions in complete sentences.

QUESTIONS

The brackets around the text indicate questions/instructions an adult should read to the children. Examples of how the children may answer the questions are included in parentheses.

- **[What do you see on this page?]**
- **[Is the dog running or walking? How do you know?]** (Its legs are off the ground, indicating that it's in the air. The dog is running.)
- **[Is the adult running or walking? Why?]** (I think the adult is walking because it's difficult to run in snow. The footprints are close together, so I think the adult is walking.)
- **[Do you think the adult and the dog are using their senses to find the young child? Why or why not?]** Write down the children's comments on a piece of paper and save this for later. (I think the adult would use their eyes to try and find the young child. I think the dog would use his or her nose to try and smell the child.) See Writing #1 and Science #1.
- **[What are the five senses?]** Write the children's responses on a piece of paper and save this for later. See Science #2.
- **[Would the young child be able to signal the adult and dog where she is located? Why or why not?]** (The young child could use her voice, but the sound might not travel very far. The young

child fell asleep in the snow, so she might still be asleep. She wouldn't be able to yell at the adult and the dog.)

- **[Do you think the flashlight is the greatest rescue device used in this situation? Why or why not?]** Put a large piece of paper on the board. Give each child a sticky note and have them print their name on it. Have each child place the sticky note on either "yes" or "no." See Writing #2.

- **[Do you think the light from the flashlight could travel a long distance?]** See Science #3.

- Have the children look at the snow falling. **[Do you think it is a heavy or a light snowfall? Why or why not?]** See Art #1 and #2.

- Note that the dog has no protective gear on. **[What things might protect the dog?]** Write the children's responses on a piece of paper. (Dog booties could help. A dog blanket/covering could protect the dog from the cold.) See Art #3.

- **[What adverse conditions might exist for finding the young child?]** Write the children's responses on a piece of paper and save this for later. (The snow is constantly falling. There could be animals hiding in and around the trees. The rescuers could be limited by the fading light. The child falling asleep in the snow could make it hard to find her). See Science #4 and #5.

- **[How would you know which direction to go?]** Write the children's responses on a piece of paper and save this for later. (The adult using the flashlight could see the surrounding area. The dog would use his or her nose.). See Science #6.

ACTIVITIES

Art

#1. Discuss whether the snowfall is heavy or light. Make snowflakes.

- **Objective.** Connecting. Anchor Standard #10. Synthesize and relate knowledge and personal experiences to make art. Synthesize. Create art that tells a story about a life experience.

- **Level of difficulty.** Moderate. (This task may take several days to complete.)

- **Materials needed.** Large and small squares of white paper, scissors, blue construction paper, glue, hole punch, and string.

- **Before the activity.** Place a large piece of white paper on the board. Have a black marker available for writing the children's responses. Go to the internet and type, "Snowfall for kids." Choose an age-appropriate website for the children.

- **Begin the activity by saying,** "Earlier, we discussed whether the snowfall was heavy or light. We noticed that the snow had covered the ground, as well as the trees, so, it must be a heavy snowfall."

- **Review the children's responses.** (Sometimes when I play in the snow, it's falling fast. At other times, the snow falls slowly. I think it's a heavy snow when the snow is coming down fast.)

- **Introduce the activity.** "Today, we're going to learn additional information about the snow falling and then we'll make snowflakes."

  1. "We noticed that the snow had covered the ground, as well as the trees, so, it must be a heavy snowfall." To have the children learn additional information about the snow falling, go to the internet and type, "Snowfall for kids." Select the age-appropriate website you chose. Read and discuss the information on this website. Write some of the facts from this website onto a piece of paper for the children to copy later. In addition, there are several videos

320

the children will enjoy watching. Preview these videos before you show them.

2. "Today, we're going to make some snowflakes. We'll make a few large snowflakes, as well as some small snowflakes. We'll hang the large snowflakes from the ceiling, and we'll glue the small snowflakes onto a piece of paper."

3. Have large and small squares of paper ready for this project. Demonstrate how to fold the square into a triangle, matching the corners. Fold the triangle again, matching the corners. They may not be able to fold the triangle again, so demonstrate cutting the triangle after two folds. You might let them try a third fold, but it's difficult to cut the paper with the third fold. Have the children make several snowflakes. Glue the small snowflakes onto a piece of dark blue or gray construction paper. Make sure they put their name on the back of their picture. Have the children write one fact they learned from the website and glue this to their snowflake paper.

4. Have the children print their name on the large snowflakes so they can be returned. Put a piece of tape at the top of each snowflake to reinforce it. Punch a hole at the top and put thread or string through the hole. Attach the string to a paper clip. Hang the large snowflakes from the ceiling. In some schools, you may have to use tape to hang them from the ceiling.

#2. Illustrate this page with a "paint wash."

- **Objective.** Creating. Anchor Standard #2. Organize and develop artistic ideas and work. Investigate. Explore uses of materials and tools to create works of art or design.
- **Level of difficulty.** Moderate. (This task may take several days to complete.)

- **Materials needed.** White construction paper, pencils, paints, paintbrushes, and crayons.
- **Before the activity.** Prepare the materials.
- **Begin the activity by saying,** "Earlier, we discussed whether the snowfall was a heavy or light snowfall. We looked at the page and decided that the snow was really coming down. We decided that it was a heavy snowfall."
- **Introduce the activity.** "Today, we're going to recreate this picture and do a paint wash over the picture."
1. Have the children print their name on the back of a piece of white construction paper. Explain to the children that they must thoroughly press the crayons onto the illustrated area. If any area that they've colored isn't thoroughly covered, the paint wash will seep through the paper. They should color the snowflakes with a white crayon. The sky portion should be left blank, except for the snowflakes falling on the trees. The sky will be painted with a watery gray / dark blue / black paint mixture.
2. The watery paint mixture should be brushed over the sky area. The paint mixture should be watery enough to easily cover the sky area. You can use a watery gray, dark blue, or black paint combination for the picture. When they've covered the sky area with the wash, have the children move the picture to an area where it can dry. The paint wash process can be done one or two children at a time.
- **Extension of the activity.** If you're in an area that has snowfall, you might want to extend this lesson by having the children measure the amount of snowfall at different times (measuring the snowfall in three hours, in four hours, overnight, or in two days). Use a ruler or yardstick to measure the snowfall and record it on a piece of paper. (At 9:00 a.m., the snow was three inches. At 10:00 a.m., the snow was four inches.)

#3. Create a dog covering for the dog in the story.

- **Objective.** Creating. Anchor Standard #2. Organize and develop artistic ideas and work. Investigate. Explore uses of materials and tools to create works of art or design.
- **Level of difficulty.** Moderate. (This task may take several days to complete.)
- **Materials needed.** Dog covering (see resource section), pencils, crayons, paints, paintbrushes, colored pencils, and glue.
- **Before the activity.** Place a large piece of white paper on the board. Have a black marker available for writing the children's responses.
- **Begin the activity by saying,** "Earlier, we discussed the fact that the dog wasn't wearing any protective gear. We thought of some things that might protect the dog."
- **Review the children's responses.** (The dog could wear a sweater. The dog could wear a blanket covering around his body. The dog could wear booties.)
- **Introduce the activity.** "Today, we're going to create a covering for the dog."
  1. Give each child a copy of the dog covering. (See resource section.) Have the children practice drawing some designs on a separate piece of paper before they draw their final design on the covering.
  2. Have the children tell a friend why they chose that design. (I chose this design because it looked like the forest area. I chose this design because it shows snow falling on the tops of the trees.)
  3. Staple or glue the side sections together (the short flaps). If possible, bring in some dog coverings, as well as booties for them to see. Explain to them that these booties protect the dogs'

paws. Some of the children may have booties for their dog(s), so ask them to bring the booties to class for everyone to see.

4. Display their dog coverings on a bulletin board, along with various facts about protective gear.

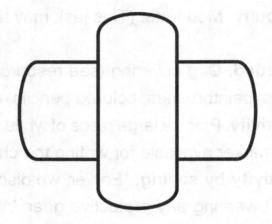

Writing / Oral Language

#1. Discuss which senses the adult and the dog might use to find the young child.

- **Objective.** Speaking and Listening Standards. Presentation of Knowledge and Ideas. Report on a topic or text, tell a story, or recount an experience with appropriate facts and relevant descriptive details, speaking clearly at an understandable pace.

- **Level of difficulty.** Moderate. (This task may take several days to complete.)

- **Materials needed.** Sticky notes and pencils.

- **Before the activity.** Place a large piece of white paper on the board. Have a black marker available for writing the children's responses.

- **Begin the activity by saying,** "Earlier, we discussed whether the adult and the dog were using their senses to find the young child."

- **Review the children's responses.** (The dog used its sense of smell to find the young child. The dog used its sense of sight to find the young child. I think the adult used her sense of hearing to find the young child.)

- **Introduce the activity.** "Today, we're going to decide which senses the adult and the dog might use to find the young child."

  1. Put up a piece of paper, with the words "dog" and "adult" written on it. (See the example included here.) Ask the children what sense(s) they think the dog and the adult used to find the young child. Let them relay as many senses as they'd like. Later, you can explain to them that not all senses might be used. (They wouldn't necessarily use their sense of taste or touch.)

Dog	Adult
Sight	*Sight*
Smell	*Hearing*
Hearing	

  2. "Which sense do you think would be the most important for the dog?" Give each child a sticky note and have them print their name on it. Allow them to put their sticky note next to their choice.

  3. "Which sense do you think would be the most important for the adult?" Give each child another sticky note, have them print their name on it, and allow the children to place their sticky note next to their individual choice. (See the example included here.)

			Dog	Adult				
Tom	Joe	Karen	*Sight*	*Sight*	Tom	Joe	Amy	Luke
Mike	Susan	Tim	Amy	*Smell*				
	Luke	John	*Hearing*	*Hearing*	Tim	John	Karen	
					Mike	Susan		

  4. Review the results of the vote. The dog's sense of sight got three votes. Its sense of smell got four votes. Its sense of hearing got two votes. Most of you thought that the dog's sense of smell would be the most important sense to find the young child. The

adult's sense of sight got four votes. The adult's sense of hearing got five votes. Most of you thought the adult's sense of hearing would be the most important sense to find the young child.

5. "Do you agree with the results of this vote? Why or why not?"

Science

#1. Discuss whether a dog's sense of smell would be a better rescue device than a flashlight.

- **Objective.** Engineering Design. Life Science. Structure, Function, and Information Processing. Construct an argument that plants and animals have internal and external structures that function to support survival, growth, and reproduction.
- **Level of difficulty.** Easy.
- **Materials needed.** None.
- **Before the activity.** Place a large piece of white paper on the board. Have a black marker available for writing the children's responses. Go to the internet and type, "A dog's sense of smell." Choose an age-appropriate website for the children.
- **Begin the activity by saying,** "Earlier, we wondered if the adult and the dog were using their senses to find the young child or whether the flashlight would be a better rescue device in this situation. Some of you thought the flashlight would be a better rescue device, while others of you didn't think it would be the greatest device."
- **Review the children's responses.** (I think a dog has a very good sense of smell. A dog can smell things that we can't. A flashlight can be seen for a very long distance. I think the light can be seen by the young child.)
- **Introduce the activity.** "Today, we're going to discuss whether a dog's sense of smell would be a better rescue device than a flashlight."

1. "We know that dogs have an excellent sense of smell, so it could be that the dog's sense of smell was a better rescue device than the flashlight." Go to the internet and type, "A dog's sense of smell." Select the age-appropriate website you chose. Read and discuss this information with the children.

2. Put a piece of paper on the board, dividing it into two halves. On one side of the paper write "Dog's Sense of Smell." On the other side of the paper write "Flashlight." Give each child a sticky note and have them write their name on it. Have them put their sticky note on their individual choice. Discuss the results. Six of you thought the dog's sense of smell would be the greatest rescue tool, while four of you thought the flashlight would be the greatest rescue tool in this situation. (See the example included here.)

Dog's Sense of Smell	Flashlight
6	4

3. Invite the children to the front of the room to relay why they voted for either the dog's sense of smell or the flashlight. (I think the flashlight would be the greatest rescue tool in this situation because the rescuers could see where they were going. I don't think the flashlight would be the greatest rescue tool in this situation because the dog's sense of smell would probably be a better rescue tool.) Have the children relay their favorite fact about a dog's sense of smell to a friend.

#2. Learn about and discuss our five senses.

- **Objective.** Life Science. Structure, Function, and Information Processing. Read texts and use media to determine patterns in behavior of parents and offspring that help offspring survive.
- **Level of difficulty.** Easy.
- **Materials needed.** None.

- **Before the activity.** Place a large piece of white paper on the board. Have a black marker available for writing the children's responses. Go to the internet and type, "Our five senses." Choose an age-appropriate website for the children.
- **Begin the activity by saying,** "Who can name one of our five senses?" Write down the children's responses. Continue until they can name all five senses.
- **Review the children's responses.** (We use our eyes to see, so that must be one of our senses. We use our sense of smell, to smell things. When I hear birds singing, I'm using my sense of hearing. I can feel my dog's fur, so that must be my sense of touch. When I eat an orange, I'm tasting it.)
- **Introduce the activity.** "Today, we're going to learn about the five senses." Go to the internet and type, "Tell me about the five senses." Select the age-appropriate website you chose. Read and discuss this information with them. There are several videos they will enjoy seeing/hearing. Preview these videos before you show them to the children. You might want to try some experiments with the five senses.

#3. Discover and discuss whether light from a flashlight can travel a long distance.

- **Objective.** Engineering Design. Physical Science. Energy. Make observations to provide evidence that energy can be transferred from place to place by sound, light, heat, and electric currents.
- **Level of difficulty.** Easy.
- **Materials needed.** None.
- **Before the activity.** Place a large piece of white paper on the board. Have a black marker available for writing the children's responses. Go to the internet and type, "How far can light travel?" Choose an age-appropriate website for the children.

- **Begin the activity by saying,** "Earlier, we wondered whether the light from the flashlight could travel a long distance?"
- **Review the children's responses.** (I think light can travel a long way, because I can see the streetlight from my house. I stood in some trees, and my brother shone a light off in the distance, and I could see it. I think light can travel a long way.)
- **Introduce the activity.** "Today, we're going to discover how far light can travel."
  1. "We wondered whether the light from the flashlight could travel a long distance." Go to the internet and type, "How far can light travel?" Select the age-appropriate website you chose.
  2. "The distance that a light can travel is so far it's hard to imagine." Have the children clap their hands. Tell them that, during that time, light would travel over 186,000 miles. Have the children orally relay their thoughts to a friend about this incredible fact. (It's amazing that light can travel that fast! I could never run as fast as light.)

#4. Learn and discuss what might make it difficult for the adult and the dog to find the young child in the snow.

- **Objective.** Earth and Space Science. Weather and Climate. Use and share observations of local weather conditions to describe patterns over time.
- **Level of Difficulty.** Easy.
- **Materials Needed.** None.
- **Before the activity.** Place a large piece of white paper on the board. Have a black marker available for writing the children's responses. Go to the internet and type, "Winter safety—advice for parents and kids." Choose an age-appropriate website for the children.
- **Begin the activity by saying,** "Earlier, we discussed what adverse conditions might exist for finding the young child."

329

- **Review the children's responses.** (The snow constantly falling, animals hiding in and around the trees, the limitation of light, the child being asleep in the snow.)
- **Introduce the activity.** "Today, we're going to talk about some things that might make it difficult for the adult and the dog to find the young child." Go to the internet and type, "Winter safety—advice for parents and kids." Select the age-appropriate website you chose. Read and discuss this information with the children. Talk about why taking these actions would be an important safety measure.

#5. Watch animals playing.

- **Objective.** Engineering Design. Life Science. Interdependent Relationships in Ecosystems. Construct an argument that some animals form groups that help members survive.
- **Level of Difficulty.** Easy.
- **Materials Needed.** None.
- **Before the activity.** Place a large piece of white paper on the board. Have a black marker available for writing the children's responses. Go to the internet and type, "Show me a polar bear sliding in the snow." Also, go to the internet and type, "Wolves playing together." Choose age-appropriate websites for the children.
- **Begin the activity by saying,** "Do you think animals play with each other?"
- **Review the children's responses.** (I think animals do play with each other. I've watched my cats run after things, and they roll over and play with each other. My dog loves to fetch a ball, and he brings it back to me. My bird "dances" when I put on the music.)
- **Introduce the activity.** "Today, we're going to watch a video that shows some polar bears having fun in the snow."
  1. "We enjoy many activities in the snow, and it's exciting to see how animals enjoy themselves as well." Write down some of

the snow activities children enjoy (e.g., sledding, cross-country skiing, downhill skiing, snowball fights, making snow angels, and making snowmen).

2. Go to the internet and type, "Show me a polar bear sliding in the snow." Choose an age-appropriate website for the children that includes a video. Let the children watch this video and discuss how the animals seem to enjoy playing in the snow.

3. You can also find a video showing wolves playing together. Go to the internet and type, "Wolves playing together." Choose an age-appropriate website with a video for the children.

4. There are several other videos you can find online, including penguins sliding on the ice, that the children might enjoy seeing. Preview these videos before you show them to the children.

#6. Discuss how we would get to a specific location, using a compass.

- **Objective.** Engineering Design. Earth and Space Science. Earth's Systems. Processes that Shape the Earth. Analyze and interpret data from maps to describe patterns of Earth's features (e.g., land, ocean floor, mountains, volcanoes, and earthquakes).
- **Level of difficulty.** Easy.
- **Materials needed.** A compass, compass rose sheet (see resource section), crayons, and pencils.
- **Before the activity.** Place a large piece of white paper on the board. Have a black marker available for writing the children's responses. Go to the internet and type, "Tell me about a compass." Choose an age-appropriate website for the children.
- **Begin the activity by saying,** "Earlier, we discussed how the adult and the dog would know where to go."
- **Review the children's responses.** (The adult was using the flashlight, so maybe he or she could tell in which direction they were headed. The dog was using its nose.)

- **Introduce the activity.** "Today, we're going to talk about how we know where to go when we're looking for a specific location."

1. What if I wanted to go to the park, and I knew it was to the left of my house. What would be some ways I could find my way there? Emphasize that they should never leave their house without adult / older child supervision. They should also tell someone where they're going and when they'll be home.

2. Write and review the children's comments. (I could call a friend to get good directions. I could ask a friend to show me where the park was located. I could look on a local city map.) Show a compass and explain to the children that it's like a compass rose. It shows you north, south, east, and west. Review what they've learned from prior activities.

3. "How do we know in which direction we're headed when we go outdoors?" (Some people use maps. Some people ask for directions. Some people use a compass.) Go to the internet and type, "Tell me about a compass." Select the age-appropriate website you chose. Read and discuss this information with them.

4. Show the children a real compass and let them move in different directions, watching as the compass needle moves. Give the children a compass rose sheet (see resource section) and have them review / write in the directional markings. (See the example included here.) There are games on the internet that the children can play to reinforce directional understanding. Preview these videos before showing them to the children.

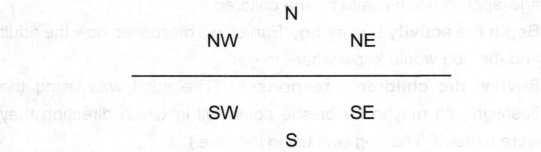

332

Wolf in the Snow illustration: The family in front of the fireplace

Direct the children's attention to the page where you see the family in front of the fireplace. Encourage them to answer the following questions in complete sentences.

QUESTIONS

The brackets around the text indicate questions/instructions an adult should read to the children. Examples of how the children may answer the questions are included in parentheses.

- **[What do you see on this page?]** Write the children's responses on a piece of paper and save this for later. (I see an oval rug in front of the fire. I see a fire in the fireplace. I see objects on the mantel.) See Art #1 and Writing #1.

- Ask the children to tell you all the things they see on this page. Write the children's responses on a piece of paper. (I see their clothing hanging on the wall. I see mugs on the rug. I see boots near the wall.) Explain to the children that observing details is an important skill when reading, it helps you understand and predict what might happen in a story.

- **[What words could describe the family?]** Write the children's responses on a piece of paper and save this for later. (The family is warm. The family looks happy. The family is smiling.) See Writing #1.

- **[What is the dog doing?]** (The dog is licking the young child's face.) See Science # 1.

- **[If the dog in this picture was the dog that helped find the child, what kind of reward could the dog receive for helping** to find the child?] (Special food, extra hugs, walks with the child, a new protective body covering.)

- **[Would you say this family has a lot of storage? Why or why not?]** (Well, the snow outfits are hanging on the wall and the boots are next to the snow outfits, so I don't think they have a lot of storage.)

- Point out that there are two chairs in this picture. **[Who do you think sits in the chairs? Where do you think the young child sits?]** (I think they probably all sit in the chairs at different times. The young child may sit on the rug and play with the dog. The young child may sit in one of the chairs when an adult is doing something else.)

- Note that the whole family is sitting on the comfortable rug. **[Why do you think they're on the rug instead of sitting in the chairs?]** Write the children's responses on a piece of paper and save this for later. Have them copy their favorite sentence on a piece of paper. If they'd like to create their own sentence, be available to help them sound out the words. (The whole family wants to be close to each other. The family is keeping warm by the fire.)

- Design a new rug for the family. See Art #2. See resource section.

- Note that there are two mugs/cups on the rug, and the young child is holding a mug/cup. **[Does the child need to drink the contents carefully? Why or why not?]** (The dog is next to the young child, so she should be careful to drink the contents of the mug/cup. It might be hot, and if the young child spilled a hot substance on the dog, it could burn the dog.) See Art #3.

- Have the children look carefully at the mantel. **[What items do you see?]** Write these items on a piece of paper and save the paper for later. (I see a wolf sculpture on a rock, howling into the air. I see books on the mantel. I see a boat.) See Math #1.

- **[Where are their snow outfits located?]** (We can see that the snow outfits are hung up on the left-hand side of the wall, and the young child's snow outfit is hung up near the fireplace.)
- **[What could you say about the storage in this house?]** (There's not a lot of storage.)
- **[How many chairs do you see in the room?]** (It looks like there are two chairs in the room.)
- **[Where do you think the young child sits?]** (She probably sits on the rug.)
- The dog must get cold during the winter. **[What protective outerwear could it use?]** Write the children's responses on a piece of paper and save it for later. (The dog could wear snow booties. The dog could have a covering for its body).
- Point out that it looks like the fire in the fireplace is burning brightly. **[How much wood would it take to keep this family warm for the winter?]** Write the children's responses on a piece of paper and save this for later. See Science #2.
- Note that the family's house looks like it's isolated in the woods. **[How would they obtain the items they need to survive?]** (They could hunt animals for food. They could plant a garden in the spring. They could fish throughout the year. They could chop down trees for firewood. They could purchase important tools they needed when they go to a major town.)
- Have the children write down ten things they think would be the most important for the family (e.g., a water supply, wood, warm clothing, food supplies). When all the children have written down what things they think would be the most important, have them rank these items. (I think water would be first. I think wood would be second). Ask them to explain why they thought their items should be ranked in the order they chose. (I think water would be first because you can't

live very long without it. I think wood would be second because your body needs warmth to survive.)

- **[How could this family travel in the snow?]** (They might have snowmobiles. They might have other vehicles that could travel in deep snow.)

- **[Can you imagine how much planning it would take to live in an isolated area? What items would be most important to you?]** See Writing #2.

- Choose one of the items on your "important list" and try to determine how much of that item you'd use in a day, a week, and a month. See Math #2.

ACTIVITIES

Art

#1. Create a mural of the family sitting in front of the fireplace.

- **Objective.** Creating. Anchor Standard #1. Generate and conceptualize artistic ideas and work. Investigate, Plan, Make. Brainstorm collaboratively multiple approaches to an art or design problem.

- **Level of difficulty.** Challenging. (This task will take several days to complete.)

- **Materials needed.** A mural-sized piece of white paper, white construction paper, paint cloth for the floor, old shirts for painting the mural, paints, paintbrushes, pencils, and cardboard strips.

- **Before the activity.** Place a large piece of white paper on the board. Have a black marker available for writing the children's responses.

- **Begin the activity by saying,** "Earlier, we discussed what we saw on this page." Write and review the children's comments."

- **Review the children's responses.** (The family is warm beside the fire. They're happy. The dog is licking the young child.)
- **Introduce the activity.** "Today, we're going to create a mural of the family sitting in front of the fireplace."
  1. Have each child pencil in their portion of the drawing until they're satisfied that it's finished.
  2. Put down a paint cloth to protect the floor. Have each child put on an old shirt to protect their clothing.
  3. Allow the children to come to the mural, a couple of children at a time. Have them carefully paint the portion they sketched on the mural. Continue this process until the mural is complete. Let it dry.
  4. Cut out six-inch wide sections of cardboard and brush it with brown paint to resemble wood. You could also paint in some wood knots. Let this dry.
  5. Glue these strips around the mural to resemble the outer window covering shown on the page.
  6. Some children may want to paint individual pictures, so give them time to complete their own paintings. Save the individual drawings and the mural for the writing activity that follows. Make sure the children have written their name on the back of their picture.

#2. Design a new rug for the family.

- **Objective.** Creating. Anchor Standard #1. Generate and conceptualize artistic ideas and work. Investigate, Plan, Make. Elaborate on an imaginative idea.
- **Level of difficulty.** Moderate. (This task may take several days to complete.)

- **Materials needed.** White construction paper, pencils, rug template page (see resource section), crayons, paints, paintbrushes, and colored pencils.
- **Before the activity.** Place a large piece of white paper on the board. Have a black marker available for writing the children's responses.
- **Begin the activity by saying,** "Earlier, we described how the family looked sitting by the fireplace." Write and review the children's comments.
- **Review the children's responses.** (The family looks warm beside the fire. They're happy. The dog is content and is licking the young child's face.)
- **Introduce the activity.** "Today, we're going to design a new rug for the family."
    1. Give each child a piece of drawing paper so they can practice drawing various patterns for their rug. When they've made their final design choice, have them copy the design onto the rug template. (See resource section.)
    2. "Do you think the family would enjoy the rug you created?" Tell a friend why you think this family would enjoy the rug you designed.
- **Extension of the activity.** You might want to have the children write on a conversation bubble (see resource section) what they think the family is saying on the rug. (Dad: "I know you were very brave in the snow." Mom: "You must have been very cold in that storm." Dog: "I'm so glad my best friend is safe.")

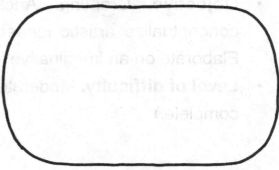

#3. Design and make a mug.

- **Objective.** Creating. Anchor Standard #1. Generate and conceptualize artistic ideas and work. Investigate, Plan, Make. Elaborate on an imaginative idea.
- **Level of difficulty.** Moderate to challenging. (This task may take several days to complete.)
- **Materials needed.** Clay, knife, paper towels, covered plastic container(s), and plastic wrap.
- **Before the activity.** Place a large piece of white paper on the board. Have a black marker available for writing the children's responses.
- **Begin the activity by saying,** "Earlier, we noticed that the family was drinking something from mugs. What do you think they were drinking?" Write and review the children's comments.
- **Introduce the activity.** "Today, we're going to design and make a mug."

  1. Get some clay from a hardware store and cut it into individual portions. Cover each clay portion with wet toweling. Place the clay into a covered plastic container. When you're ready to do this project, take out individual portions of clay from the plastic container and give them to the children. An adult or older student could help the children.
  2. Have them pull off a large chunk of clay and roll it into a snakelike strip. The width of the strip should be the same size. This long strip will be the outer portion of the mug. Take another small piece of clay and roll it into another snakelike strip. This strip will be the bottom section of the mug.
  3. Have them put a piece of plastic wrap on the table. Then they should take the small snakelike strip (the bottom section of the mug) and put it on the plastic wrap. The plastic wrap will prevent it from sticking to the surface. Tell them to gently smooth the

bottom section of the mug with some water, using their fingers for this process.

4. Now guide them through these steps: Start placing the snakelike strip around the bottom section of the mug. Use water to moisten the strip as you attach it to the bottom section. Continue placing the rolled strip around the mug, attaching the strip as you move up and around the mug. Continue this process until you've created a small mug, smoothing out the strip with water. You may or may not want to add a handle. Let this dry.

5. If you have access to a kiln, allow the children to put glaze on their mug before firing. If you don't have access to a kiln, simply allow the children to paint their mug after its dried.

6. Have the children tell a friend why they chose to paint their mug in the way they did. (I chose this design because it looked like the forest area. I chose this design because it shows snow falling on the tops of the trees.)

Writing

#1. Use adjectives to describe the family sitting by the fireplace.

- **Objective.** Language Standards. Conventions of Standard English. Demonstrate command of the conventions of standard English grammar and usage when writing or speaking. Use frequently occurring adjectives.
- **Level of difficulty.** Easy.
- **Materials needed.** Strips of lined paper and pencils.
- **Before the activity.** Place a large piece of white paper on the board. Have a black marker available for writing the children's responses.
- **Begin the activity by saying,** "Earlier, we described how the family looked sitting by the fireplace."

- **Review the children's responses.** (We said they looked warm beside the fire. They're happy. The dog is content and is licking the young child's face.)
- **Introduce the activity.** "Today, we're going to use adjectives to describe the family sitting by the fire." We call descriptive words "adjectives." Adjectives tell us valuable information about objects. Adjectives tell us that the family looks content, safe, loving, and happy. Allow the children to write their favorite adjectives on strips of paper and attach the strips of paper to the mural they created, as well as their individual pictures.

#2. Discuss household items that would be needed on a regular basis and then rank these items in order of importance.

- **Objective.** Writing Standards. Text Types and Purposes. Write informative/explanatory texts in which they name a topic, supply some facts about the topic, and provide some sense of closure.
- **Level of difficulty.** Easy.
- **Materials needed.** Lined paper and pencils.
- **Before the activity.** Place a large piece of white paper on the board. Have a black marker available for writing the children's responses.
- **Begin the activity by saying,** "Earlier, we discussed how much planning it would take for this family to live in an isolated area."
- **Review the children's responses.** (The family would need to get wood, food, water, clothing, tools, and equipment.)
- **Introduce the activity.** "Today, I want you to think of the things that would be important to you if you lived in this isolated area (e.g., games, books, or your favorite food)." Write down some of the items that the children relay.
1. Give each child a piece of lined paper. Have them write down at least ten items they'd want to have if they lived in this area.

2. Have the children rank these items in numerical order of importance. (My favorite cereal would be first. My boots would be second. My favorite candy would be third.)

3. Discuss the results with the children. Does everyone value the same thing?

Science

#1. Learn about a dog's tongue. Learn about our tongue.

- **Objective.** Life Science. Structure, Function, and Information Processing. Read texts and use media to determine patterns in behavior of parents and offspring that help offspring survive.
- **Level of difficulty.** Easy.
- **Materials needed.** None.
- **Before the activity.** Place a large piece of white paper on the board. Have a black marker available for writing the children's responses. Go to the internet and type, "Tell me about a dog's tongue." Choose an age-appropriate website for the children.
- **Begin the activity by saying,** "Earlier, we noticed that the dog was licking the young child."
- **Review the children's responses.** (My dog licks my face, and it feels funny. My dog has little bumps on his tongue. I have these bumps on my tongue.)
- **Introduce the activity.** "Today, we're going to learn about a dog's tongue."
  1. "We noticed that the dog was licking the young child. Go to the internet and type, "Tell me about a dog's tongue." Select the age-appropriate website you chose. Read and discuss this information with them. You will be able to find several videos online that the children might enjoy watching. Preview these videos before showing them to the children. Discuss this information with them.

2. Have the children choose a partner and sit facing that person. Have each set of partners choose which of the children will be number 1 and which will be number 2. Tell the children they're going to examine each other's tongues. Their tongue is like a dog's tongue. Tell them they'll both have an opportunity to carefully examine each other's tongue. Emphasize to the children that they're not to touch their partner's tongue.

3. Tell the 2's to stick out their tongue. The 1's will examine their partner's tongue. "What do you see on the tongue?" (There are bumps on the top of the tongue.)

4. Repeat this process so the 1's can stick out their tongues and have them examined by the 2's.

5. "Do you know what these bumps on the tongue are called?" (They're called taste buds.) "Do you think dogs have these same bumps on their tongue?" (Well, dogs taste their food, so they must have similar taste buds.)

#2. Learn how much wood would be required to warm a one thousand-square foot house in a cold location.

- **Objective.** Engineering Design. Physical Science. Energy. Obtain and combine information to describe that energy and fuels are derived from natural resources and their uses affect the environment.
- **Level of difficulty.** Easy.
- **Materials needed.** Paper and pencils.
- **Before the activity.** Place a large piece of white paper on the board. Have a black marker available for writing the children's responses.
- **Begin the activity by saying,** "Earlier, we noticed that the family had a fire burning in the fireplace. We wondered how much wood it would take to keep this family warm for the winter."
- **Review the children's responses.** (I think it would take a lot of wood to keep a house warm during the winter. I think it would take

several logs in the fireplace to keep the house warm. I think it would take half of a tall tree to keep the house warm for a week.)

- **Introduce the activity.** "Today, we're going to learn how much wood it would take to keep this family warm for the winter."

1. Have the children write and review the amount of wood they think it would take to warm the house for the winter. Go to the internet and type, "How much wood would it take to warm a 1,000-square foot cabin in a cold location?" Choose an age-appropriate website for the children. Read and discuss this information with them. "For a 1,000 square-foot home, it would take approximately three cords of wood to keep it warm during the winter." A single cord of wood is four feet tall, eight feet wide, and four feet deep.

2. "If one cord of wood costs $200, how much would three cords of wood cost?" Explain that not all families purchase wood from a company. Some families use the trees on their property to keep them warm. "What difficulties might arise if they had to cut down their own trees?" Write the children's responses on a piece of paper. (They'd have to have strong tools. They'd need a lot of strength. They'd need to know how to properly cut down a tree. They'd need to properly maintain their tools.)

Math

#1. Vote on whether the items on the mantel belong to the adults or the young child.

- **Objective.** Measurement and Data. Represent and interpret data. Draw a picture graph and a bar graph (with single-unit scale) to represent a data set with up to four categories. Solve simple, put-together, take-apart, and compare problems using information presented in a bar graph.

344

- **Level of difficulty.** Moderate. (This task may take several days to complete.)
- **Materials needed.** Graph paper, pencils, sticky notes, and crayons.
- **Before the activity.** Place a large piece of white paper on the board. Have a black marker available for writing the children's responses.
- **Begin the activity by saying,** "Earlier, we looked at the items that were sitting on the mantel. We wondered whether they belonged to the adults or to the young child."
- **Review the children's responses.** (There's a boat on the mantel. I think it belongs to the dad. There are books on the mantel. These could belong to either the adults or the young child. There's a wolf statue howling on top of a rock. I think it belongs to the young child.)
- **Introduce the activity.** "Today, we're going to vote on whether the items on the mantel belong to the adults or the young child."
  1. Explain that the items could belong to either of the adults, but the children will simply choose between the adults or the young child.
  2. Place a large piece of paper on the board and list the items (a circular rock, books, a wolf howling on a rock, a catlike creature, a boat, and a triangular shape). Below each item, write "Adults" or "Young Child."
  3. Give each child a sticky note and have them put their name on it. Ask each child to put their sticky note in one of these two locations ("Adults" or "Young Child"). Only do one item at a time (starting with, say, the circular rock). Do this same process for each item on the mantel. Tally the number of adult or young child votes. Keep this paper for later.
  4. Discuss what the children see. (Most of us thought the circular rock belonged to the adults. We thought the books belonged to the adults. We thought the wolf howling on the rock belonged to the young child.)

#2. Determine how much of a specific item (e.g., games, books, or a favorite food) you'd need in a day, week, or month.

- **Objective.** Operations and Algebraic Thinking. Represent and solve problems involving addition and subtraction. Use addition and subtraction within 100 to solve one-and two-step word problems involving situations of adding to, taking from, putting together, taking apart, and comparing with unknowns in all positions (by using drawings and equations with a symbol for the unknown number to represent the problem).

- **Level of difficulty.** Moderate. (This task may take several days to complete.)

- **Materials needed.** Paper and pencils.

- **Before the activity.** Place a large piece of white paper on the board. Have a black marker available for writing the children's responses.

- **Begin the activity by saying,** "Earlier, we wondered about the things that would be important to you if you lived in this area."

- **Review the children's responses.** (Games, books, favorite food.)

- **Introduce the activity.** "Today, we're going to find out how much it would take to supply us with one of the items on our 'important' list for a day, week, and a month."

1. Have the children choose one item on their "important" list and have them try to determine how much of that item they'd use in a day, a week, and a month. Demonstrate an example. "If the important item on my list is cereal, I'd have to first find out how much I eat in a single serving. Let's say I eat 1 cup of cereal at a time. If I eat cereal four times a week, I'd have to multiply 1 cup times four days (1 x 4), which would equal 4 cups per week. To determine how much cereal I'd use in a month, I'd have to multiply the weekly amount (4 cups per week) by the number of

weeks in a month, which is four (4 x 4). Now, I've determined that I eat 16 cups of cereal in a month."

2. Have the children try to make this determination for several items on their list. Talk about the need to plan for these important purchases, as they might not go to the market on a regular basis.

Direct the children's attention to the back cover of the book. It shows a wolf standing on a rock, howling into the air. Encourage them to answer the following questions in complete sentences.

QUESTIONS

The brackets around the text indicate questions/instructions an adult should read to the children. Examples of how the children may answer the questions are included in parentheses.

- **[What do you see on this page?]**
- **[Do you think it's the same wolf who was in the story or a different wolf? Why or why not?]** See Math #1.
- **[Do you think the wolf is howling to its pack, or do you think it's howling to the young child?]** Write the children's responses on a piece of paper and save this for later. See Art #1 and Writing #1.
- **[What are the reasons a wolf would howl?]** (A wolf might howl to call the pack together. A wolf might howl to let the other members of the pack know it's in the area.) Write the children's responses on a piece of paper and save this for later. See Science #1.

ACTIVITIES

Art

#1. Recreate an illustration in the book, using a sponge technique.

- **Objective.** Presenting. Anchor Standard #4. Select, analyze, and interpret artistic work for presentation. Select. Categorize images based on expressive properties.

- **Level of difficulty.** Moderate. (This task may take several days to complete.)

- **Materials needed.** Sponge, paints for illustrations, plates for paint, gray/black paint, pencils, small pins, knife, white construction paper, crayons, and colored pencils.

- **Before the activity.** Place a large piece of white paper on the board. Have a black marker available for writing the children's responses.

- **Begin the activity by saying,** "Earlier, we discussed whether we thought the wolf standing on the rock was howling to its pack or to the young child." Write and review the children's responses.

- **Review the children's responses.** (Well, it has dark fur like the wolf in the story. I think it's the same wolf.)

- **Introduce the activity.** "Today, we're going to create a sponge painting of the wolf standing on the rock."

    1. Draw a simple picture of a wolf on posterboard and carefully cut around it. Place the wolf on a sponge, putting several small straight pins into the wolf so it will stay in place on the sponge. Draw around the wolf with a black marker and carefully cut off the excess sponge. Only an adult should do this. Dip the sponge wolf into the gray/black paint mixture, gently blotting it onto a piece of paper towel. The paint should be thick enough to absorb the paint.

2. Give each child a piece of paper and have the children draw the rock in the middle of the paper, along with the surrounding forest.

3. When they've finished their drawing, have the children come one at a time to a table area where they can press their wolf onto their picture. Have them gently dip the sponge into the paint mixture, and carefully stamp their wolf on top of the rock. Let their pictures dry. Attach the writing assignment that follows to their picture.

Writing

#1. Discuss whether the wolf standing on the rock is howling to the pack or to the young child.

- **Objective.** Reading Standards for Literature. Integration of Knowledge and Ideas. Use information gained from the illustrations and words in a print or digital text to demonstrate understanding of its characters, setting, or plot.

- **Level of difficulty.** Moderate. (This task may take several days to complete.)

- **Materials needed.** Lined paper and pencils.

- **Before the activity.** Place a large piece of white paper on the board. Have a black marker available for writing the children's responses.

- **Begin the activity by saying,** "Earlier, we discussed whether or not the wolf standing on the rock was howling to the pack or to the young child." Write and review the children's responses.

- **Review the children's responses.** (I think the wolf standing on the rock is the mother of the young cub. I think she's howling to the young child to thank her for helping her cub. I don't think it's the same wolf because the other wolves aren't nearby.)

- **Introduce the activity.** "Today, we're going to discuss whether the wolf standing on the rock was howling to the pack or to the young child." Write and review the children's responses. (I think the wolf standing on the rock was howling to the young child because it wanted to say goodbye. I think the wolf standing on the rock was howling to the pack because it knew that the young child was safe.) Have the children write their thoughts about who the wolf is howling to. Have the children attach their writing to the picture they created in the previous art activity (the sponge painting of the wolf on top of the rock).

Science

#1. Learn and discuss why wolves howl.

- **Objective.** Engineering Design. Life Science. Interdependent Relationships in Ecosystems. Construct an argument that some animals form groups that help members survive.
- **Level of difficulty.** Easy.
- **Materials needed.** None.
- **Before the activity.** Place a large piece of white paper on the board. Have a black marker available for writing the children's responses. Go to the internet and type, "Why do wolves howl?" Choose an age-appropriate website for the children.
- **Begin the activity by saying,** "Earlier, we discussed the reasons why wolves howl."
- **Review the children's responses.** (Wolves howl to let the members of their pack know where they're located. I think wolves howl to let the other wolves know where prey is located. I think wolves howl for fun.)
- **Introduce the activity.** "Today, we're going to find out why wolves howl." Write and review the children's responses. Go to the internet and type, "Why do wolves howl?" Select the age-appropriate website you chose. Read and discuss this information with the children. Have them tell a friend their favorite reason wolves howl.

Math

#1. Survey the children on the following question. Do you think the wolf standing on the rock is the same wolf as the one in the story (the mother wolf)?

- **Objective.** Measurement and Data. Represent and interpret data. Draw a picture graph and a bar graph (with single-unit scale) to represent a data set with up to four categories. Solve simple, put-together, take-apart, and compare problems using information presented in a bar graph.

- **Level of difficulty.** Moderate. (This task may take several days to complete.)

- **Materials needed.** None.

- **Before the activity.** Place a large piece of white paper on the board. Have a black marker available for writing the children's responses.

- **Begin the activity by saying,** "Earlier, we discussed whether or not the wolf standing on the rock was the same wolf as the one in the story."

- **Review the children's responses.** (Well, it looks like one of the wolves in the story. I think it's the same wolf.)

- **Introduce the activity.** "Today, we're going to decide if the wolf standing on the rock is the same wolf in the story or a different wolf." We'll take a survey to determine who thinks it's the same wolf and who thinks it's a different wolf.

  1. Give each child a sticky note and have them write their name on it. Place a large piece of paper on the board and write the words "same" and "different" on it. Have each child come up to the paper and place their sticky note on one of the choices.

  2. Have one child come up to the board and count the number of sticky notes for "same." Have another child come up and count

the same number of sticky notes. If the two numbers are the same, write the number below the word "same."

3. Do this same process for "different."

4. Relay the survey results. (Six children thought the wolf was the same, and five thought the wolf was different.)

5. Have the children relay why they thought the wolf on the rock was either the "same" or "different."

RESOURCE SECTION

Permission Slip (to Drink Hot Chocolate)

Dear Parent(s),

Our class has been reading the Caldecott medal-winning book *Wolf in the Snow* by Matthew Cordell. It's a story about a young child and a young wolf meeting in the forest. The family is living comfortably in a small cabin in the woods. They're enjoying a beverage inside the house, next to a blazing fire. We took a survey to determine the possible beverages this family might be enjoying and graphed the results.

As a culmination of our survey, we'll be enjoying one of the beverage choices. We'll be having hot chocolate. Please mark which permission you give and then sign the form at the bottom of the page.

Please return it to school as soon as possible. Your child will not be allowed to participate in this activity without this permission form. Thank you in advance for completing and returning the form.

_____I give permission for my child to have the hot chocolate.

_____I do not give permission for my child to have the hot chocolate.

_____

Parent Signature

Permission Slip (to Consume Pine Nuts)

Dear Parent(s),

Our class has been reading the Caldecott medal-winning book *Wolf in the Snow* by Matthew Cordell. It's a story about a young child and a young wolf meeting in the forest. We've been learning about evergreen trees, which have pine cones attached. We've examined, smelled, and touched a pine cone. We'll soon be tasting pine nuts.

Please mark which permission you give and then sign the form at the bottom of the page. Please return it to school as soon as possible. Your child will not be allowed to participate in this activity without this permission form. Thank you in advance for completing and returning the form.

_____I give permission for my child to taste a pine nut.

_____I do not give permission for my child to taste pine nuts.

_____My child has a nut allergy, so he or she cannot be in the same room.

_____

Parent Signature

Weather calendar

Window for inside/outside view

Mug design

Thermometer

Permission slip to consume hot chocolate.

Mitten

Conversation bubbles

Shape

Dogs

Permission slip to consume pine nuts

Boots

Compass rose.

Clock

Wolf ears

Wolf tracks

Wolf cards

Snow globe / base

Weather sheet

Picture frames

Trees for diorama

Coat for young child (diorama)

Wolf print for potato

Covering for dog

Rug

ABOUT THE AUTHOR

Claudia Krause, a native of Los Angeles, was raised in a small, rural community in California. She earned a bachelor's degree in psychology from California State University at Long Beach, California, and a master's degree in education from Redlands University at Redlands, California. She is an author and teacher.